PORTRAIT OF LORD COLLINGWOOD.

THE LIFE OF ADMIRAL LORD

COLLINGWOOD

BY

W. CLARK RUSSELL

AUTHOR OF "THE WRECK OF THE 'GROSVENOR'," "MY DANISH SWEETHEART,"
"A MARRIAGE AT SEA," ETC.

WITH ILLUSTRATIONS BY F. BRANGWYN

NEW AND CHEAPER EDITION

METHUEN & CO.
36 ESSEX STREET, STRAND
LONDON
1895

TO

IDA BLACKETT.

PREFACE.

WHAT may be termed the "ocean-seclusion" of Lord Collingwood lasted so many years that there is probably no man of his, or any other time, who rose to eminence and filled a great public position, of whom less is known; or, as I should prefer to say, about whom less has been written. His contemporaries seldom refer to him. Here and there in the biography of an officer who served under him may be found some dry, insipid, official letters communicating the proceedings of the ship; but there are no "asides," so to speak, nothing of that sort of gossip which furnishes to a writer a basis for a theory of character, or which helps him as a glancing of light over a canvas on which the painted lineaments lie hidden in darkness or in dust.

The only account of Collingwood with which I am acquainted, that aims at any sort of fullness, is the memoir of him written by his son-in-law, G. L. Newnham Collingwood. But it is a very meagre relation, even less useful perhaps than the thin narrative of the Admiral's career which was published in the 15th volume of the *Naval Chronicle.* It is little more than a thread designed by the able gentleman who penned it, for the stringing together into the best attainable form of coherency of a large number of Collingwood's letters. Much of the man may be gathered from these letters, but not all, not nearly all, that one could wish to know. We obtain but the briefest glimpse of him on board ship. Nothing that is specially characteristical of a most noble, gallant, and original nature is indicated or preserved; I mean in those directions to which Collingwood would not think of referring in writing to his wife, to his father-in-law, and others. And then, again, there is little doubt that Newnham Collingwood suppressed much, and revised and sub-edited much, which, in its entirety, would have enabled us to gain a clearer view of his great relative than his anxiety not to offend the living—for his volumes were printed in 1828—suffers us to obtain.

Yet Collingwood's *Memoir and Correspondence* is an excellent book, and posterity owes the memory of the son-in-law of the Admiral a large debt of gratitude for compiling and issuing it. Many of the letters are compositions of wonderful elegance and spirit, full of high and wise thoughts, of prudential deliverances, uttered in a style so captivating that one is tempted to think that if Collingwood had not been foremost amongst the greatest naval Captains and Commanders-in-Chief of his time, he would have led the van—and not the van of the lee division either !—of the best writers of his age. I have not scrupled to quote freely from these delightful letters. Newnham Collingwood's book is not known as it should be; it has not, to my knowledge, been reprinted for many years; to naval students it is of course a familiar work; but the average reader can scarcely, I think, be called a naval student, and it may be quite likely that he is not acquainted with Collingwood's letters; therefore, whoever gives him a substantial helping from this rich repast, cannot, I think, but be greatly obliging and improving him.

I am happy, however, in being able to add to the published correspondence of Lord Collingwood. A number of original letters, addressed by him to Sir Edward Blackett, Bart., whose niece Lord Collingwood married, are in the possession of Sir Edward's grandson, John Blackett, Esq., late R.N., of Thorpe Lea, Egham, Surrey, and his courtesy privileges me to communicate them for the first time to the public. My thanks are also due to Joseph Cowen, Esq., of Stella Hall, Blaydon-on-Tyne; to Robert Blair, Esq., of North Shields; to W. E. Adams, Esq., of the *Newcastle Weekly Chronicle;* and to Richard Ruddock, Esq., of Newcastle-on-Tyne.

So much being said, this story of the career of a great British Sailor goes forth to plead for itself. I have spared no pains to obtain original information; but Collingwood has been dead eighty years. Local tradition is silent about him. Indeed, it is not too much to say that very few people in and round about Morpeth, where his house was, appear to have any knowledge even of the name of Collingwood. An old resident writes: "Lord C. was always spoken of as a man of plain, simple habits, who often walked down to my grandmother's, and stood with his back to the fire for a long gossip. He was fond of his garden, and had some trees

planted on Lord Carlisle's castle banks, which could be
then seen from his house. I remember best his gardener."
Much as I am obliged for such communications, the reader
will not require to be told that something more is needed
to make out, and to make up, the story of a man's life.

W. Clark Russell.

CONTENTS.

CHAPTER I.

CHAPTER II.

CHAPTER III.

CHAPTER IV.

CHAPTER V.

CHAPTER VI.

CHAPTER VII.

CHAPTER VIII.

CHAPTER IX.

CHAPTER X.

CHAPTER XI.

CHAPTER XII.

LIST OF ILLUSTRATIONS.

COLLINGWOOD.

CHAPTER I.

CUTHBERT COLLINGWOOD was born in the year 1748 at Newcastle-on-Tyne, in a street called the Side. The house where he first saw the light still stands; it is of brick, three stories high, with a basement; and it was no doubt in its day a genteel, commodious residence. Since Collingwood's time, however, it has been gutted by fire and put to somewhat base uses—hired for the sale of tobacco, of liquor, of old clothes, and it has, I believe, been a tramps' lodging-house.

The entry of Collingwood's baptism in the register of

the Church of St. Nicholas at Newcastle-on-Tyne runs thus: •

"*1748. October 24, Cuthbert, son of Cuthbert Colling-wood, Merchant, and Milcah, his wife.*"

His family was one of the most ancient in Northumberland. The Collingwoods in their generations had numbered amongst them Border Chieftains and Cavaliers, Kings' Commissioners, County Sheriffs and Justices of the Peace.[1] Royalty itself is imported into the genealogy, and the son-in-law of Lord Collingwood boldly introduces us to the Earl of Kent, Joan of Plantagenet, King Edward I., and the Black Prince as ancestors of the Admiral.[2] We shall be going far enough back for all purposes if we start with our hero's father, Cuthbert Collingwood, who married Milcah, daughter of Reginald Dobson of Barwise, in Westmoreland, and had by her three sons and four or five daughters, Cuthbert being the eldest of the sons.

Mr. Collingwood in his youth was bound apprentice to a Merchant Adventurer and Boothman in Newcastle, and after obtaining his freedom, started in business in that house in the Side where his son, the future admiral, was born. He was unfortunate, and his affairs were wound up. His creditors were distillers, oilmen, soap-boilers, druggists, and so forth, whence the character of his business may be inferred. It was manifestly a hard struggle for the parents, and but for the assistance of friends they must have found it difficult to feed, clothe, and educate their large family. The father died in February 1775, and the property that had been mortgaged for the benefit of the widow, when sold by her, realized nine hundred pounds,[3] so that, as we may see, Cuthbert, when he began

[1] Richard Welford : *Newcastle Monthly Chronicle.*
[2] *Collingwood's Public and Private Correspondence*, by G. L. Newnham Collingwood, 1829, p. 3.   [3] J. Clayton in *Archæologia Æliana.*

his sea career, had little or nothing to expect in the shape of money-help from his home.

Education was happily cheap at Newcastle-on-Tyne in those days, as it still is. Cuthbert was sent to the Grammar School, the head-master of which was the Reverend Hugh Moises, a person whose fame as a teacher was more than local; for it was related by Lord Eldon that when George III. read Collingwood's account of the Battle of Trafalgar he expressed surprise that a naval officer should be able to write so excellent a dispatch; "but," added the King, "I find he was educated by Moises." [1] The two Scotts, John and William, afterwards

[1] Twiss's *Life of Lord Eldon*, vol. ii. p. 119. The eloquent Mr Joseph Cowen, for many years senior Member for Newcastle-on-Tyne, has been good enough to send me the following interesting note on Moises :—

"Beyond the mural monument in St. Nicholas' Church, there is no visible memorial of Mr. Moises in Newcastle. He is only known to the present generation as the schoolmaster of Lords Eldon, Stowell, and Collingwood ; of Sir Robert Chambers, the Indian judge ; Brand, the antiquarian ; and Burdon, the philosopher. Yet in his day he was a man of great influence, and engaged a large share of public attention. Half a century ago his name was one to conjure with. His authority was acknowledged, and his opinions deferred to on all local and literary subjects. Mr. Moises was a born teacher. He loved his profession, and he laboured in it with enthusiasm. He had the faculty of constituting himself the companion as well as the master of his pupils. He was a strong disciplinarian, and, when in school, was supreme. He took his seat at his desk with as much dignity as a judge takes his seat upon the Bench. Every one bowed to him. But when their tasks were over, his relations with his scholars were of the most cordial character. He invited them to his house, assisted them with their lessons, walked with them in the country, and counselled them not only as to the work of the day, but as to the work of their lives. He advised his pupils to read only the works of great authors as much with the view of learning their style as their doctrines. He had himself a passion for the classics, but he always strove to ascertain the special aptitude of his scholars, and urged them to pursue only such studies as they were likely to excel in. A friend of mine, when a boy, was engaged with Mr. Moises after he left the Grammar School. He spoke of him

Lords Eldon and Stowell, were amongst Collingwood's
schoolfellows under Moises. No youth ever profited more
from his school. His diligence still lingers as a tradition.
Probably when he went to sea his Greek and Latin were
hove overboard; I find few or no hints of an acquaintance
with those languages in his letters; but in general knowledge there was probably not a man in the Service
throughout his long career that could have matched him.
He loved books, and suffered nothing but his professional
duties to interrupt the delight they yielded him. He
was perfectly well informed in what may be called polite
letters, was a student of everything good in English
literature, and had such an art of expressing himself with
his pen as brings many of his letters in polish, sweetness
of language, and archness of humour, very close to some
of the happiest compositions of Addison. His fine taste
was the gift of nature, but Moises must claim the merit of
cultivating and directing it.

I have been unable to collect any anecdotes of Collingwood's school-days. Lord Eldon would speak of him as
having been "a pretty boy." "Collingwood," said the
Earl, "at school was a mild boy; he was in the same class
as my brother Harry; but he did not then give promise
of being the great man he afterwards became; he did not
show any remarkable talents then. Lord Collingwood
and I," Lord Eldon told the Hon. Henry Legge soon after
the Battle of Trafalgar, "are memorable instances of the
blessings to be derived from the country of our birth and
the constitution under which we live. He and I were

---

with unbounded admiration. His youthful admiration was most
impressed with Mr. Moises' gentleness and generosity. The good old
man was at every one's call, and he showed his kindness, not merely
in aiding deserving persons with money (according to his means),
but with what is more difficult to give—useful service and advice."

class-fellows at Newcastle. We were placed at that school because neither his father nor mine could afford to place us elsewhere; and now if he returns to this country to take his seat in the House of Lords it will be my duty to express to him, sitting in his place, the thanks of that House (to which neither of us could expect to be elevated) for his eminent services to his country." [1]

The quality of reserve we find in his manhood he probably possessed as a lad, and it would be heightened in him by the sensitiveness that poverty creates. Yet poverty might have helped him, too, by causing him to be determined in his studies. It was certain that whatever his future was to hold must be of his own manufacture; this the quiet, high-spirited lad would understand, and the perception that made his career noble in after days for valour and for dutifulness, animated him as a lad to the degree of rendering him one of the most resolved, patient, and honest scholars that the old Grammar School of Newcastle ever dismissed into the world.

It is not stated that he exhibited as a lad any marked taste for the sea, though born in a district that has been famous for centuries for its breed of sailors, and that is charged with scores of just such maritime inspirations as would fix the fancies of a boy whose leaning was in any degree oceanwards. A sister of his mother had married Captain, afterwards Admiral, Brathwaite, and no doubt this connection caused Mr. and Mrs. Cuthbert Collingwood to choose the sea as a profession for their son. Brathwaite had entered the naval service in 1743 under the patronage of his relative, Sir Chaloner Ogle, and on the recommendation of Sir Edward Hawke was made lieutenant in 1755. A year later he was promoted Commander, and in the

---

[1] Twiss's *Life of Eldon*, passim.

spring of 1761 posted into the *Shannon* frigate.[1] In a notice of his services, written by himself, dated January 7th, 1806, Collingwood says: " I went into the Navy at a very early period of my life, in the year 1761, in the *Shannon*, under the protection and care of a kind friend and relation, the late Admiral Brathwaite; to whose regard for me, and to the interest which he took in whatever related to my improvement in nautical knowledge, I owe great obligations." [2]

He entered as a volunteer. In the memoir published by his son-in-law, it is said that when he first went on board the *Shannon* he sat crying over his separation from home. The first lieutenant observed him, and "pitying the tender years of the poor child," addressed a few words of encouragement and kindness to him. The boy was so grateful that he took the officer to his sea-chest and offered him a large piece of plum-cake which his mother had stowed away with his clothes. [3]

For a number of years young Collingwood continued with Brathwaite, first in the *Shannon*, then in the *Gibraltar*, and afterwards in the *Liverpool*. In a narrative of his life, published in 1806, it is stated that he served as midshipman in the *Gibraltar* in 1766, and as master's mate in the *Liverpool* from 1767 to 1772. He was then taken into the

---

[1] He died Admiral of the White, June 28th, 1805, at Greenwich, aged 80.

[2] *Naval Chronicle*, vol. xxiii. p. 380.

[3] *Correspondence and Memoir*, p. 6. Mr. J. Clayton remarks upon this : " In Mr. Newnham Collingwood's *Biography*, Cuthbert Collingwood is stated to have been only eleven years old, which is obviously an error, and the anecdote of his having invited the first lieutenant to eat plum-cake with him in his berth is more likely to have really occurred if he had been in fact eleven years old instead of thirteen, his actual age." But even at the mature age of thirteen, boys have been known to cry on leaving home, and to share their cakes with those who were kind and sympathizing.

Lenox, guard-ship at Portsmouth, commanded by Captain Roddam, who also received his brother Wilfred. Roddam was one of the most seasoned mariners of his day. He was at sea in the *Lowestoffe* frigate some thirty-six or thirty-seven years before young Collingwood joined the *Lenox*, had served in expeditions in the West Indies under Vernon, had experienced as a prisoner of war the horrors of a San Domingo jail, and in one fashion or another had seen or suffered pretty nearly everything that entered into the vocation of the sea in those wild, exciting, fighting times.

We may believe that the conversation and recollections of such a man would provide an extraordinary entertainment. The association to the two Collingwoods was, in its way, a liberal marine education. Cuthbert and his Captain were not as yet related; but the spirit of the north country was strong in them both: it must bring them together in a sense of sympathy that would be impossible to the ordinary relations between the commander of a ship of war and his midshipmen. As we think of the lumbering old guard-ship at Portsmouth, the vessels of those distant times rise before the mind's eye—utterly phantom ships now—the crews, the science, the navigation, the ordnance as ghostly, as completely gone, metaphorically and absolutely, as the *Flying Dutchman* with her sakers, her poop-lanthorn, and her sprit-topsail. What ponderosity of conformation you find in such craft as young Collingwood was now going to sea in! They floated with the grace of casks, and yet they possessed a certain quality of majesty too, thanks to the embellishment of lines of artillery and to the spacious heights of canvas which, even when on a bowline, and when blowing a single-reef topsail breeze, could scarcely heel them. And the navigation! Hear old Mungo Murray, who was writing but a few years before young Collingwood had strapped a dirk to his hip: "After the latitude is thus found by a good observation, if it agrees with the latitude by the account, it may be presumed that your longitude by account is true; but if there be any considerable difference, it may be feared there will likewise be an error in the longitude; to correct which there can be no certain rule. . . . If after all this, the observed latitude and that by account do not agree, the only thing that can be done is to let the longitude go as by his account, or make a remark what the longitude would have been, provided the error was in the course, and supposing the distance true."[1] Is there a nautical Charles Lamb amongst us? There should be as much relish for his palate in the above sentences as ever Elia found in the most felicitous quaintnesses of old Fuller or Burton.

Collingwood remained with Roddam in the *Lenox* until the latter was relieved in December 1773.[2] In the following February we find our hero aboard the *Preston*, bound to Boston. The magnificent struggle for independence in North America had begun. The materials for a mighty blaze had been sullenly and obstinately accumulating, and "the insignificant duty of threepence a pound upon tea" was the torch that was to put fire to the heap. On

---

[1] *A Treatise on Ship-building and Navigation*, by Mungo Murray, 1754, p. 254.

[2] Long afterwards, when Roddam was above four-score years old, when the Battle of Trafalgar had been fought and won, and the names of Nelson and Collingwood were in everybody's mouth, the brave and hearty veteran wrote thus of the man who, in his youth, had served under him : " His private worth equals the splendour of his well-known public value. He is in every respect a great and good man : and in every circumstance, both professionally and otherwise, he has finally proved himself deserving of the high opinion I early formed of him, and which I always hoped would in time render him as much approved by his country as he was valued by me."—*Naval Chronicle*, vol. xv. p. 381.

December 18th, 1773, a number of men disguised as
Indians had boarded three tea ships lying at Boston and
pitched their cargoes overboard. This was followed by the
detestable Bill which aimed to extinguish Boston's privi-
lege as a port—a law that dated the decisive resolution of
Parliament to proceed to extremities with the province of
Massachusetts Bay ; and the *Preston*—bearing the flag of
Vice-Admiral Samuel Graves—with other ships of war, was
despatched to Boston to strengthen the naval force in
America.

"In 1774," says Collingwood, in the modest narrative of
his career, which I have before quoted from, "I went to
Boston with Admiral Graves, and in 1775 was made a
lieutenant by him on the day the battle was fought at
Bunker's Hill, where I was with a party of seamen supplying the army with what was necessary for them." He
used to say that he had never witnessed a fiercer struggle.[1]
In the darkness of the night, and in wonderful silence, the
Yankees, or Provincials, as they were then termed, con-
structed a small but immensely strong redoubt, with
entrenchments and a breastwork, in some parts cannon-
proof. Many ships of war floated near, but not a sound of
what was going on was heard by them. When the dawn
broke and disclosed the almost magical achievement of the
night, the guns of the *Lively* man-of-war—whose people
were the first to see what had been done—broke forth in a
sort of roar of astonishment. Then followed a heavy and
continual fire of cannon, howitzers, and mortars from the
ships, from the floating batteries, and from the height of
Cop's Hill. The Americans were bayoneted out of their
stronghold at last, but at a fearful cost of life to our side.

---

[1] "Some gentlemen, who had served in the most distinguished
actions of the last war, declared that for the time it lasted it was the
hottest engagement they ever knew."—*Annual Register*, 1775, p. 135.

Collingwood's share in this affair of slaughter he himself related, as we have seen. The writer of the *Memoir* of him in the *Naval Chronicle*, states that he was promoted to the rank of fourth lieutenant in the *Somerset*. Nothing is then heard of him until March 1776, when we find him appointed to the *Hornet* sloop, Captain Haswell, and sailing in her to the West Indies. The conduct of the captain induced a trifling sulkiness of demeanour in Collingwood. He seemed wanting in alacrity, and there appeared a spiritlessness in him that gave offence. In the autumn of 1777, at Port Royal, a court-martial was held upon him; but on every charge he was fully acquitted. The recollection of this unpleasant passage of his life seems to have been present to him ten years later, when he addressed a letter full of beauty and wisdom to a young friend named Lane: "A strict and unwearied attention to your duty," he says, "and a complaisant and respectful behaviour, not only to your superiors, but to everybody will ensure you their regard; and the reward will surely come, and I hope soon, in the shape of preferment: but if it should not I am sure you have too much good sense to let disappointment sour you. Guard carefully against letting discontent appear in you; it is sorrow to your friends, a triumph to your competitors, and cannot be productive of any good. Conduct yourself so as to deserve the best that can come to you; and the consciousness of your own proper behaviour will keep you in spirits if it should not come."[1] The whole composition is a masterpiece of grave, touching, all-important advice, the fruits, no doubt, of many a long mood of introspective meditation.

His close professional association, but not his acquaintance, with Horatio Nelson dates from this period. He tells us in his *Memoir* that he "had been long before

[1] *Correspondence and Memoir*, p. 14.

in habits of great friendship" with Nelson. But now begins the story of their intermingled careers. The *Lowestoffe*, with Nelson on board as a lieutenant, arrived at the station where Collingwood was, and on Nelson being removed, Collingwood succeeded to the vacancy; and when Nelson's next step was into the *Hinchinbrooke*, his friend was made commander in the *Badger;* and on Nelson's promotion to the *Janus*, Collingwood was posted into the *Hinchinbrooke*. The most noticeable feature of his career at this time was the San Juan expedition. The Governor of Jamaica, General Dalling, had projected a scheme for cutting off the communication of the Spaniards between their northern and southern dominions in America, by seizing Fort San Juan on the Rio San Juan, and then obtaining possession of the cities of Granada and Leon. The command of the naval force was given to Nelson, but nothing could withstand the climate. The season, too, was wrongly chosen. " Had the expedition," wrote Nelson, "arrived at San Juan's harbour in the month of January, the violent torrents would have subsided, and of course the whole army would not have had occasion, which was the case in April, to get wet three or four times a day in dragging the boats." [1] Nelson fell dangerously ill; but the death of Captain Glover of the *Janus* provided a vacancy. Sir Peter Parker gave the command to Nelson, and Collingwood was posted in Nelson's place into the *Hinchinbrooke*.

"My constitution," says Collingwood, referring to this San Juan expedition, " resisted many attacks, and I survived most of my ship's company, having buried, in four months, 180 of the 200 who composed it." The transports were converted into derelicts by death, and they sank at their anchors as they lay in the harbour. Dr. Moseley,

[1] *Clarke and M'Arthur*, vol. i. p. 157.

who refers to this expedition in a treatise on tropical diseases, says that out of 1800 people who were sent to different posts at different embarkations, not more than 380 returned.   Men dropped dead in the march, and their bodies putrified before their companions missed them. Corpses lay unburied on the banks of the river, or were devoured by wild beasts in sight of the helpless survivors. Numbers of the poor fellows lost their minds.   Collingwood's north-country constitution bore up stoutly against the accumulated miseries and perils of this time.   Happily neither he nor Nelson was to be destroyed by General Dalling's theory of harassing the Spaniards.

"From this scene," he says, " I was relieved in August 1780."   And in the following December he was appointed to a small frigate, the *Pelican*, of 24 guns.   It is stated that under his command the *Pelican* captured the French frigate, *Le Cerf*, of 16 guns, and recaptured the *Blanford*, a richly-laden vessel from Glasgow, "under circumstances that reflected the highest credit upon the captain and crew." [1]   Of this event, however, I find no mention in the several short notices of Lord Collingwood which have been published at intervals since his death.   But it is certain that he was wrecked in this ship, and came very near to losing his life.   He has himself briefly told the story: " In August in the following year (*i. e.* 1781) there was a severe hurricane, in which she [the *Pelican*] was wrecked, being cast on the rocks of the Morant Cays in the middle of a most tremendous night.   The next day, with great difficulty, the ship's company got on shore on rafts made of the small and broken yards ; and upon those sandy islands with little food we remained ten days, until a boat went to Jamaica and the *Diamond* frigate came and took us off."

[1] *Memoir of Vice-Admiral Lord Collingwood in Clarke and M'Arthur*, part vii. p. 271.

The Morant Cays consist of four low islets in the form of a crescent, surrounded by a dangerous reef. They lie about thirty-five miles distant from Morant Point; they stand about eight feet above the water, and have bushes on them, and, in Collingwood's time, there were probably a few cocoa-nut trees to be met with ; but there is none now, save perhaps on Savanna Cay. In a publication of 1843 I find a reference made to Collingwood's disaster; but the writer was evidently an old man, whose memory misled him. He speaks of the *Pelican* as the *Badger*, and says that she went ashore near the Marley Hill, between the church and the town, and that she ultimately stranded on the soft mud and sand at the south-west end of the harbour of Montego. But though there is an inaccuracy here, the writer adds the following item of domestic interest : " There were some female relatives of Lord Collingwood residing at Lucea, immediately over the scene of his disaster. The house was conspicuous as standing alone and higher than others upon the ridge to the westward. One of these ladies was married to Doctor Corral, a physician practising in the place; it is probable that not a remnant of the family remains at this day in the island." [1]

The hurricane in which the *Pelican* was lost is historic. Above a hundred merchant ships were driven ashore in Port Royal harbour, and two men-of-war, the *Ulysses* and *Southampton*, were entirely dismasted.

Collingwood's next appointment was to the command of the *Sampson* of 64 guns. At the peace of 1783 this vessel was paid off, and shortly afterwards he was sent, in command of the *Mediator*, a frigate, to the West Indies, on which station his friend Nelson was at that time commanding the *Boreas*. Captain Wilfred Collingwood was

[1] *Nautical Magazine*, 1843, p. 243.

also on this station in command of the *Rattler*. We hear
all too little of this fine young fellow in the accounts of his
illustrious brother, though Sir Harris Nicolas tells us that
the extensive correspondence preserved at the Admiralty
respecting the illicit traffic which Nelson was now dealing
with in his defiant, instant, headlong way, shows that he
was an able and zealous officer.[1]   Collingwood's main
occupation during this second West Indian experience of
his seems to have lain in co-operating with Nelson and
Wilfred in enforcing the operation of the Navigation
Laws.   The West Indian seas swarmed with American
traders who claimed, or pretended to claim, all the advantages conferred by their vessels' registers, which dated
before their Independence, when, therefore, the Americans
were British subjects.   But under our Navigation Laws
they were now foreigners, and Nelson properly treated
them as such.   In his honourable struggles to suppress
this illegal traffic, which was connived at not only by the
planters, merchants, and officers of the Customs of the
different islands, but by the Commander-in-Chief himself,
Admiral Sir Richard Hughes, he was ably assisted by
Captain Wilfred, and in a lesser degree by Captain Cuthbert Collingwood.   There are many references to both
brothers in Nelson's letters written at this time.   "Collingwood," he writes, September 24th, 1784, referring to
Cuthbert, "is at Grenada, which is a great loss to me,
for there is nobody that I can make a confidant of."
"What an amiable good man he is!" he writes again; and
in 1786 he declares of the West Indian station, that "had
it not been for Collingwood it would have been the most
disagreeable I ever saw."

Wilfred Collingwood died at sea of consumption on the
21st of April, 1787, on board the *Rattler*, whilst heading

[1] Nelson's *Dispatches and Letters*, vol. i. p. 116.

for Grenada. Cuthbert was at home at the time, and Nelson thus wrote to his old friend about Wilfred's death: "To be the messenger of bad news is my misfortune, but still it is a tribute which friends owe each other. I have lost my friend—you an affectionate brother; too great a zeal in serving his country hastened his end. The greatest consolation the survivor could receive is a thorough knowledge of a life spent with honour to himself and of service to his country. If the tribute of tears be valuable, my friend has it." The following sentences are characteristic of Nelson: "The esteem he stood in with his Royal Highness[1] was great. His letter to me on his death is the strongest testimony of it. I send you an extract from it. 'Collingwood, poor fellow, is no more. I have cried for him; and most sincerely do I condole with you on his loss. In him his Majesty has lost a faithful servant, and the Service a most excellent officer.' A testimony of regard so honourable is more to be coveted than anything this world could have afforded, and must be a balm to his surviving friends." What wonderful loyalty there was in those days! It is said of Sam Pellew, Lord Exmouth's father, that it was his custom to make his children drink the King's health on their knees every Sunday![2] Nelson did not exaggerate; I can conceive Collingwood acquiescing with emotion in his friend's assurance that nothing in the world was to be more coveted than a sympathetic sentence from Royalty!

A glimpse of the character of Collingwood at this time is obtained from a letter written many years afterwards by Mrs. Moutray to Mrs. Newnham Collingwood: "Although," says she, "the vigour of his mind was soon discovered, there was a degree of reserve in his manner which pre-

[1] The Duke of Clarence (afterwards William IV.).
[2] Osler's *Life of Exmouth*, p. 4.

vented the playfulness of his imagination, and his powers
of adding charms to private society from being duly appreciated. But the intimacy of a long passage in his ship
gave us the good fortune to know him as he was, so that
after our arrival at Antigua, whenever he was at St. John's
or in English Harbour, he was as a beloved brother in our
house." [1]

The *Mediator* returned to England towards the close of
1786, from which date to 1790, Collingwood tells us he
was in Northumberland, "making my acquaintance with
my own family, to whom I had hitherto been as it were a
stranger." What is known in history as the Spanish
Armament, called him from the North to the command of
the *Mermaid* frigate. An officer in charge of two Spanish
ships-of-war had seized some British vessels lying at
Nootka Sound on the north-western coast of America,
and the crews of the ships were sent as prisoners to a
Spanish port. This act threatened a rupture with Spain.
Great Britain at once prepared for war, but the subsequent
conduct of Spain preserved the peace that then subsisted
between the two countries: at a cost, however, to this
country of three millions, though, as Brenton justly says,
the money was not uselessly spent, "since it brought
forward the naval service, which in a peace of seven years
had fallen much into disuse." [2] Collingwood in the *Mermaid* made one of a small squadron under Cornish (afterwards Admiral Sir Samuel Cornish), and sailed to the
West Indies; then returning, was paid off. Perceiving no
immediate prospect of obtaining employment at sea, "I
went into the North," says he briefly, "and was married."

[1] Mrs. Moutray was the wife of the Resident Naval Commissioner
at Antigua. Nelson's affectionate references to her will be found in
his correspondence.
[2] *Naval History*, vol. i. p. 71.

Portrait of Lady Collingwood.

In the *Newcastle Chronicle*, June 18th, 1791, appeared the following :—

"*Thursday, Captain Collingwood, of his Majesty's frigate* Mermaid, *to Miss Blackett, daughter of John Erasmus Blackett, Esq., the Right Worshipful Mayor of Newcastle.*"

The Blacketts are a distinguished family, who, as Mr. Clayton informs us, have for some centuries held the highest position in the commercial and mining transactions and territorial investments in the north of England.[1] Several baronetcies have belonged to the family, but all are extinct save that now held by General Sir Edward William Blackett, of Matfen. The Admiral's wife's grandfather was a younger brother of Sir Edward Blackett, fourth baronet.[2]

After his marriage Collingwood took a house at Morpeth, a pleasant little town, near which flows the river Wansbeck. This house he purchased some years later (in 1802). Writing to his wife's uncle, Sir Edward Blackett, from Spithead in that year, he says: "My wife has been very busy lately in making the purchase of our house at Morpeth; it was to be sold, and we must either have bought it or turned out. The situation is convenient for us, and so we bought it, and I feel a satisfaction now that we are not subject to be removed at the will of a landlord. On examining the house they tell me it is good

---

[1] *Archæologia Æliana.*

[2] Mrs. (afterwards Lady) Collingwood's mother was Miss Roddam, a daughter of Captain (afterwards Admiral) Roddam, who had received Cuthbert and Wilfred Collingwood on board the *Lenox.* There is an interesting account of John Erasmus Blackett in the autobiography of the Rev. Dr. Alexander Carlyle, who speaks of him as "a very handsome young man of about thirty, who had been bred at Liverpool with Sir — Cunliffe, and was now settled partner with Mr. Alderman Simson, an eminent coal-dealer in Newcastle. John Blackett was called Erasmus after Erasmus Lewis, who was secretary to Lord Oxford in Queen Anne's time."

and strong built, and will be a good house after our time." [1]
All who love and respect the memory of Collingwood
think with interest of his house at Morpeth. He saw but
little of it; but it was the home of his wife and his two
daughters, to whom he was for ever sending blessings in
the fond letters he addressed to them from distant seas.
No sailor's home that I can think of has such an atmosphere of pathetic association as this of Collingwood.
His heart was always there: his thoughts were for ever
with his beloved Sarah and his two little girls—on the
eve of battle—amidst the wretched monotony of blockading
—in the hour of decisive victory. Let us remember that
of the fifty years he passed in the navy, forty-four were
spent away from home; and that from 1793 till his death
in 1810, he was only for *one year* in England! One knows
not where to look for the like of such an absence in naval
annals, and it is this that communicates to Collingwood's
home the tenderness and beauty of sentiment one finds in
the thought of it. The house is still to be seen—of a
plain aspect, brick-built, a typical, commodious north-
country structure. The stream of the Wansbeck flows
near. In Lady Collingwood's time the country was open,
and the prospect from the windows just such a picture as a
man far away at sea would recall and muse upon with
delight and love.

His wife bore him two children, Sarah, born in May
1792, and Mary Patience in 1793; so that at his death
they were respectively eighteen and seventeen years old,
and had seen so little of him that it is almost possible to
imagine them meeting and not knowing him.

Nelson was also at home at this time devouring his
noble heart in the long spell of idleness forced upon him,

[1] From unpublished letters in possession of John C. Blackett, Esq.,
Thorpe Lea, Egham.

asking for even the command of a cock-boat, and getting nothing save soul-chilling replies from the Admiralty. "You must not be displeased," says Collingwood to his old friend, dating his letter at Morpeth, November 14th, 1792, "that I was so long without writing to you. I was very anxiously engaged a great part of the time, and perhaps sometimes a little lazy; but my regard for you, my dear Nelson, my respect and veneration for your character, I hope and believe will never be lessened. God knows when we may meet again, unless some chance should draw us to the seashore." [1]

For that chance he had now not very long to wait. On the 2nd of January, 1793, the British 12-gun brig-sloop *Childers*, commanded by Captain Robert Barlow, having stood in shore to Brest harbour—where, by the way, as Captain Brenton justly points out, she had no right to be [2]—was fired into by the batteries which guard the entrance to that port. This act of hostility confirmed the fears which had been current for months that war with France was inevitable. On the 21st of the same month Louis XVI. was beheaded, and M. Chauvelin, the French Ambassador at London, was ordered to quit England. The National Convention declared war (February 1st) against Great Britain and the United Netherlands. As though the French feared that these programmes would not provide

[1] Collingwood's tastes and perhaps his occupation to a certain extent, whilst he was at home at this time, are suggested in the following. Writing from Plymouth (December 24th, 1799) to Sir Edward Blackett, Bart., after speaking of the prospects of peace: "Then will I plant my cabbages again and prune my gooseberry trees, cultivate corn and twist the woodbine through the hawthorn hedge with as much satisfaction in my improvement as ever Diocletian had, and with the same desire and hope that the occasion never may occur again to call me back to more important but less pleasurable duties." (MS. letters in possession of J. C. Blackett, Esq.)
[2] *Naval History*, vol. i. p. 80.

them with throats enough to cut, they proceeded in the month of March to declare war against Spain; next against Portugal; and in a short time the kingdom of the two Sicilies was involved. Meanwhile, and before they had declared against Great Britain, they were at war with Austria, Prussia, and Sardinia. At the close of February, or in the beginning of March, a number of French line-of-battle ships assembled in Quiberon Bay, and by the end of August, the number amounted to 21 sail of the line; but they continued to lie at anchor in the Road of Belle-Isle, weighing at long intervals for a stretch across to the island of Groix. Owing to the demands made upon our naval forces by distant stations, this country was unable to assemble a fleet fit to cope with the French in Quiberon Bay until the month of July, when, on the 14th, Admiral Lord Howe set sail from St. Helen's with 15 ships of the line and some frigates and sloops.

Shortly after the breaking out of the war with France, Collingwood was called to the command of the *Prince*, carrying the flag of Rear-Admiral Bowyer. On July the 22nd, 1793, dating his letter on board the *Prince* at Spithead, he writes thus to his wife's uncle, Sir Edward Blackett :—

"I have been a tedious time in getting from Plymouth, and am at last arrived here very short of men, which seems a difficulty insurmountable. Lord Howe stripped everything here of their men to enable his ship to go to sea, to cover and protect the West Indian convoy which may be expected within this week from the Leeward Islands; Admiral Bowyer is left here to get his ship manned when he can, and then to join Lord Howe with such other ships as may be ready for sea. I do think (and it grieves me) that we do not manage our ships with that alacrity and promptness that used to distinguish our navy. There is a tardiness everywhere in the preparation, and a sluggishness in the execution that is quite new The effect is obvious to everybody, and the moment the ships are put in motion they feel it. Lord Howe cannot get down the Channel in fine weather, and the middle of summer, without an accident. Two ships ran foul of each other, and the *Bellerophon* has lost her foremast and bowsprit, and gone to Plymouth a cripple. This was not the fault of the weather, but must ever be the case when young men are made officers who have neither skill nor attention, and there is scarce a ship in the navy that has not an instance that political interest is a better argument or promotion than any skill. Sir John Laforey[1] is just arrived from the West Indies, and brings accounts from them, very different from our expectation. Instead of Martinique surrendering on the appearance of the English fleet, as had been represented by the aristocratic party, they found the Republicans so completely masters of the island, except of some very inconsiderable places, that nothing was likely to succeed but a regular attack by an army, and the last accounts to be had from Admiral Gardner's fleet were in an imperfect way, that the British troops had landed, been repulsed in several skirmishes, and again re-embarked. The *Duke*, a 90-gun ship, had her mainmast rent by lightning, and so ill-provided were our stores there, that there is not another in the country to replace it. The fleet at Gibraltar, whenever they want refitting, will find the same there. I assure you, sir, I perceive a languor in all our operations that deprives me of many a good hour's sleep."[2]

[1] Vice-Admiral Sir John Laforey, who had his flag on board the 50-gun ship *Trusty*, Captain John Drew ; "which," says James, "with a small frigate and two or three sloops, was all the British force" on the West Indian station before the arrival of Rear-Admiral Gardner, who succeeded him.

[2] From letters in possession of J. C. Blackett, Esq.

CHAPTER II.

Skirmishing—The *Barfleur*—Hood at Toulon—Fleet sails—Codrington on Howe—Howe before the Battle—Collingwood's Account of the 1st of June—No Medal—Molloy of the *Cæsar*—Sir Roger Curtis' Letter—Collingwood's Grief and Mortification.

DURING the rest of the year whilst the fleet under Howe kept the sea, there was one trifling skirmish and much cruising. Nothing of consequence, nothing in any way decisive happened. In the middle of December Howe returned with the fleet to Spithead. In a letter dated December the 27th, Collingwood gives the following account to Sir Edward Blackett of the proceedings of the fleet:—

"I should have wrote to you before this if I had not known that you would hear the history of our cruise from Mr. Henry Blackett, and indeed there is so little in it worth note that there was nothing to lament if you had never heard it. It was a series of vexations, disappointments, and bad weather. What is more mortifying than all these is to find on our return that to be unfortunate is to be criminal, and that want of success where it was

scarce to be expected is treated with all the severity of
censure of a high offence. I believe no man can serve on
a more honourable principle than Lord Howe does. To
do good service to his country is the first ambition of his
life, but he has no supernatural powers, on a winter's day,
to make the sun stand still, or make an English ship sail
fast and a French ship ill. Considering the great distance
they were from us in the morning, some great stroke of
good luck only would have brought us up with them. It
is true two or three of our very fast sailers did get near
them, but in doing that they lost our own fleet and never
joined us again.[1] There was no want of exertion. The
Admiral made every signal that the case seemed to require,
and the ships carried sail until three of them lost their
topmasts and were disabled. The French got round us
very cleverly, and the next day it seems, while we were
chasing them to the southward, they were jogging on to
the north, having passed us in the dark. I hope the next
time we meet we shall have better luck. The *Prince* is
the most miserable sailer in the fleet, for ever in the rear,
and has been a constant fret and torment to us. We have
tried every means, to no purpose—always bad—but, however, now we are done with her. Admiral Bowyer has
influence with Lord Chatham to get another ship, which
is reckoned a better; we are about changing her for the
Barfleur. I am already appointed to her, but shall not
take up my commission until this ship is cleared, which I
hope will be next week, and that we shall have the *Barfleur*

---

[1] This refers to the skirmish on November 18th, when the French
ships, mistaking Lord Howe's fleet for a merchant convoy, bore down
and were chased by the *Russel, Audacious, Defence, Bellerophon,*
and *Ganges*. The only ship that seems to have got near the enemy
was the *Latona* frigate. Several of the pursuing craft sprung their
spars, and the ships in consequence were obliged to bear up for the
Channel.

ready to sail with the fleet. I assure you amongst them I have as much business as I can manage." After a touching reference to his wife and family in the North—"all my troubles here seem light when I look northward and consider how well I am rewarded for them "—he adds: "I consider the railing at Lord Howe, who is no favourite with the ministers, and firing the Tower guns for successes which appear to me very trifling, a trick to engage the attention of the people and keep them from prying into miscarriages of more consequence. Our trade has been totally cut up on the coast of America by two large ships and six frigates, French. I believe we saved Sir J. Jervis and a convoy from Lisbon by dispersing the squadron we met." [1]

In March Collingwood was still at Spithead, but by this time the *Barfleur* [2] is ready for sea, Admiral Bowyer has shifted his flag to her, and our hero, dating his letter in this ship on the 2nd of that month, writes thus to Sir Edward Blackett:

"For this month past I have been in daily expectation that I should have been able to tell you what was to be our destination; but as it is yet as little known to us as ever, I will no longer delay to thank you for your very

---

[1] Letters in possession of J. C. Blackett, Esq.

[2] An interest of a peculiar kind attached to this ship, which was built at Chatham in 1768. When George III. visited Portsmouth in 1773 to inspect the fleet that had assembled there in force, he went on board the *Barfleur*, "where he kept his table for some time." It is said that the King had never before seen his ships assembled in any force. The French Ambassador, who accompanied him, exclaimed, "I have now seen two of the most famous sights in the world : the King of Prussia at the head of his army and the King of England at the head of his fleet." The *Barfleur* was Sir Samuel Hood's flagship in his action with Du Grasse. She also, as we shall see, bore Bowyer's flag on the 1st of June. She was in the action of the 23rd, 1795, and bore Admiral Waldegrave's flag on the 14th February, 1797. She was, in a word, an historic bruiser of the old sort, her tonnage, 1947, and her length a few inches over 177 feet.

kind letter. I have lately had a great deal of employment and trouble in dismantling the dull *Prince* and equipping this ship, which, however, was accomplished long before she was wanted. I hope her good qualities will reward our trouble. Admiral Bowyer has command of eight sail of the line to be ready to go out on the shortest notice; but of what nature our service is to be, whether to convoy the trade out or to execute any other scheme, we have no hint. The trade has hitherto been generally left to the care of Providence, and our plans are so often varied that it is not improbable that we may stay here for the summer sun to gild our achievements. This war is certainly unlike any former, both in its object and execution; the object is a great and serious one—to resist the machinations of a mad people, who, under the mask of freedom, would stamp their tyranny in every country in Europe, and support and defend the happiest constitution that ever wisdom formed for preserving order in civil society. The execution is quite mysterious; great fleets are prepared and lay totally inactive; schemes of conquests are formed and relinquished at the moment when execution is expected. Lord Moira's army and Admiral Gardner's fleet are both withdrawn from their intended purpose, and it seems now we are to abandon all other plans and stand on our defence. By all accounts we are to expect an attack, and I expect it will terminate as happily as can be wished in so total a discomfiture of the enemy that they will sue for peace." He then refers to the proceedings of the British fleet at Toulon: "Our miscarriage at Toulon is truly provoking, the more so as gross mismanagement alone could have prevented its being totally destroyed. Lord Hood was in good luck to get possession of it, but was not general enough to discover how critical his situation was there, nor I believe were they at all aware of it until O'Hara arrived.

No preparation was made for the destruction either of ships or arsenal; and at last perhaps it was put into as bad hands as could be found—Sir Sidney Smith, who arrived there a few days before, and had no public situation either in the fleet or army, but was wandering to gratify his curiosity—you know how it was executed. The ships should have been prepared for sinking as soon as he got possession of them, loading them deep with ballast and stones, and making a porthole in them near the edge of the water; and then place the ships in those parts of the harbour which would most effectually injure it. If the necessity for sinking the ships did not arise they would be uninjured: if it did they might have all been put under water in half an hour." [1]

The judgment exhibited in these remarks is a striking proof of the qualities and genius which Collingwood would have exhibited had he been entrusted with enterprises of great moment. To distress the enemy to the very uttermost degree, yet to render his distress subservient in the most practical sense to British interests: this is the true signification of Collingwood's reference to the destruction of the French ships at Toulon. And that he should have thus written and thus thought must surely satisfy us that he perfectly well knew what he was about when after the Battle of Trafalgar he ordered the prizes to be sunk and otherwise destroyed. "The squadron in the Mediterannean are very much in the dumps," he adds. "Lord H.'s [2]

[1] According to James's *Amended Statement* the number of ships burnt was 14; but in Steel's *Naval Chronologist* (1793—1801) it is stated that eight ships were destroyed by Captain C. Hare, two by Lieutenants Middleton and Stiles, one by Lieutenant Miller, two by Lieutenants Pater and Miller, and four by Captain W. Edge and Lieutenant Tupper—17 in all, exclusive of those burnt by the Spaniards and Sardinians.

[2] Hood. Yet Nelson spoke of Lord Hood as the greatest sea-officer of the age.

ambition far exceeding his abilities, gives rise to many unpleasant circumstances. Sir Hyde Parker, his first captain,
has left him, and hoisted his flag in the *Bedford*.   In all
our operations there is nothing pleasurable to be found."

On the 2nd of May, probably one of the finest spectacles
ever witnessed was to be seen at St. Helen's, where there
having happened a shift of wind into the north-east, 148
sail, of which 34 were of the line, got under way.   They
were formed of the fleet under Lord Howe and a convoy.
When, on the 4th, the merchantmen had parted company,
Howe's fleet was reduced by the detachment of Rear-
Admiral Montagu, with six line-of-battle ships and two
frigates, to convoy the traders to the latitude of Cape
Finisterre.   Howe's force now consisted of 26 sail of the
line, seven frigates, and a few other craft of several de-
nominations.   Collingwood, as we have seen, had shifted
from the *Prince* into the *Barfleur*, that was flying Rear-
Admiral George Bowyer's flag.   Nothing material happened
till the 16th, when the French fleet of 25 ships of the line
under Villaret-Joyeuse, with whom as deputy or spy was
Jean-Bon Saint-André, sailed from Brest; and next day,
as it turned out, in so dense a fog that the forecastle of a
ship was not to be seen from her poop, the enemy passed
close enough to the British fleet to hear the bells and
drums which were being rung and beaten as fog-signals;
yet when the weather cleared on the following morning
the two fleets were out of sight of each other.

On the 28th, twenty-six sail of French liners with five
frigates hove into view, and on this and the following day
there was some hard fighting.   Howe seems to have gone
into battle as though suspicious of his captains.   On one
of these two days Lieutenant Codrington said to him, " I
suppose, my Lord, from what you were saying lately, if we
come up with the French fleet at night you will attack

them at once ? " Howe replied, " No; I require daylight
to see how my own captains conduct themselves." [1] It is
not necessary to read very far into the life of Sir Edward
Codrington to discover his willingness that the world should
believe the battle of the 1st of June was almost entirely
won by the *Queen Charlotte*, Howe's flag-ship, aboard
which Codrington was junior lieutenant in the action.
On the morning of the 30th the fog was still very thick,
and the British ships scattered in consequence. The
French had vanished; but on the 31st the weather again
cleared, and the English ships of war made sail for their
stations.

Whilst this was doing the French were descried in the
North, and though some of them had suffered more or less
severely in the previous engagements, nearly the whole of
them, to the surprise of the British, appeared in a perfect
state.[2] Codrington paints a lively picture of the scene as
it appeared to him on the morning of the 31st—"Upon
Sir Roger Curtis going into the cabin at daylight on the
31st to make his report to Lord Howe, I, being officer of
the watch, lifted up the canvas screen by which alone the
cabin (then cleared for action) was divided from the
quarter-deck, for him to enter. Lord Howe was in his
great-coat, sitting in an arm-chair, his only resting-place
from the time of our falling in with the enemy, and the
following dialogue took place: ' Well, sir, how is the
weather ? ' ' My Lord, I am sorry to tell you that the fog
is now so thick that we cannot see anything beyond our
own ship;' adding, ' and God knows whether we are standing into our own fleet, or that of the enemy.' I can never
forget the contrast of Lord Howe's answer: ' Well, sir,
it can't be helped; we must wait with patience till the

[1] *Memoir of Sir Edward Codrington*, p. 21.
[2] *James*, i. 160.

weather improves.' Instead of shyness or nervousness in these trying circumstances, Lord Howe evinced a heroic fortitude which may have been equalled but never can have been exceeded. Upon the fog clearing up about one o'clock in the afternoon, the French fleet were seen to leeward, showing every symptom of determination to sustain a battle. I watched Lord Howe's countenance when this report brought him to the quarter-deck to look at them; it expressed an animation of which, at his age and after such fatigue of body and mind, I had not thought it capable." [1] It would be interesting to know what sort of expression Lieutenant Codrington expected to find in the old Admiral's face, at which he appears to have stared.

The memorable battle was fought next day, the 1st of June. The following is Collingwood's account of it in a letter to Sir Edward Blackett: " *Barfleur*, June 15th, 1794. Dear Sir,—Thank you for your kind letter and congratulations. I supposed you were probably gone into Northumberland or would have wrote to you immediately on my arrival, for well am I assured of the pleasure you have in my welfare and success. We have, with God's blessing, obtained as complete a victory as ever was won at sea; and I hope it will be happy in its consequences to this country. But at the time we have so much to rejoice at, I have much to lament in the sufferings of my friends, particularly Admiral Bowyer, whose misfortune [2] has quite checked joy in me. He is a brave and gallant man, and was so raised by the success of the day that he made his own misfortune of little consideration; and I believe he would have done himself material injury by his spirits if I had not at last shut him up and prohibited everybody but the surgeon and necessary attendants going near him. We carried him on shore yesterday,

[1] *Memoir of Sir Edward Codrington*, p. 28.
[2] The loss of his leg.

D

and I hope he is in a favourable way. It was early in the action when he was wounded by a great shot, and I caught him in my arms before he fell to the deck. It is a great misfortune to me: for the more we were engaged in business the more we were attached, and I believed he had full and implicit confidence in me. We who were seamen were well acquainted with the great professional abilities of Lord Howe; but he has outdone all opinion that could be formed. The proceedings of the 1st of June were like magic, and could only be effected by skill like his. I scarce know how to give you an account of it. You have seen in his letter what information he had previous to our meeting the evening the 28th of May. They were to windward, and that day we were employed in getting near them. Our advanced squadron, commanded by Admiral Pasley, in the evening brought their rear into action. Not more than five of our ships were engaged, but after dark the *Révolutionnaire*, of 120 guns,[1] struck; though, from unlucky circumstances, she was afterwards lost to us.[2] On the 29th, in the morning, they were still about four miles to windward of us, and showed no disposition to come to close action, but to attack us in their way at long shot. That would not do. At 12 o'clock the Admiral made the signal for our van to tack and pass through their line. They could not pass their line, but Admiral Gardner, who now led the line, closed with their rear, who sustained the whole fire of our line in passing them, and suffered very much; three of them were quite wrecks.

"*Barfleur* was at that time in the rear, but on our closing

[1] 110?

[2] James says the *Révolutionnaire* became no prize to the British, owing partly to the disabled state of the *Audacious*, but chiefly because the *Thunderer*, on approaching the latter and being hailed to take possession of the French ship, made sail after her own fleet.—Vol. i. 147.

with one of their ships our fire was such that it is astonishing how she swam after it. They returned very little, and we sustained no injury of consequence. The French made a good manœuvre by which they covered the ships we had bore hard on, and made a bold push at the *Queen* and *Invincible*, two of ours that had suffered. Admiral Graves wore, and we after him—closing with the enemy's van, and turning them to leeward of the disabled *Queen*, so that she did not receive a shot from them. Foiled in this attempt, they bore away to repair their ships, three of which were quite like wrecks. It was then too late in the day to do anything decisive, and the various movements we had made had put us out of order. The 30th and 31st were foggy days, and superior as the French were, they would have gone off, I believe, had not the guillotine hung over their heads. We were now to windward, and time and manner of engaging was at our command. The afternoon of the 31st was fine weather, and both sides were employed in forming their order of battle—and in the evening we were ready—about three miles to windward, they impatiently waiting the morning to destroy us, which their superiority in force made them confident of; we—to do our duty faithfully to our country.

"After closing our line, and putting in order, between eight and nine the Admiral made the signal for each ship to engage that opposed in the enemy's, Came close [1]—and in an instant all the ships altering their course at the same time, down we went on them. 'Twas a noble sight! Their fire soon began, we reserved ours until we were so near that it was proper to cloud our ships in smoke. However, we were determined not to fire until Lord Howe had, and he is not in the habit of firing soon. In three minutes our whole line was engaged—and a better fire was never. It

[1] So in original.

continued with unabated fury for near two hours, when the
French broke. When we had engaged for three-quarters
of an hour they called from the forecastle that the ship to
leeward of us was sinking. Up started all the Johnnies
from their guns and gave three cheers. I saw through the
smoke a wreck lying—but she was covered in an instant
with the smoke. I did not see her sink. Nine of their
ships had not a stick left as long as my finger. Three
others had lost two masts each; their frigates got hold of
them and towed them off; seven were left to us, but the
Vengeur sank in the evening. You may suppose we were
not in a condition for pursuit. We reckon they had 300
guns more in their line of battle than we had." [1]

In one of the most charming letters in the language,
Collingwood, writing at sea June 5th, ten days earlier than
the date of the above communication, tells the story of the
famous fight to his father-in-law, Mr. J. E. Blackett: "The
night," he says, "was spent in watching and preparation
for the succeeding day; and many a blessing did I send
forth to my Sarah, lest I should never bless her more;"
and a little later on he adds, referring to the morning of
the 1st: "It was then near ten o'clock. I observed to
the Admiral that about that time our wives were going
to church, but that I thought the peal we should ring
about the Frenchmen's ears would outdo the parish
bells." [2]

[1] From letters in the possession of J. C. Blackett, Esq. I congratulate myself on the privilege of printing for the first time this graphic and admirable description of the battle.

[2] The great novelist, W. M. Thackeray, after quoting from this letter, exclaims: "There are no words to tell what the heart feels in reading the simple phrases of such a hero. Here is victory and courage, but love sublime and superior. Here is a Christian soldier spending the night before battle in watching and preparing for the succeeding day, thinking of his dearest home, and sending many blessings forth to his Sarah, 'lest he should never bless her more.'

In Lord Howe's dispatch supplementing his letter of
the 2nd of June, the names of a number of officers. were
given who had, as he said, a particular claim to his attention. To these officers medals were presented, but Collingwood's, together with some other names, did not appear
in the list, and these officers received no medals. The
Admiral in his dispatch explained that the commander of
a fleet is unavoidably so confined in his view of the
occurrences in time of battle as to be little capable of
rendering personal testimony to the service of officers who
distinguish themselves. "To discharge this part of my
public duty," Howe says, "reports were called for from the
flag-officers of the fleet for supplying the defects of my
observance." It seems clear from this that it was in the
power of Rear-Admiral Bowyer to have so named Collingwood to the Commander-in-chief as to ensure him a medal.
What Bowyer thought of Collingwood's conduct during
the action may be gathered from his letter to Admiral
Roddam, in which he says, dating from Cowes, October
11th, 1794: "I write you this letter that I may not lose
the satisfaction I always feel in doing justice to the merit
of a friend of yours, which I hardly do, in saying that I do
not know a more brave, capable, or a better officer in all
respects than Captain Collingwood. I think him a very
fine character; and I told Lord Chatham when he was at
Portsmouth, that if ever he had to look for a first captain
to a commander-in-chief, he would not find a better than
our friend Collingwood." [1] This being so, why did not
Bowyer say as much to Lord Howe in June, instead of
waiting until October to privately communicate his senti-

Who would not say Amen to his supplication? It was a benediction
to his country—the prayer of that intrepid, loving heart."—*The
Four Georges.*
[1] *Correspondence and Memoir of Lord Collingwood*, p. 24.

ments to Roddam? It is true the gallant officer had lost his leg; he might for some weeks after the action have been too ill to make any sign; but even when he had recovered, he, who as one of the flag-officers in the battle had surely the power to influence by his representations and obtain justice for Collingwood by a plain and direct avowal of fact, does not appear to have exerted himself to the extent of penning or dictating a syllable. He had been disabled early in the action, and during the remainder of the engagement the *Barfleur* was fought by Colling-wood; yet one of the most heroic of the captains in that famous fight received no mention, obtained no medal, and was mortified and insulted by a slight amounting, to his sensitiveness at all events, and in the opinion of his friends, to the imputation of undutifulness—to say no more.

Bowyer received a medal; he was perhaps an econo-mist in his theories of honours and rewards, and might hold that the gift of two medals to one ship would be an extravagance. "If Collingwood," Captain Packenham of the *Invincible* said, "has not deserved a medal, neither have I, for we were together the whole day."[1] Captain Anthony J. P. Molloy, of the *Cæsar*, was one of the officers whose names were omitted; and he demanded a court-martial. His request was that he should be tried for his behaviour on the 29th of May. Lord Howe wished that Molloy's conduct on the 1st of June should be in-cluded. The significance of the Admiral's reference to the *Cæsar* in his supplementary letter justified Captain Molloy's demand for a court-martial. After saying that the signal for passing through the enemy's line was renewed, Lord Howe continued: "It could not be for some time seen, through the fire from the two fleets in the van, to what extent that signal was complied with. But

[1] *Correspondence and Memoir*, p. 24.

as the smoke at intervals dispersed; it was observed that
the *Cæsar*, the leading ship of the British van, after being
about on the starboard tack, and come abreast of the *Queen
Charlotte*, had not kept to the wind ; and that the appointed
movement would consequently be liable to fail of the
purposed effect." An order for a court-martial was granted,
but it was not held until April 1795. Molloy's personal
courage was pronounced unimpeachable, but his behaviour
on the 29th of May was disapproved of, and he was
dismissed from the command of the *Cæsar*.

The remarks of Captain Isaac Schomberg on this unfortunate business are full of dignity and wholly to the
point : " The meritorious conduct of these officers (meaning
those who received the medal) was no doubt highly deserving of so distinguished a mark of Royal favour; how
far such selections may be consistent with the well-being
of so important a service as that of the British Navy, in
which every officer is supposed on like occasions to act to
the best of his abilities, needs no comment; if in the
presence of an enemy or in action a commander appears
deficient either in courage or conduct, it is more candid
and decided in a commander-in-chief to have such
conduct investigated before a public tribunal than leave
a doubt on the minds of his country by such oblique
insinuations as that some have fallen short in their
duty." [1]

We shall now see what Collingwood thought of Howe's
treatment of those whose names he had omitted :

To Sir Edward Blackett, Bart.

"*Barfleur, June 30th*, 1794.

" Dear Sir,

" I hope you will excuse my not having answered
your very kind letter before this, but really I have been

[1] *Naval Chronology*, 2, p. 270.

so engaged, first in preparing for the King and lately in
attending him, that I have scarce had time to write a note
to Sarah to tell her I was well. But now to answer the
latter part of your letter. I will take Mr. Wise into my
ship with a great deal of pleasure, rate him midshipman,
and do everything in my power to bring him forward in
the service, and doubt not, notwithstanding Lord Howe's
supplemental letter, he may learn his duty in my ship as
an officer as well as any other. That extraordinary pro-
duction of Sir Roger's[1] pen threw the fleet into the
utmost consternation and astonishment. There was not
a cool heart amongst us before, except Molloy's, whose
conduct is past defence; and though the situation of the
ships in so large a fleet must necessarily be very different
on such a day, there was not, I believe, a suspicion in the
mind of any man that all had not done their duty well.
The appearance of that letter had nearly broke my heart;
but I still trusted that facts would stand their ground
against any insinuations to their disadvantage. I went
immediately to Sir Roger Curtis and demanded to see
Lord Howe (who, however, I have not yet seen with
opportunity to talk of the subject). I told Sir Roger that
I considered the conduct of the *Barfleur* had merited
commendation when commendation was given to zeal and
activity; and that an insinuation that either had been
wanting was injurious and unjust. Nor do I believe any
ship was more warmly or effectively engaged than the
Barfleur from the beginning of the action to the end of it.
That the Frenchmen did not knock our masts away was
not my fault.

"He assured me that no disapprobation was meant to be
implied, but that in the selections the Admiral was pleased

[1] Sir Roger Curtis. He was first captain to Lord Howe on board
the *Queen Charlotte.*

to make he must stop somewhere, and the good conduct of
the fleet was summed up in a latter sentence. All that
could be said to that was that it was a most unfortunate
style.[1]

"Those who are mentioned in his letter were almost as
much offended at the manner as those who were omitted.
The King arrived on Thursday, and we all attended in our
barges to escort his Majesty, the Queen, &c., to Lord
Howe's ship in great parade. There, I understand, great
ceremonies passed of congratulation, and Lord Howe was
presented with a diamond sword. In the evening we
attended him on shore, and it was notified that the King
would have a levée the following day on shore. The
better (not being admitted on board his Majesty's ship
whilst his flag was flying) to pay our duty to him, and
witness the honour he was doing the Admiral, had soured
the minds of everybody;[2] and while the nation were
rejoicing in a great victory, those who had won it seemed
alone dejected and sad. On Friday morning, when we
were assembled in a room to be first presented to his
Majesty, Lord Hugh Seymour represented to Lord Howe
how justly the officers of the navy were dissatisfied with
their treatment. They had hoped that when his Majesty
did them the honour to hoist his flag in the fleet, they
should not have been by order excluded from his presence;
that nothing could have been more gratifying to them
than to witness the honours conferred on *him* which he

[1] Nothing indeed could be more unfortunate, for, after condemning
the behaviour of officers by the negative censure of silence, Howe's
letter proceeded: "These selections, however, should not be construed to the disadvantage of other commanders who may have been
equally deserving of the approbation of the Lords Commissioners of
the Admiralty, although I am not enabled to make a particular
statement of their merits."

[2] So in original.

had so justly merited; that the world understood the King was come to do honour to his fleet; that while officers of inferior rank in other corps had been received into his ship, *they* were positively excluded, and he knew of no honour the officers of the navy had received by his presence, unless sitting in a boat four hours was an honour.

"Lord H. defended himself as well as he could, and in conclusion said he would remain no longer in the fleet than he could give general satisfaction. We were then introduced to the King and Queen, and had the honour of kissing hands. On Saturday he sailed in a frigate, and they ran her on shore near the Isle of Wight.[1] On Sunday we all dined with his Majesty, and, surpassing my expectation, had a very pleasant day. He was cheerful and good-humoured to all, and there was as little ceremony as at the table of a private gentleman. This morning they went in a frigate to Southampton, and there I understand were to proceed for Windsor. He has made a promotion to Captain John Harvey, who, however, poor man, is dead to-day of his wounds. Admiral Graves is to be made a peer if he chooses, and Sir Alex. Hood

---

[1] Lady Mary Howe, writing to her sister, Lady Altamont, from Portsmouth, July 2nd, in this year, says: "The next day the King held a levée at the governor's, where all the officers of the fleet were presented separately to the King and Queen, and the gold chains given to the Admirals, after which the King gave a dinner to the Admirals —mamma, Lady Pitt, and I dining with the Queen; and in the evening the Royals went on board the prizes in the harbour; but there mamma and I did not attend them. On Saturday they sailed about and dined on board the *Aquilon*, which struck upon the Motherbank, and we were obliged to come home in boats about nine o'clock, having passed a most delightful day and with the finest weather possible."—Barrow's *Life of Earl Howe*, p. 283. There is a wonderful freshness in the whole of this letter. It might have been written yesterday. One lives and moves in the past in reading such compositions; and as illustrations of naval history they are incomparable—only unhappily they are few.

a peer of Ireland. They intended Admiral Bowyer to be created a baronet, but as he is already in succession to an old baronetage, he declines. Admiral Gardner is made Major-General of Marines, a new appointment with twelve or fourteen hundred a year. There are also some promotions of captains and lieutenants—an Admiral will certainly come to this ship, and Lord Chatham has promised that I shall have a good ship of such rate as my rank entitles me to.

" Lord Howe is less blamed for his letter than his captain, who has ever been an artful, sneaking creature, whose fawning, insinuating manner creeps into the confidence of whoever he attacks, and whose rapacity would grasp all honours and all profits that come within his view.[1] The letter was an attempt upon the credulity of the world to make them believe the *Queen Charlotte* with very little help defeated the French fleet. It may be considered a libel on the fleet." [2]

The story of Collingwood's life at this period is continued in the following letter, dated Portsmouth, August 7th, 1794, and addressed to Sir Edward Blackett:

"I cannot tell you how very thankful I am for your two very kind letters which I have received since I wrote to you last; the first was a great comfort to me, and came

[1] Sir Roger Curtis is here meant. Lord Howe, in his private letter to Lord Chatham, says: " Being very much fatigued with our last five or six days' (and I may without impropriety add as many nights') employment, I must beg you will allow me to refer you to Sir Roger Curtis for any particulars you may desire to be informed of, which are unnoticed respecting the late operations of the fleet in my official letter."—Barrow's *Life of Earl Howe*, p. 250. Codrington, too, has his fling at Sir Roger: " The *Pegasus* never got any credit from Sir R. Curtis, Captain Barlow being one of Lord Howe's favourites, and Sir R. C. always wishing to detract from them and not allow them to be favourites."—*Memoir*, p. 16.

[2] Letters in possession of J. C. Blackett, Esq.

to me at a time when I very much wanted it, for in my life I never met with any circumstance that gave me such mortification and exquisite pain of mind as that ill-conceived report of Lord Howe's. It was as much as I could bear, and had I not trusted the truth and facts that had evidence enough in the fleet would stand their ground against any injurious insinuations, I should have sunk with grief, and I really had not spirits to write to anybody until my sky opened out a little.

" Lord Chatham, when at Portsmouth, took some pains to get information on the subject, and before he left sent me a message that I should be employed in a ship proper to my rank. When I went to London, he sent for me, and offered me the command of any 74 that was vacant. *Hector* and *Edgar* were quite ready, and I chose the *Hector* as being at this port. Admiral Montagu was to remove from her, which would probably take ten days or a fortnight, and I was determined at that time to see my good little wife and family in Northumberland. Short as my visit was, I was rewarded by finding them in great comfort, and my little daughters as fine healthy children as ever the sun shone on. We had scarce time to express our joy at meeting, before I received an order from the Admiralty to repair hither and take the command of my ship. I fully intended to pay a visit to you in my way, but when I came to London found my commission sent to Portsmouth, waiting to be dated for my arrival, when the other officers of the ship were to be appointed. I did not choose, particularly at this time, to be missing for an hour, and so made the best of my way and have now taken possession of my ship. We have no men; but as all the ships we can muster will be wanted, I am in hopes it will not be long before I get out.

" I went yesterday to visit Lord Howe at Spithead, who

received me very graciously; lamented that the Admiralty had put new officers into the fleet who were unacquainted with his signals and general discipline, and hoped my ship would soon be in a condition to join him. I have told him how much I have been disappointed and hurt after all the exertion I was capable of by not having obtained that testimony of his approbation which he had given to others, and which I hoped for; but doubted not on some future day it would not be denied. He talked of the disadvantages the fleet laboured under by the windward situation of the enemy, and what we should have done if we had had the good fortune to have had the wind of them at first meeting —steering clear of any explanation which related particularly to me. I believe he heartily wishes his letter had never been wrote."[1]

I can find nothing of interest in relation to Collingwood's command of the *Hector*. His next ship was the *Excellent*, of 74 guns, eight years old at this time, and of a burthen, according to the measurement of that period, of 1614 tons. In August 1795 he arrived at Leghorn, and in a letter dated the 31st of that month, congratulates himself on having "Brought all my convoy safe without damage of any kind or loss of one." Elsewhere in this letter he says: "We do not know what to make of the Spaniards. We hear they have 18 sail of the line cruising off Cape St. Sebastian. I feel exceedingly relieved that I have got my convoy safe off my hands. I seldom slept more than two hours at a time all the way out, and took such true care of my charge that not one was missing. All the masters came on board my ship to thank me for my care and attention to their safety."[2]

[1] Original in possession of J. C. Blackett, Esq.   [2] MS. letters.

CHAPTER III.

THE anxiety and worry of convoying is scarcely to be realized in these days of peace and of steam. Figure seventy or eighty sail of ships: many of them heavy, lumbering, round-bowed old merchantmen, so shaped in beam and length that they might have been built by the league and sawed off as customers required them. A dozen ships at a time would be lagging; the naval officer in command would signal them—but to no purpose: the sour old merchant skipper, wrapped up in pilot-cloth, eyed the epaulet askant, and sulkily went to work to give as much trouble as possible. Meanwhile there was not only an enemy's fleet to be feared, but swarms of privateersmen who hovered on the skirts of the slow-sailing commercial craft, cutting off one after another in the dead of night, and often in the full glare of day, yet with such agility, with such skilful ocean manœuvring, as to keep the naval officer sweeping the sea-line with a telescope at his eye in perplexity, until the sudden staggering away of the captured vessel on an easy bowline left him in no doubt as to what had happened.

Having filled his fresh-water casks at St. Fiorenzo, at which place the *Excellent* had arrived on the 23rd August, 1795, Collingwood sailed for Leghorn on the 27th, and joined the fleet under Admiral Hotham. In a letter to Sir Edward Blackett, dated at this port, he thus refers to the engagement that had occurred in the previous month :—

" On the 13th of last month they [the British fleet] had an action with the French fleet, but the issue of it has not given much satisfaction to the officers. I have heard little from them, because sensible people are guarded in their conversation when there is no subject for praise ; but I can understand it was one of those fortunate opportunities which do not often happen, to strike a strong and decisive blow, and was not made all the use of that might have been. I understand our fleet saw the French between three and four o'clock in the morning, before daylight. It blew hard, and the French were to the leeward, about four miles ; in the night they had separated so as to make two distinct parts, and it appeared easy to place the English fleet so as to prevent their junction, if not to stop them all. They stood towards the land ; we stood from it ; several of our ships had split their sails in the night—and the position of the English fleet was not altered till about six o'clock, by which time they had increased the distance so much that it was one o'clock before our head-most and best-sailing ships got up, and as they drew towards the land the wind fell away almost calm. The *Alcide* struck, was set on fire by accident, and burnt ; near 300 of her men were saved by the English boats; the rest of the enemy's ships got in with the shore, and our ships were called in.

"We should be careful and slow in censure, because men of weakest judgment are most prompt to question what perhaps their want of intelligence makes them not comprehend—and in this instance because the commander [1] has been esteemed a skilful and good officer—yet the opportunity seemed a good one to ruin the French naval forces in this country."

His life at this time, whilst the *Excellent* formed one of the fleet that was guarding Corsica and blockading Toulon, is to be gathered in part from passages in his correspondence. On March the 14th he writes from Ajaccio, Corsica, to his father-in-law that there were 17 sail of the line lying at Toulon, apparently ready for sea; that on the night of the 27th of February, in a squall, when it was very dark and wet, the *Princess Royal* ran into the *Excellent* and almost wrecked her aloft. He was on deck, and luckily saw the liner thundering into him, with foam to the hawsepipe, and a shift of the helm saved the *Excellent* from being cut down to the water's edge. His skill as a seaman served him well here; it may be said, indeed, that in the art of handling a ship, in the knowledge of every professional essential that could qualify a man whether for the work of an able seaman forward or for the duties of a commander on his quarter-deck aft, Collingwood had not his equal in the navy. The two ships had scarcely gone clear, and the *Excellent* had barely cut away the wreck of her masts, when it came on to blow a hard gale of wind that drove her into the Gulf of Lyons on a

[1] Vice-Admiral, afterwards Lord, Hotham. "By dint of sheer interest he got himself made an Irish peer," says James or his editor. *Naval History*, i. 306.

lee-shore. The fleet dared not stay, and a frigate was left to attend the liner. After many attempts Collingwood got his ship's head round, and then, under jury-masts, succeeded in making the port of Ajaccio on the 3rd of March. "Since that time," he adds, "my cares and anxiety to get ready have really been very painful to me. I have been forty-eight hours on deck, and scarce sat in that time to eat; I am not much the fatter for it, nor a bit the worse, thanks to a good hard constitution."

Admiral Hotham struck his flag on the 1st of November, 1795, and returned to England. Both Collingwood and Nelson, in a contemptuous sort of way, regarded him as a very good sort of man, of talents, as a sea-officer, merely respectable. He was succeeded by Vice-Admiral Sir Hyde Parker. On the 30th Admiral Sir John Jervis arrived in the frigate *Lively*, and on the 3rd of December shifted his flag to the *Victory*, and ten days later sailed with the fleet for Toulon. The dullness of blockading speedily made itself felt. No man was to have a larger share in this wretched monotonous work than Collingwood. "It is not a service on which we shall get fat," he writes to his father-in-law, May 11th, 1796, "and often do I wish we had some of those bad potatoes which old Scott and William used to throw over the wall in the garden, for we feel the want of vegetables more than anything."[1]

Writing on August 27th to Sir Edward Blackett, and dating his letter aboard the *Excellent*, still off Toulon, Collingwood says: "The enemy seems to have given up all naval operations in this sea. Since we came here in April we have kept our station so close to the port that the moment they pass from under the protection of their forts we are ready for them. So impatient does the Admiral appear to get at them, that were they to venture

[1] *Correspondence and Memoir*, p. 29.

E

from their anchorage the protection of such forts as they have along the shore would not much avail them. They have had an equal number of ships to ours when the detachments were away, but I fancy find it easier to discipline men to their army than qualify them for the various duties of the navy. Our fleet is in excellent order, well provided with everything, in which the Admiral, Sir J. Jervis, takes wonderful pains, and the consequence is we are remarkably healthy after being twenty-eight weeks at sea." [1]

The ships' companies, however, aboard the British liners at this time appear to have been somewhat oddly recruited. The French were collecting all the Austrian deserters and prisoners at Genoa for their army, but the British stopped the ships in which they were carried, took them out, and made sailors of them; so that, writes Collingwood, " in my ship's company I have some of all the States in Germany —Austrians, Poles, Croats, and Hungarians—a motley tribe !" [2]

A treaty of alliance, offensive and defensive, between France and Spain was ratified at Paris on the 12th of September, 1796, and on the 15th, news having been received of this treaty, an embargo was laid on all Spanish ships at anchor in English ports. This was followed early in October by a declaration of war by Spain against England. On the 2nd of November in this same year, the evacuation of Corsica having been completed as far as was practicable, Sir John Jervis sailed with the fleet to Rosia Bay, where he learnt that on the preceding day the Spanish fleet, accompanied by a French squadron under Villeneuve, had put to sea. Later came intelligence that the Spanish Admiral, with 26 sail of the line and a number of frigates,

---

[1] Letters in possession of J. C. Blackett, Esq.
[2] *Correspondence and Memoir*, p. 23.

had entered the port of Carthagena, and that Villeneuve with his squadron was making his way to Brest. On the 16th of December Jervis sailed with his fleet for the Tagus, and on January 16th, 1797, Collingwood writes as follows to Sir Edward Blackett, from Lisbon :—

" I have not heard from my wife or any one belonging to me for nigh three months, but hope now we have drawn a little nearer home that ere long I shall have good tidings of my family. We have had but a lamentable winter. Political events have gone very much against us : abandoning the Mediterranean—leaving our army behind which was not likely to effect anything without us. But the elements, the dreadful and almost constant gales of wind, have done us infinitely more harm, and reduced our little fleet to the strength of a cruising squadron. The *Courageux* and *Bombay Castle* are lost; with the *Courageux* most of her men perished. The *Gibraltar* and *Zealous* have had miraculous escapes, and have injured their bottoms so much on the rocks that the fleet is coming to England to repair. The other is in dock here. We have but tardy allies in these Portuguese. They take everything perfectly easy ; seem to say, ' Well, if you will protect us, you may.' They have a few fine ships here, which I am persuaded the French might have taken without opposition if they had come in and asked for them." [1]

Two days after this letter was written, Jervis stood for the mouth of the Tagus with his line-of-battle ships—eleven in all—partly for the purpose of escorting some Brazilian merchantmen and Portuguese men-of-war to a safe latitude, and partly to effect a junction with a reinforcement from England off Cape St. Vincent. The reinforcement consisted of five sail of the line and one frigate under Rear-Admiral W. Parker, detached by Lord Bridport from

[1] Letters in possession of J. C. Blackett, Esq.

the fleet that had been watching Brest. Owing to a
disaster that had befallen the *St. George*, a 98-gun ship,
Jervis's force consisted now of 15 instead of 16 sail of the
line. On the 19th of August in the preceding year, Nelson
had written to the Duke of Clarence: "As to our fleet,
under such a commander-in-chief as Sir John Jervis,
nobody has any fears. . . . I will venture my life Sir John
Jervis defeats them; I do not mean by a regular battle,
but by the skill of our Admiral, and the activity and spirit
of our officers and seamen."[1]

Lieutenant Parsons, who was a midshipman on board
the *Barfleur* in the Battle of St. Vincent, introduces us to
Collingwood at this time in a humorous experience of his
own, which must be introduced in a work that aspires
mainly to present the character of the hero of it: "We,
one morning," he says, referring to an early day before the
battle, "went on board the *Excellent*, Captain Cuthbert
Collingwood, not then so celebrated as he afterwards
became, and I being tired of seeing John Marlingspike
and Tom Rattling smooth down his front hair and hitch
up his trousers preparatory to scraping his feet with his
best sea jerk as he passed in review before the bigwigs,
and pressed to go down by a brother mid. who felt proud
of feasting the Vice-Admiral's[2] aide-de-camp—I forgetting
my proud station, stole from the Vice-Admiral's side, and
was well employed in stowing my hold, in the most ex-
peditious manner, with beef and pudding, when all at once
I heard: 'Pass the word for the Vice-Admiral's midshipman; his Admiral and Captain are towing alongside
waiting for him.' This alarming information nearly caused
me to choke by endeavouring to swallow a large piece of

[1] Nelson's *Dispatches and Letters*, vol. ii. p. 246.
[2] Vice-Admiral the Hon. William Waldegrave, afterwards Lord
Radstock.

pudding I had in my mouth, and with my cocked hat placed on my head the wrong way, I crossed the hawse of Captain Collingwood, who, calling me a young scamp and some other hard names, which I have long since forgiven, assured me in not a very friendly tone he would treat me with a dozen by marrying me to the gunner's daughter." [1]

Collingwood's name as a taut disciplinarian would no doubt be familiar to young Parsons, and his fears might well account for the haste, as he tells us, with which he leaped into the boat alongside, crushing his Captain's old-fashioned cocked hat as he alighted.

During the night of the 13th of February some heavy guns were heard to windward. It was thick on the morning of the 14th; but at about the hour of half-past six, the *Culloden* signalled five sail in sight, and by nine o'clock in the morning, when the fog had lifted, a fleet of 31 sail altogether had been counted from the masthead of the *Victory*, Jervis' ship. Parsons tells us that the British ships formed one of the most beautiful and close lines ever beheld. On the other hand, the Spanish fleet is described as having made the most awkward attempts to form their line of battle. "They looked a complete forest huddled together; their commander-in-chief, covered with signals and running free on his leeward line, used his utmost endeavours to get them into order; but they seemed confusion worse confounded." [2]

Yet their very disorder heightened the magnificence of the picture they submitted to the gaze of the British. The towering *Santissima Trinidad* loomed in colossal proportions amongst them: she was the largest ship at that time afloat, and Brenton, in writing of her years after,

---

[1] *Nelsonian Reminiscences*, by G. S. Parsons, Lieut. R.N., p. 319.
[2] *Parsons*, p. 323.

seems to hold his breath as though with astonishment and awe induced by recollection of her dimensions !

This grand fleet of Spain was under the command of Admiral Don Josef de Cordova. His flag-ship, the *Santissima,* carried 130 guns; several others were of 112, two of 80, and the remainder 74's. Collingwood's share in this battle is in great part to be read in the story of Nelson's brilliant achievement. It is doubtful, indeed, whether Nelson would have captured his two huge Spaniards without the help of Collingwood. Colonel Drinkwater, who watched the battle from the deck of the *Lively* frigate, says, referring to the behaviour of Collingwood in passing on to the support of Nelson's ship, the *Captain :* " His interference here was opportune, as the continual and long fire of the *Captain* had almost expended the ammunition she had at hand, and the loss of her fore-topmast and other injuries she had received in her rigging, had rendered her nearly ungovernable." [1]

The *Excellent,* after engaging the *Salvador-del-Mundo* for a few minutes, headed for the next Spanish ship, the *San-Ysidro,* and closely engaged her for some twenty minutes, until she hauled down her colours; then passed on to the 80-gun ship *San Nicolas,* with which huge craft Nelson was in hot action. Steering within a few feet of the *San Nicolas'* starboard side, Collingwood poured in a heavy and destructive fire, then filled and stood on, in obedience to the signal at that time flying. This is the historian's cold review of the proceedings of the *Excellent;* but one discovers the true theory of Collingwood's noble conduct in the letter that Nelson afterwards wrote to him, and in the narrative which he sent to the Duke of Clarence: " My dearest friend," Nelson said, " ' a friend in need is a friend indeed ' was never more truly verified than by your

[1] *Narrative of the Battle of St. Vincent,* 1840, p. 40.

Collingwood in *Excellent* off St. Vincent helping Nelson.—p. 54.

most noble and gallant conduct yesterday in sparing the *Captain* from further loss; and I beg, both as a public officer and as a friend, you will accept my most sincere thanks." And to the Duke of Clarence Nelson wrote: "Captain Collingwood, disdaining the parade of taking possession of beaten enemies, most gallantly pushed up with every sail set to save his old friend and messmate, who was, to all appearance, in a critical situation, the *Captain* being actually fired upon by three first-rates and the *San Nicolas*, the 74 within about pistol-shot distance of the *San Nicolas*. The *Blenheim* being ahead, and the *Culloden* crippled and astern, the *Excellent* ranged up, and hauling up her mainsail just astern, passed within ten feet of the *San Nicolas*, giving her a most awful and tremendous fire." [1]

The gallant Jervis appreciated to the full Nelson's and Collingwood's spontaneous manœuvre. His first Captain (Calder) suggested, in the course of a conversation with Jervis, that the behaviour of Nelson and Collingwood was an unauthorized departure by Nelson, in the first instance, from the prescribed mode of attack. "It certainly was so," replied Jervis, "and if ever you commit such a breach of your orders, I will forgive you also." [2] Collingwood's pride in and appreciation of Jervis' skill are indicated in a sentence included in a letter from Nelson to the Admiral: "A letter from a humbler pen came to me at Gibraltar— Collingwood; and his sentiments are, I am confident, those of the whole fleet—'I have a great desire our Admiral should be a Marquis this summer; his bright honours will reflect on all of us.'" [3]

There is a letter from Lady Collingwood, addressed to

[1] *Correspondence and Memoir of Lord Collingwood*, pp. 40 41.
[2] Tucker's *Memoirs of Earl St. Vincent*, vol. i. p. 263.
[3] Nelson's *Dispatches and Letters*, vol. ii. p. 389.

Sir Edward Blackett, referring to this memorable Battle of St. Vincent, that remarkably exhibits the wonderful modesty of Collingwood. The part he had borne in the battle wanted indéed the brilliance, one might almost call it the theatrical brilliance, of Nelson's achievement, to which the *Excellent* had materially contributed; yet those who carefully study the details of the fight will discover that the services rendered by the *Excellent* were not less splendid and remarkable than those performed by the *Captain*. Certainly Nelson took no pains to conceal the part that he had borne in that day; he writes enthusiastically of his own performances to friends ranging from the Duke of Clarence down to William Suckling. The egotism of these letters is sublime indeed, but egotism it is all the same. Lady Collingwood writes thus to her uncle:

"CHARLOTTE SQUARE, NEWCASTLE,
"*March* 14*th*, 1797.

"I return you and my aunt many thanks for your very kind letter of congratulations on the late glorious victory, and on the safety of my husband, who has indeed gained great honour on that day, and I feel not a little thankful and proud in being wife of so deserving a man, and I trust he will be preserved to be a comfort and happiness to his wife and family. I intended to have sent you a copy of my husband's letter, with an account of the victory, but I find you have heard from him. He inclosed some letters he had received of thanks for his gallant conduct from Captain Grey (Sir John Jervis' second captain), Commodore Nelson, and Admiral Waldegrave and Captain Dacres, his captain. My husband desired I would not show them, but they are such flattering marks of approbation that I cannot resist copying them on the other side for your perusal and my aunt's; but you will be so good as not to show them, as it was my husband's desire. When you have read them you will not wonder at my wishing you and Lady Blackett to see them."[1]

Mr. Newnham Collingwood has printed these testimonies to Collingwood's professional skill and noble behaviour, but they must also find a place in these pages. Captain J. W. Dacres wrote, dating from the *Barfleur* on the day following the action : " I have just time to request you will accept of my congratulations upon the immortal honour gained by the *Excellent* yesterday. The Admiral joins very sincerely in my ideas. God bless you, and may we all imitate you. Yours ever sincerely." Admiral Waldegrave wrote thus : " My dear Collingwood—Although Dacres has in a great degree expressed all I feel on the subject, yet I cannot resist the satisfaction of telling you myself that nothing in my opinion could exceed the spirit and true officership which you so happily displayed yesterday. Both the Admiral and Nelson join with me in this opinion, and nothing but ignorance or a bad heart can think otherwise. God bless you, my good friend, and may England long possess such men as yourself! 'Tis saying everything for her glory." Nelson's letter I have already quoted in part. Captain Grey's contribution to this applause savours somewhat of officialism after the warm-hearted letters of Nelson and Dacres and Waldegrave. He names the ships which had struck, and says he is desired by the Admiral (Jervis) to mention how sensible he is of Captain Collingwood's gallant conduct, with that of his officers and ship's company, and every other ship in the fleet.

Medals were distributed on this occasion. One might figure Swift musing upon an engraving of this medal,

---

[1] Original in possession of Miss Blackett.

reading that the flag-officer's was to be suspended by a blue and white ribband round the neck, and the captain's in the third and fourth button-hole on the left side, moralizing upon the heart-burnings caused by this symbol of victorious combat, and introducing some philosopher out of the territory of Laputa or the tribe of the Yahoos to deliver his views on the circle of gold stamped with the representation of Britannia in the act of being crowned by some quite Hogarthian theory of a winged goddess. Yet was the medal the professional pole-star of that age. The sailor steered his course by it; legs, limbs, and eyes were light in comparison with it. Indeed, with many it would have weighed more than the head itself could it have happened that the time *had* passed when, if the brains were out, the man would die.

On Lord St. Vincent informing Collingwood that he was to receive a medal for the 14th of February, he answered with emotion that he would not consent to take one whilst a medal for the 1st of June was withheld from him. "I feel," he exclaimed nobly, "that I was then improperly passed over; and to receive such a distinction now would be to acknowledge the propriety of that injustice." St. Vincent replied: "That is precisely the answer which I expected from you, Captain Collingwood." Both medals were sent to him.

It would seem from Lord Spencer's letter, in which their transmission was announced, that Collingwood's claim for a medal for the Glorious First had been admitted some months before the Battle of St. Vincent. The apology is awkward and insufficient. "I congratulate you most sincerely," said Lord Spencer, "on having the good fortune to bear so conspicuous a part on two such glorious occasions, and have troubled you with this letter only to say that the former medal would have been transmitted to you some months ago if a proper conveyance had been found for it." There is every reason to believe that the 1st of June medal would *not* have been sent had the Battle of St. Vincent never been fought, or its medal not been deserved by Collingwood; yet Lord Spencer distinctly mentions the conspicuous part Collingwood acted on the 1st of June! Sir John Barrow is very angry with Collingwood for having said, in a letter dated February 22nd, 1797: "I cannot help feeling an almost spiteful satisfaction that Lord Howe is outdone. His 1st of June (grand as it was) bears no proportion in any respect to this." But viewing the matter from Collingwood's standpoint, it is impossible not to sympathize with this expression of scornful elation. "The observation," says Sir John Barrow, "is only that of an angry man, and is worth nothing more."[1] The observation is that of a wronged man, and has all the significance that can be communicated by the emotions of a fine spirit vexed and depressed by neglect.

Collingwood's description of Nelson's heroic conduct in the Battle of St. Vincent is full of generous appreciation and sincere admiration: "After I had driven the *San Nicolas* on board the *San Joseph*, and left them on their fire ceasing to be taken possession of by somebody behind, they fell on board my good friend the Commodore, and as they had not surrendered, he, in his own little active person (for he could almost go through an alderman's thumb-ring), at the head of his ship's company, boarded them, driving the Spaniards from deck to deck at the point of their swords; and they at last both surrendered, and the Commodore, on the deck of the Spanish first-rate *San Joseph*, received the swords of the officers of the two ships; while a Johnny, one of the sailors, bundled them

---

[1] *Life of Lord Howe*, p. 242.

up with the same composure he would have made a faggot, and 22 of their line still within gunshot. We have had the Spanish fleet off here to look at since we came in; but I dare say they would rather see us at a distance than near. The Spaniards always carry their patron saint to sea with them. I have given St. Ysidore a berth in my cabin—the least I could do for him after he had consigned his charge to me. It is a good picture, as you will see, when he comes to Morpeth."[1]

For the next two years Collingwood remained with the fleet under Jervis watching Cadiz. It would weary the reader to follow closely the incidents of the tedious weeks and months of blockading. So early as June 1797, we find him complaining of the wretchedness of incessant shipboard life: "I had the pleasure," he writes to his father-in-law, "to receive your letter, and am quite happy to hear that Sarah, our children, and all your family are doing well. This is the only thing like comfort that can reach us here; for it is a dreary life we lead, pent up in a ship for such a length of time. God help us! There is nothing to gratify the mind but the hope that we may render essential service to our country, and the consciousness that we deserve it."[2] In this time the mutiny at the Nore had happened, and it was not long before

---

[1] This passage is quoted in a letter from Mr. J. E. Blackett to his brother, Sir Edward, dated at Newcastle, 15th March, 1797. He writes: "I had a letter from Captain Collingwood by this day's post, dated Lagos, 22nd February. He was very well, and in a part of his letter says," &c. On comparing this fragment with the text of Collingwood's communication as it is to be found at page 38 of the *Correspondence and Memoir*, it will be seen that Mr. Newnham Collingwood, the Editor, has erased two or three highly characteristic sentences; whence it is to be feared that he may have practised the same art of "improvement" on others, if not on all of Collingwood's letters.

[2] *Correspondence and Memoir*, p. 47.

there was disaffection among the crews of the ships cruising off Cadiz. It is said that in the months of May and June some letters were brought from home by the *Alcmene* frigate; they were addressed to the captains of the forecastle and other non-commissioned officers, were well expressed, and written in a clear and business-like hand. One of these letters came to the knowledge of Captain Dacres of the *Barfleur*, who immediately dispatched an officer to Lord St. Vincent for instructions. The Commander-in-Chief ordered the intercepted letters to be given to the persons to whom they were addressed. Two men belonging to the *St. George* had been tried for a breach of the 29th Article of War. The ship's company riotously demanded that they should be set at liberty; two of the officers rushed at the men, who bundled headlong below, leaving their principals behind them—four seamen, who were forthwith conveyed prisoners to the *Ville de Paris*, that had recently arrived to receive St. Vincent's flag. The unfortunate men were tried next day, Saturday, and hanged at nine o'clock next morning.[1]

This decisive measure effected much, but not everything. In point of discipline, however, the *Excellent* was unquestionably the model ship of the fleet. It was St. Vincent's frequent practice to draft the worst and the most menacing of the seamen into her. " Send them to Collingwood," he used to say, " and he will bring them to order." Yet there was probably no captain afloat who was more sparing in the use of the lash—the odious instrument with which the morals and opinions of the pigtailed mariner were chastened and directed. It was Collingwood's custom to keep a record of the punishment he inflicted, and from the table printed by the editor of his correspondence, I find that in the year 1793 the greatest

---

[1] Brenton's *Life of the Earl of St. Vincent*, vol. i. pp. 363-4.

number of lashes ordered from May 21st down to September 12th was twelve—in two instances twelve; first for the culprit absenting himself from duty; second for disobedience of orders in bringing liquor into the ship and contemptuous behaviour. The lowest number was six.

Captain Brenton is astonished by Collingwood's mercifulness. "What shall we say," cries this old-fashioned officer, whose books with their anecdotes, their egotism, their obsolete views, and above all their predictions, are to say the least as amusing as any old sea-story—" What shall we say," he cries, " to the officer who, having turned the hands up and gone through all the ceremony of punishment—quartermaster's gratings, foxes, cats, and boatswain's mates—gives to the most atrocious of these offenders twelve lashes, and to the least six? I am no friend to punishment, but I must say that here Captain Collingwood showed himself to be the most unfit man in the navy to have charge of such a ruffian as we have seen described." St. Vincent thought otherwise. Probably Brenton himself would change his opinion could he rise from his grave, step aboard an ironclad, and observe the sort of discipline that is now contrived without any assistance from foxes, cats, or quartermaster's gratings.

The ruffian to whom he refers was a seaman that had been sent to the *Excellent* from the *Romulus*. This man had loaded a forecastle gun, and so pointing it as to command the quarter-deck, stood by it with a match, swearing that he would fire at the officers unless a promise was made him that he should not be punished. Collingwood, on the scoundrel's arrival, is represented to have addressed him thus: "I know your character well, but beware how you attempt to excite insubordination in this ship, for I have such confidence in my men " (many of whom were listening) "that I am certain I shall hear in an hour of everything you are doing. If you behave well in future I will treat you like the rest, nor notice here what happened in another ship; but if you endeavour to excite mutiny, mark me well! I will instantly head you up in a cask and throw you into the sea." [1]

That this was said I do not for a moment doubt; that it was *meant* is quite another matter. The forecastle sea-lawyer was not in existence in those days; Collingwood might rely on the fellow not knowing whether this threat of a cask could or could not be executed; he meant to have the benefit of his fears, very well aware that there was the yard-arm as well as the cask, and that the alternative provided him with all he needed.

[1] *Correspondence and Memoir*, p. 50.

CHAPTER IV.

MUCH of the mutineering spirit amongst the sailors in the Royal Navy at this time was due to bad food, and, in many ships, to an abominably cruel discipline. I have somewhere read of a captain whose practice was to flog the last man off a yard after reefing or furling a sail. As there must always be a last man, so there was always a sailor to flog, and the cat and the topsail halliards went together. The boatswain's mates, too, were inexorable ruffians for the most part, brutes who were licensed to lay about them like any Nova Scotia mate of the present day.

In short, Navy Jack's life in the last century was one of unspeakable wretchedness. He was beaten senseless by the press-gang; he was forced to lie crowded, as beasts in pens, or in railway waggons, in tenders waiting for distribution, till the atmosphere below grew so horribly fœtid with the multitude who crowded the confined space that when he was drafted he was commonly dying of fever or of some other malady born of his loathsome jail, and for days the sufferings of the impressed men were scarcely less dreadful than those of the negro slave during the Middle Passage. When sent to a ship of war the sailor might have the luck to fall in with a good captain, like Collingwood or Nelson, but the chances were heavily against him. Even if the captain were a humane man, the lieutenants were certain to furnish forth some unbearable tyrant from amongst them. It is well indeed that the cat should have been hove overboard. As an instrument of discipline it was shockingly abused by the majority of those who were unhappily empowered to direct its application.

How Collingwood abhorred it we may gather from his exceedingly mild employment of it.[1] It is said of him that, "when the offence was of such a nature that the necessity of corporal punishment was manifest, Captain Collingwood was present, as is customary, but suffering from his wounded feelings greater pain probably than the culprit himself; and on these occasions he was for many hours afterwards melancholy and silent, sometimes not

---

[1] "My friends," exclaims James Hannay, in his admirable novel *Singleton Fontenoy, R. N.*, as brilliant a book as any in the language, "read the life of Collingwood, and you will see that he maintained his ship in the most admirable order without a tithe of the flogging now carried on in any average vessel. And this was nearly half a century ago!" Hannay was writing this in about 1850, when the "cat" was still a living beast in the Royal Navy.

speaking a word again for the remainder of the day." [1]

His crew were in good hands. A whole year would pass without a stripe having been ordered aboard his ship. His lieutenant, Clavell, his friend, and deservedly a favourite with him, seems to have possessed Collingwood's humanity without knowing it. "I wish," he shouted to some men who were "sogering," and going about their work lazily; "I wish I were the captain for your sakes." He turned as he spoke the words and met the gaze of Collingwood. "And pray, Clavell, what would you have done if you had been captain?" "I would have flogged them well, sir." "No you would not, Clavell; no you would not," replied Collingwood: "I know you better." He exacted for his youngest midshipman the same instant obedience from the men that he himself looked for, and took care his crew should understand that the least show of disobedience to the little lads of the cocked hat and dirk would be dealt with with a taut hand. Sometimes a midshipman complained of a sailor and forthwith an order would be issued for the punishment of the man next day; but in the interval Collingwood would call the midshipman to his cabin and address him to the following effect: "In all probability the fault was yours; but whether or not, I am sure it would go to your heart to see a man old enough to be your father disgraced and punished on your account; and it will therefore give me a good opinion of your disposition, if, when he is brought out, you ask for his pardon." Such a hint was never likely to be lost; the boy would intercede for the man, and Collingwood, making a great show of yielding, would after a long pause exclaim, addressing the prisoner: "This young gentleman has pleaded so humanely for you, that

[1] *Correspondence and Memoir*, p. 51.

in the hope that you will feel a due gratitude to him for his benevolence, I will for this time overlook your offence."

These, to be sure, are admirable traits of character; they cannot but deepen one's admiration and love for the memory of this noble old sea-officer, this lion-hearted ocean warrior, this modest gentleman, who before all things was a good Christian, and the tenderest of husbands and fathers. He replaced the cat by a discipline of a sort very different from the bleeding back and the soul-killing degradation of the public whipping. He watered the men's grog, and this they found galling enough, but it was better than the lash. He would order an offender to be excluded from his mess and to be put to all sorts of mean duties, so that at all moments he was being called up on deck to do boy's work, and worse than boy's work, amid the jeers and laughter of his shipmates. It is declared that the sailors would often say that sooner than be put to such contemptible laughter-moving jobs they would take three dozen. There was something paternal in Collingwood's care of his crew. He was constantly devising amusements for them to occupy their minds and kill the painful tediousness of the hours. "My wits," he writes in January 1798, "are ever at work to keep my people employed, both for health's sake, and to save them from mischief. We have lately been making musical instruments, and have now a very good band. Every moonlight night the sailors dance; and there seems as much mirth and festivity as if we were in Wapping itself. One night the rats destroyed the bagpipes we had made by eating up the bellows; but they suffered for it, for in revenge we have made traps of all constructions and have declared a war of extermination against them." He visited the sick daily, and took care that they were fed with little comforts from his own table, and when they got better the lieutenant of the morning watch brought them to him that he might examine and cheer them, and satisfy himself on the doctor's report. "If you do not know a man's name," he used to say to his officers, "call him 'sailor,' and not 'you—sir,' and such other appellations. They are offensive and improper."

He had the strongest objection to the use of the word mutiny. He could fully appreciate its significance in its application to the navy during such a time as our country was then passing through. It was a word of awful import never to be lightly used as an expression of what might prove no more than a forecastle murmur, justified, yet to be easily silenced. "Mutiny, sir, mutiny in my ship!" he would exclaim, on a complaint being made to him of the sailors' conduct. "If it can have arrived at that, it must be my fault and the fault of every one of the officers. It is a charge of the gravest nature, and it shall be most gravely inquired into."

Though a strict disciplinarian, Collingwood was essentially a gentleman in his relations with his officers and men. He was never known to swear. This seems incredible, but it is confidently asserted. Most of his contemporaries—Nelson amongst them—could whip out with a hearty "sea-blessing" in a moment of vexation or hurry; but if Collingwood could look the word, his lips never delivered it. This capacity of smothering maledictions I regard as something very astonishing in a man forced to keep the sea for months and years. Why do sailors swear? It is because the food they have to live upon afflicts them with indigestion; the liver and the brain are intimately connected, and what is called "language," such as one hears upon the ocean, is simply mahogany-hard lumps of salt-beef and biscuits full of worms metamorphosed into expletives. Feed sailors on tender roast mutton, light digestible puddings, and sparkling bitter ale, and you shall not find their equals in any calling in the world for sweetness of manner and decorum of speech.

Collingwood resembled Nelson in the interest he took in his midshipmen. Every week he examined them in their studies, and was constantly directing their attention when on deck to the minutiæ of ship-board routine. An anecdote, the probability of which has been much disputed, belongs to this period. The *Excellent*, being at anchor off Cadiz, was signalled to weigh and to close with the Admiral's ship. Whilst approaching the flag-ship Collingwood was signalled several times to shift his course, first to port, then to starboard, and finally the signal for a lieutenant was run aloft. Collingwood, who had been looking on in silence, on perceiving this last signal, ordered his boat to be manned, and said he would go too. On his arrival he desired the lieutenant when the order was copied to bring it to him; and read it whilst he walked the quarter-deck with Lord St. Vincent and Sir Robert Calder. It was an order for the *Excellent* to receive two bags of onions for the use of the sick. " Bless me !" cried Collingwood, " is this the service, my Lord ? Is this the service, Sir Robert? Has the *Excellent's* signal been made five or six times for two bags of onions? Man my boat, sir, and let us go on board again." Lord St. Vincent pressed him to stay to dinner, but he refused, and went over the side.[1]

Brenton seems to credit the tale: calls Collingwood's behaviour peevish, and a violation of the 22nd Article of War. The story carries an air of *vraisemblance* that makes one unwilling to disturb it as, at all events, a naval tradition. Supposing the incident true, Collingwood might

[1] *Memoir and Correspondence*, p. 56.

find justification for his temper in St. Vincent's well-known love of practical jokes. On Brenton's own showing there was a degree of brutality in this fine old Admiral's theory of humour that must often have occasioned bitter mortification to subordinates who dared not openly resent his lordship's coarse fooling. One or two characteristic anecdotes may well find a place.

Dr. Morgan was St. Vincent's chaplain, and one Sunday after Divine Service, the Admiral seemed to think that the parson had not enough to do. He asked the signal-lieutenant if there was a black flag on board. He was told that there was a black and white one. "That will do, sir; make the signal for all lieutenants." When the officers arrived the order was given that whenever the black and white flag was displayed with the red pendant over it, it was the signal for all chaplains. A few days after this it came on to blow half a gale of wind from the west-south-west. The inshore squadron lay six miles from the flag-ship, dead to leeward. In the thick of this weather up went the signal for all chaplains. A high sea was running, and when the parsons reached the quarter-deck of the *Ville de Paris* they were drenched to the skin. On their making their appearance, shivering, and in the last degree wretched, after their long pull through six miles of stormy waters, the Admiral, "with a leer," presented them to "Bishop Morgan," as he called his chaplain, and desired that they would go down into the ward-room and hold a conclave. The point of the joke lay in drenching the chaplains, and in putting Dr. Morgan to the cost of "standing" half a dozen of sherry to his chilled and trembling brother-workers.

Another joke. One night, feeling very restless, St. Vincent rang his bell and ordered the officer of the watch to his bedside. This officer was Lieutenant Cashman, described as a fine, rough, unlettered sailor, of the true breed. "What sort of a night, sir?" "A very fine night, my Lord." "Nothing stirring? no strangers in sight?" "No, my Lord." "Nothing to do on deck?" "No, my Lord." "Then you may take a book and read to me." Cashman would rather have been in the boat with the chaplains, but escape was impossible. "What book shall I read, my Lord?" "Oh, any book—take the Admiralty Statutes." The lieutenant pulled out the huge quarto, placed the lantern on the table, sat down in his watch coat, and began to stammer through the Acts of Parliament. St. Vincent in telling the story used to say: "Sir, I thought I should have suffocated myself, I was forced to keep my head so long under the bed-clothes to conceal my laughter at the manner in which he stumbled and hobbled through his task."

Again, one night, or rather at half-past two in the morning, he sent for Colonel Flight, the commanding officer of Marines. The Colonel arrived, fully armed in readiness for the enterprise he expected to hear of. "I have sent for you," said Lord St. Vincent, "that you might smell, Colonel, for the first time in your life, the delicious odours brought off from the shores of Andalusia by the land-wind. Now take a good sniff, and then you may go and turn in again."

A lieutenant came on board to answer a signal. He was a fat man, and St. Vincent looked at him. "Calder," said he to his Captain of the Fleet, "all the lieutenants are running to belly. They have been too long at anchor. Block up the entering port, except for admirals and captains, and make them climb over the hammocks." Brenton, who relates these anecdotes, explains the purport of this stroke of humour thus: after describing the height of a line-of-battle ship from the water-line to the hammocks, and the prodigious climb it involved, he proceeds: "There was also a great inconvenience and even expense attending this painful operation, namely, that whereas in those days all officers wore white knee-breeches, or shorts, as they were called, the consequence was that many useful garments which could not so readily be replaced were torn and spoiled in this attempt at juvenile activity."

Other anecdotes of a like sort could be quoted, but those already given will be thought sufficient. It is strange that Brenton should not have perceived that in relating these stories as illustrations of St. Vincent's character, he was making out the strongest possible case for Collingwood, whose behaviour in the matter of the bags of onions he very severely handles. The austerity and dignity of Collingwood's nature would be sure to find something very objectionable in such grinning through a horse-collar, as Brenton represents his idol, St. Vincent, to have repeatedly indulged himself in. Always supposing the two bags of onions to be a true story, Collingwood doubtless witnessed such a taste for fooling in the Admiral's signals and requirements as he was assuredly right not to encourage at his own expense.

In May 1798, Lord St. Vincent placed a small squadron under the command of Nelson, and despatched him to the Mediterranean to ascertain by every means in his power the object of a projected expedition by the French. The Admiralty instructions to St. Vincent were that he should lose no time in detaching twelve sail of the line and a few frigates under the command of *some discreet flag-officer*. Lord Spencer, however, in a private letter to the Commander-in-Chief, suggested that the command should be given to Nelson, "whose acquaintance," he added, "with that part of the world, as well as his activity of disposition, seemed to qualify him in a peculiar manner for that service." St. Vincent, in writing to Nelson, expressed himself thus: " You, and you alone, my dear Admiral, shall command the important service in contemplation; therefore make the best of your way down to me. . . . You shall also have some choice fellows of the inshore squadron." [1]

Sir John Orde and Sir William Parker, who were Nelson's seniors, were greatly angered by his appointment over their heads. Sir John's resentment was heightened by the indignity, as he held it, of Sir Roger Curtis having taken command under Lord St. Vincent in the second post, lowering him, Sir John, to the fourth. A copy of a letter he addressed to Earl Spencer, written on board the *Princess Royal*, off Cadiz, and dated June the 16th, 1798, was forwarded to Lord St. Vincent, who informed Sir John in reply, "That those who are responsible for measures have an undoubted right to appoint the men they prefer to carry them into execution." Disputes followed; there was much ill-feeling, misrepresentation, whisperings amongst the captains and officers of the ships which were watching Cadiz. The quarrel between St. Vincent and Sir John Orde resulted in the Commander-in-Chief ordering Sir John to strike his flag on board the *Princess Royal* of 98 guns, and to hoist it on board the *Blenheim* of 90 guns, in order to return to England.

Collingwood shared in the uneasiness that was felt throughout the fleet. The captains looked strangely on one another; there seemed a general distrust; indeed, certain letters of Lord St. Vincent would lead us to suppose that the spirit of mutiny, which was by no means inactive in the forecastle, had made its way into the officers' quarters. Dating his letter July 22nd, in this year, Collingwood writes,—but in ignorance that the sug-

[1] Clarke and M'Arthur's *Life of Nelson*, vol. ii. p. 79.

gestion of Nelson's appointment came from Lord Spencer, though his own conviction was that St. Vincent could choose no other, as he could have chosen no fitter man: "This appointment of Admiral Nelson to a service where so much honour was to be acquired, has given great offence to the senior Admirals of the Fleet. Sir William Parker, who is a very excellent officer and as gallant a man as any in the navy, and Sir John Orde, who on all occasions of service has acquitted himself with great honour, are both feeling much hurt at a junior of the same fleet having so marked a preference given him, and have written to Lord Spencer complaining of this neglect of them. The fleet is, in consequence, in a most unpleasant state; and now all that intercourse of friendship, which was the only thing like comfort which was left us, is forbidden: for the admirals and captains are desired not to entertain even at dinner any who do not belong to their ships. They all complain that they are appointed to many unworthy services, and I have my share with the rest: but I place myself beyond the reach of such matters; for I do them with all the exactness in my power, as if they were things of the utmost importance, though I do not conceal what I think of them. In short, I do as everybody does—wish myself at home very much."

In a letter to the Secretary of the Admiralty, written in February 1799, St. Vincent bears testimony to Collingwood's dutifulness at this trying time: "Did you," he says, "observe in Sir John Orde's narrative an avowal of his having convened some of the senior captains to sit in judgment upon my conduct towards him? You have no conception how far these meetings went; and with the exception of Sir Roger Curtis, and perhaps Collingwood, I do not believe there was an officer of any standing who did not in some sort enter into cabals to pull down my

authority and level all distinctions."[1] I do not believe
that St. Vincent would have qualified this exception of
Collingwood but for the lack of sympathy between them.
That Collingwood held his peace, though he might
grumble aloud on his quarter-deck at times at the dull
and miserable routine of his life at this period, and that
he faithfully, if sullenly, carried on his duties in a way to
merit his Commander-in-Chief's approval, there can be no
reason whatever to doubt. He has been severely criticized
for daring to express such sentiments as I have just tran-
scribed. But to whom was he writing? To his father-in-
law. Surely a man is privileged to think aloud at his
own fireside! Nor can he be held guilty of breach of
discipline and regarded as deserving of a trial by court-
martial, for merely whispering his disappointments and
his mortifications to his wife and relatives!

Collingwood felt, and strongly and properly felt, that
he had been undeservedly overlooked by St. Vincent, and
perhaps by Nelson himself, when the Mediterranean expedition that resulted in the Battle of the Nile was planned.
"You shall also have some choice fellows of the inshore
squadron," wrote St. Vincent to Nelson, as we have seen.
What choicer man than Collingwood was there in the
whole fleet, no matter in what squadron his ship was?
His claims were peculiar, the glory of them recent. He
had helped Nelson to his noble achievement on the 14th
of February, and the battle had gained in lustre as the
victory had gathered in completeness by the magnificent
behaviour of the *Excellent*. When news of the Battle
of the Nile reached him, his over-wrought feelings broke
forth: "I have been almost broken-hearted all the
summer," he wrote to Captain Ball, who had fought
under Nelson in that famous conflict; "my ship was in as

[1] Brenton's *Life of Earl St. Vincent*, vol. i. p. 421.

perfect order for any service as those which were sent;[1] in zeal I will yield to none; and my friendship—my love for your admirable admiral gave me a particular interest in serving with him. I saw them preparing to leave us, and to leave me, with pain; but our good Chief found employment for me, and to occupy my mind, sent me to cruise off St. Luccars to intercept—the market-boats, the poor cabbage-carriers. Oh, humiliation! But for the consciousness that I did not deserve degradation from any hand, and that my good estimation would not be depreciated in the minds of honourable men by the caprice of power, I should have died of indignation."[2]

Nevertheless his warm heart beat strong in his letter of congratulation to Nelson: "I cannot, my dear friend," he writes, "express how great my joy is at the complete and glorious victory you have obtained over the French—the most decisive, and in its consequences perhaps the most important to Europe that was ever won; and my heart overflows with thankfulness to the Divine Providence for His protection of you through the great dangers which are ever attendant on services of such eminence. Say to Lady Nelson," he adds, "when you write to her, how much I congratulate her on the safety, honours, and services of her husband. Good God! What must be her feelings! How great her gratitude to Heaven for such mercies."

Collingwood sailed from off Cadiz for England at the close of October 1798. On the eve of his withdrawal he had written to Captain Ball: "I am tired of it; and you will believe that to-morrow I am glad that I depart for

---

[1] Captain Brenton denies this; but the reader will perhaps agree with me that Collingwood would, better than Brenton, know the condition of his ship. The *Excellent*, at all events for fighting purposes, was in as good a state as most of the British ships which were engaged in the Battle of the Nile.

[2] *Correspondence and Memoir*, p. 73.

England." Shortly after his arrival at Spithead, he addressed the following letter to Sir Edward Blackett, dating it on board the *Excellent*, December 3rd, 1798: "Your letter, which I had the pleasure to receive to-day, made me very happy to hear you, Lady Blackett, and family were well, and safely arrived from your long journey. All the accounts I have of my family are comforting to me, and I am now suffering a painful impatience to see them. The moment the destination of my ship is determined, I shall ask for leave of absence and hasten to them. If there is any impediment to that, which I do not apprehend, my Sarah must come to me wherever I am, for I am restless and unfit for anything until I see her. . . .

"I am feeling very happy that I am once again in England, for the station I have been on has not latterly been very agreeable. The disagreement between the Chief and other flag-officers, and his impetuous conduct towards several others on trifling occasions, shut the door to the few comforts that were to be found there. I had, however, the good fortune to keep clear of all disputes, but could not help feeling disquietude at many violences and innovations which I witnessed. The Admiralty, I find, have entirely disapproved of his sending Sir John Orde home. It seemed to everybody an unwarrantable stretch of power; and I think the Admiralty cannot consider it otherwise than a hardy stroke at their authority in sending the officers of *their* appointment home to them without even the slightest charge of misdemeanour. Sir John Orde is proud and carries himself very high, and circumstanced as he was, it needed not great sensibilities to feel indignities. They were generally gross enough for the roughest minds. They drew from him expressions of what he felt—and discussion was crime enough. He wrote for a court-martial on the Commander-in-Chief. When Lord St. Vincent showed me his letters I was sorry for it, because it would have been more judicious in him to have left the Board of Admiralty to defend themselves and their appointments, than to make *himself* the opponent of the Chief.. They have given him leave to come to England, perhaps before he asked it, and offered Sir John Orde immediately a command in the Channel fleet.

"The only great mortification I suffered was in not going with Admiral Nelson. He[1] knew our friendship; for many, many years we had served together, lived together, and all that ever happened to us strengthened the bond of our amity. But my going would have interfered with the aggrandisement of a favourite to whom I was senior, and so he sent me out of the way when the detachment was to be made. After all this what joy am I feeling in the hope of soon seeing my most excellent wife and precious darlings. I hope I shall never again be so long separated from them."[2]

On the 14th of February, 1799, on the promotion of flag-officers, Collingwood was raised to the rank of Rear-Admiral of the White, and on the 12th of May following he hoisted his flag on board the *Triumph*, one of the ships under the command of Lord Bridport on the Channel station.[3] In a letter to Sir Edward Blackett, written a week before he was called away from Morpeth, he says: "Here I am now settled in my own house with as many comforts and sources of happiness about me as anybody could reasonably wish. We are all in very good health and have constant amusement in the improvement of our children, whom we brought with us from their school at Newcastle, and who, I think, will do better under our own instruction, at their age, than at school. The change of air and good exercise, for which

[1] *i. e.* Lord St. Vincent.
[2] Letters in possession of J. C. Blackett, Esq.
[3] *Naval Chronicle*, 15, p. 367.

I am in great part indebted to your good horse, has made me stronger and better than I have been for some time; and had we but Peace I could be content indeed. But I cannot in the present state of things suppress an impatience to be in the exercise of my profession, and this will increase when the newness of my present situation wears off. There is a nothingness in a sailor ashore at such a time that will, if it lasts long, weary me; but I rather think that it will not last long.

" I called on Lord Spencer the day I left London, when he told me it was his wish and intention to employ me, but that I would not be so immediately as to prevent my going into the country. I know how much he is pressed by numbers who are as anxious as I am; so having done what was proper on the occasion, I must now wait his time. The papers to-day tell us the French fleet have got to sea in greater force than was expected; but as their strength · consists less in their numbers than in their condition, I think whenever Lord Bridport meets them he will not wait to count them. . . . Affairs in Ireland, between the threatened invasion of the French and the Union, are exceedingly critical. The Archduke and Austrians in all quarters are acting a noble part; and would to God that those successes would humble the French, bend their minds to peace, and restore to those powers the possession and right of which they have wronged them. The French must make great exertions to recruit their army, which will increase the discontent of the people with the war and with their tyrants who wage it. I have great hopes in the result of this campaign." [1]

In this same letter, referring to his home-life at this period, he says: " Our Morpeth neighbours are very gay and good-humoured to us; but when I tell you the dining-

[1] Letters in possession of J. C. Blackett, Esq.

room where we dined yesterday was ornamented with pictures of Tom Paine and Horne Tooke, you will conclude we have strange characters amongst us. It was at young Burdon's—the son of him who lives at Newcastle; he was bred at Cambridge and is a philosopher."[1]

Having joined the fleet under Lord Bridport, he re-

---

[1] It is to be gathered from Collingwood's correspondence that his politics were moderate Tory ; but he never obtrudes his opinions. "Collingwood's letter [On the Battle of Trafalgar] (which is admirable) proves that it was his art to make all under him love him, and own his superiority without a ray of jealousy. He never was a *party man* himself, and there never was a party in his fleet."— *Diaries and Correspondence of the Earl of Malmesbury*, iv. 342. Of Burdon the philosopher, referred to by Collingwood, I am indebted to Mr. Joseph Cowen for the following interesting notice : "William Burdon the philosopher was a very remarkable man, and a relative of Collingwood by marriage, if I am not mistaken. Being an extremely modest and retiring man, Burdon never received his due meed of praise. He was a considerable coal-owner and landowner, managed his own estates and collieries, and yet found time to do a large amount of literary work. He was reared as a strong Tory, and became a pronounced Radical, a friend of Thomas Paine, Horne Tooke, 'The Scottish Martyrs,' Farmer, Muir, and Skirving; and indeed all the more prominent of the group of philosophical Radicals that make such a figure in public life towards the close of the last century and the beginning of this. He was intended for the Church, and was made a Fellow of his College ; but he refused to take Holy Orders, and became a Freethinker. His best known books were his *Life of Napoleon* and his *Materials for Thinking*. Like many other Radicals and Whigs of his time, he was an admirer of Buonaparte and wrote in that sense, but when Buonaparte's Imperialistic ideas developed themselves, Mr. Burdon wrote as strongly against him. He took very much the line that Carnôt, 'The Organizer of Victory,' did with respect to Buonaparte. His *Materials for Thinking* went through five or six editions in a few years, which was a remarkable thing for a philosophical book to do at that time. Not long ago I read in one of our modern publications, entitled *Words of the Wise*, or some such name, a copious extract from Burdon's book, credited to Seneca, of all men in the world ! Burdon, like his teacher Moises, was a great classical scholar. He translated a good deal of Spanish literature into English, and altogether was a man of high character, of ability, and learning. I can well imagine such a good Conservative as Collingwood being astonished at the philosophical democracy of Burdon."

mained on that station until the escape of Vice-Admiral
Bruix, on the 25th of April, with one of the most powerful
fleets that France ever sent to sea. He was then detached
with a reinforcement under Rear-Admiral Sir Charles
Cotton for Lord Keith. Sixteen sail of the line left the
Channel fleet, four of which, under Admiral Allan Gardner,
put into the Tagus; the remainder, with the *Triumph*
amongst them, joined Lord Keith on the 7th of June.
This Admiral was hunting the Mediterranean for the
French fleet with a force now augmented to 31 sail of the
line, four frigates, and a few small vessels. The chase as
a matter of history takes the aspect of an almanack; its
interest is almost wholly one of dates. Enough if it be
said here that after steering to and fro and stretching away
in wrong directions to the inspiration of false news, Lord
Keith, on the 30th of July, sailed from Gibraltar and stood
for the English Channel. On the 12th the fleet was in
soundings, and on the 14th, three ships being detached to
look into Brest, discovered the French and Spanish fleets
snugly moored in the Roads, where they had arrived on
the preceding day. The story of this Mediterranean hunt,
together with Collingwood's opinion of it, will be found
in the following letter, dated at Torbay aboard the
Triumph, August 17th, 1799, and addressed to Sir Edward
Blackett :—

"I am afraid we shall be very unwelcome to England,
returning from so fair a field for great deeds, having effected
nothing. The fleets of France and Spain seemed to be in
our power, at least to combat them; and we had a force
that promised everything. But the truth is our efforts
were not great. I do not pretend to give reasons why they
were not; the way of them was obvious to everybody, but
we did not go that way. Lord St. Vincent, sick on shore,
continued to command and give orders to the fleet at sea,

and acted on intelligence which the Spaniards chose should
be received at Minorca; whilst Lord Keith, at sea with the
fleet, daily received his information from those who had no
interest in deceiving—pursued their fleet to the Bay of
Albingo on the coast of Genoa, and when their look-out
frigate was in view from our fleet, bethought of Minorca's
safety, bore away for its protection, and left the French to
follow their schemes at their leisure. Our whole operations
were of this class, and managed with the same degree of
skill.

"It was obvious to every person that the French might
have been come up with before they left Carthagena, and
as obvious to most men that they never would be come up
with. Lord St. Vincent's sagacity and penetration I am sure
saw this man failing in everything without displeasure. He
would have ill brooked the laurels which presented themselves to us being gathered by another's hand under his
nose as it were. To those of the fleet who only looked
how best their country's interest might be supported, whose
only object was the destruction of the enemy's fleet, it has
been a continued series of vexations and disappointments.
I have been told some sharp correspondence has passed
between Lord Keith and Sir William Parker on the subject.
The short story is that the whole business had been dread-
fully marred, and the British navy suffered much in our
opinions, and no doubt will be sharply handled by our
friends on shore. I wrote to Mr. Blackett soon after our
arrival at Minorca that nothing great or good was to be
expected of us. It did not require second sight or the gift
of prophecy to discover it. . . . I suppose this combined
fleet mean to try some grand experiment upon Ireland,
and unless we manage our affairs better than we have
done, our friends there may have their hands full." [1]

[1] From letters in possession of J. C. Blackett, Esq.

This severity of criticism seems to have been due to disappointment rather than to conviction. Lord Keith was a shrewd and able commander, as gallant and conscientious a sea-officer as was ever afloat. That his efforts might to a certain extent have been hindered, not to say crippled by the directions of Lord St. Vincent, whose ill-health obliged him to administer the affairs of the Mediterranean fleet from the Rock of Gibraltar, seems possible in the face of Collingwood's assurance to that effect. The wonder is that Lord Keith should have lacked the courage of his own convictions, seeing that his theories as to the enemy's movements exhibited all needful penetration. In his Order to Lord Nelson, dated July the 9th, he says that he has reason to believe the enemy have no intention of attempting an impression on the Island of Sicily, or of reinforcing their army in Egypt and Syria, but on the contrary "that their efforts are likely to be directed against Ireland, and that they are bent towards the ocean;"[1] from which it would appear, Lord Keith was clearly of opinion that the enemy's haunt would not long be the Mediterranean. Collingwood had predicted the issue in a letter dated July the 11th. "In the meantime," he writes, "the French go where they please and we take care of Minorca. They are now with the Spaniards at Carthagena, and if you hear of their arrival at Brest you must not be surprised."

[1] Nelson's *Dispatches and Letters*, vol. iii. p. 314.

CHAPTER V.

ORD BRIDPORT resigned command of the Channel fleet off Brest, April 24th, 1800, and two days later the Earl of St. Vincent hoisted his flag on the *Namur* (90) at Spithead as Commander-in-Chief, and shortly afterwards joined. It was now Collingwood's lot to resume the old weary distasteful work of blockading; no longer, however, off sunny Cadiz, where the jaded mariner might fancy, at least, that he tasted the perfume of the orange and the citron in the off-shore breeze, but in the comfortless regions of the chops of the Channel, where the surge runs with the whole weight of the North Atlantic in it, where even on a summer's day the breeze will blow with a shrewd nip, and where in winter the gale is frequent and of terrible severity, the snow-storm blinding, the nights of a pitchy blackness.

It is difficult to realize in this age of steam what was signified by blockading in those days of tacks and sheets. No sea-labour could be more arduous and distressing. The attention was for ever on the strain, the eyes were for ever groping into the thickness where the land lay, on the look-out for any sort of smudge that might mean a ship in motion; and let it not be supposed that because a man happens to be a sailor he can endure without uneasiness and disgust the perpetual motion of his vessel, and above all such motion as a craft that was little more than three times as long as she was broad, and that sat on the water with the height of the side of a house, was capable of. The perpetual going about, the incessant making and shortening sail, the weary iteration of the sullen plunge of the round colossal bow, and the long-drawn heel to leeward to the sweep of the freshening blast into the con-cavities of the giant topsails, the monotonous round of meals and of duties, the afflicting sense of home being close at hand, and all its comforts and delights as inac-cessible as though the mariner were locked up in the ice of the North Pole; not days of this, but weeks and months, running into years! How can we realize it all in this age?

The steamer keeps her station at will. It is but the clanking of a bell in the engine-room, the pulsing of a hidden and irresistible power throughout the length and breadth of her, and the manœuvre is executed. The huge capstan around which the Jacks sprawled thrusting at handspikes, heaving in inch by inch the ponderous hempen cable—where is it? I very well remember bringing up in a fine steamer off a port on the South African coast. We let go the anchor in an ugly popple caused by the rush of a river that had been heavily swollen with rains. "This won't do!" exclaimed the captain, after watching his big ship wallowing to the line of her rails; "yonder it is smoother, and yonder we will go," and in a few minutes the steam windlass had lifted the ground-tackle clear of the ooze, the screw revolved, and all as quietly and easily as a man shifts from one chair to another, the iron fabric of hard upon 5,000 tons was at anchor half a mile further down the bay where the swell was regular and the motion comparatively comfortable.

We are accustomed to all this now; it needs a severe effort of imagination, even in a sailor bred to steam, to figure with clear perception of the truth the conditions of shipboard life in Collingwood's time—an age yet so recent that there died only the other day, at this time of writing,[1] in the person of Mr. John Clayton, a man who was eighteen years of age when Collingwood quitted this life.

On Lord St. Vincent taking command, orders were issued for ensuring a discipline similar to that which was in force in the Mediterranean. An inshore squadron of five ships were anchored near the Black Rocks, with frigates and cutters cruising close at hand; three line-of-battle ships cruised between Ushant and Black Rocks; a line-of-battle ship and a frigate guarded the Passage du Raz and the Penmark Rocks; and another ship of the line masked L'Orient to prevent supplies from Vannes. From time to time ships were sent to Cawsand Bay to replenish and bring out stores. Writing in January in this year (1800), on board the *Triumph* in Cawsand Bay, Collingwood says:

[1] July, 1890. Mr. Clayton was for many years town clerk of Newcastle-on-Tyne.

"I have been hoping that on the arrival of Sir Alan Gardner with the fleet I should be ordered up to Spithead to join the *Barfleur*, and then it was I looked for the pleasure of seeing you (Sir Edward Blackett) and meeting my Sarah at Thorpe Lea, and I should have been as happy a creature as the sun ever shone on. But I do not know when I am to be thus gratified, for on the fleet's arrival in Torbay I am ordered to join them with all the ships that are ready, and hear from them that they expect to go to sea again as soon as the wind comes easterly. I most sincerely wish peace was more in view. Buonaparte seems more moderate and reasonable, both in his acts and language, than any of the ruling factions in France hitherto have been. Whenever his powers are generally acknowledged by the French nation, monarchy is established in his person with another name, but not less absolute than in the reigns of their former kings, with a more formidable army at his command and the Council subject to his nod. Will the people (versatile as they are) submit to this usurpation after all the clamour they have been making for so many years about republicanism and liberty and equality, and wading through such scenes of bloodshed and devastation after a Phantom? And if they resist, another week may produce another new constitution and a new class to treat with; yet I pray the means of peace may be found practicable—for I think I see even here, where war is the profession, all people impatient for its termination . . . .

"The report of Lord St. Vincent commanding the fleet seems to have been dropped; yet I believe it was in contemplation.[1] Had he managed our affairs well in the Mediterranean last summer it would not have signified now

---

[1] This, it will be seen, was written on January 12th. St. Vincent hoisted his flag April 26th.

who commanded it. Lord Spencer, I believe, is a very able minister, and is as vigilant and industrious in his office as a man should be who undertakes a great public trust. But in the executive part, here in the ships, there is a languor and an indifference that is truly provoking. The officers in general are not such good seamen as they used to be, nor is there the same emulation to excel each other that did make the life and spirit of the navy. And yet there is great encouragement given to those who exert themselves."[1]

April the 8th he writes again on board the *Barfleur* at Torbay: "We are just returned from a long and tedious cruise off Brest, where we have been watching those Frenchmen, who are there in very great force, and I dare say meditating something very mischievous. Whether the ministers here are apprised of their plans I do not know; but there seemed great anxiety that we should be as watchful of them as possible—and so we were, for we stuck very close to their port. However, we have now left them to the westerly wind, which will as effectually prevent their sailing as if we were there, and are coming to replenish our ships. . . . We have been very unfortunate in loss of ships this cruise. The revolt of the *Danäe's* crew is a shocking thing, but those who knew a good deal about her are not much surprised at it.[2] There may exist a degree of violence when severity is substituted for discipline that is insupportable. I have heard that the young man who commanded her paid not long since £4,000 for having tarred and feathered a young gentleman belonging

[1] From letters in possession of J. C. Blackett, Esq.
[2] On the 15th of March the *Danäe* frigate, commanded by Captain Lord Proby, one of the ships employed to watch the French fleet in Brest, was taken possession of by part of the ship's company and given up to the enemy. The particulars of this mutiny will be found in Schomberg's *Naval Chronology*, vol. iii. p. 363.

stantly on his guard against the machinations of wicked
and designing men. "The main-hatchway berth on the
larboard side of the lower deck was ordered to be restored
to the master's mates, and the masters-at-arms were to be
established, abreast of the bitts, on the starboard side; the
Marines were to be berthed close aft without any seamen
intermixed with them, and such other precautions to be
taken as best to defeat the horrible crime supposed to be
in contemplation." Captains were ordered to report from
time to time upon the apparent disposition of the ship's
company. Markham reported that there was no sign of
ill-humour or discontent amongst his seamen.

One cannot but observe something senile in grand old
St. Vincent's scares at this time, and in his notions of
discipline. A captain of a line-of-battle ship with a party
of Marines, under its captain and a subaltern, was ordered
to keep guard at the watering-place at Brixham night and
day for twenty-four hours at a stretch. They slept under
a boat's sail; no petty-officer or man was suffered to quit
his boat on any pretence whatever; no officer was permitted to sleep on shore, and leave was extended to
between sunrise and sunset only. Officers were forbidden
to go further from the beach than Upper Brixham and
Paington.[1] Thus was the wretchedness, the weariness,
the misery, and the monotony of blockading complicated
by the suspicions, the fears, the dislikes of the Commander-
in-Chief.

Collingwood is very candid on the subject. He takes
his father-in-law by the hand, so to speak, and tells him
exactly what he thinks, and what no doubt scores of others
were thinking. There is no breach of discipline; he does
not shout his sentiments to some brother-admiral or captain
over the bulwark rail of his quarter-deck; he writes

[1] *Markham*, p. 178.

privately to his intimate friend—to his wife's father:
"*Neptune*, off Brest, August 15th, 1800. . . . We are
wandering before this port with no prospect of change for
the better. Nothing good can happen to us short of peace.
Every officer and man in the fleet is impatient for release
from a situation which daily becomes more irksome to all.
I see disgust growing round me very fast. Instead of
softening the rigours of a service, which must, from its
nature, be attended with many anxieties, painful watch-
ings, and deprivation of everything like comfort, the
contrary system is pursued, which has not extended to
me, but I see its effects on others, and deplore them.
What I feel as a great misfortune is that there is no
exercise of the military part of the duty, no practice of
those movements by a facility in which one fleet is made
superior to another. Whoever comes here ignorant in these
points must remain so; for he will find other employment,
about blankets and pig-styes, and tumbling provisions out
of one ship into another. How the times are changed!
Once when officers met the first question was—What news
of the French? Is there any prospect of their coming to
sea? Now there is no solicitude on that subject, and the
hope of peace alone engages the attention of everybody." [1]

It is impossible to read this and to appreciate the
significance of the large truth lying deep in it without
perceiving the wisdom of Lord Howe's objection to
blockading the enemy's ports. In the judgment of that
great Admiral it seemed the sheerest folly to keep a fleet
at sea watching the enemy's forests of masts snug in port,
ready to start in taut trim and hard fighting condition the
moment the weather had blown the blockading ships out
of sight. The system was ruinous to the ships themselves,
and detested by the seamen. Vessels were torn to pieces

[1] *Correspondence and Memoir*, p. 79.

by gales of wind, and Sir John Barrow tells us that as a result of these blockadings, when Lord Melville succeeded to the head of naval affairs, "he found a fleet of worn-out ships utterly inadequate to meet the combined fleets of France and Spain; but by doubling and cross-bracing and patching them up a fleet was with great exertion got together, which under Nelson fought and conquered at Trafalgar."[1] Lord Howe's notion was to keep a fleet at St. Helen's with frigates cruising to gain information; the fleet would, in case of emergency, be in readiness to put to sea at the shortest notice. The grand fleet, with a suitable number of frigates, he would station in Torbay, equally ready to start in the event of the enemy sailing from Brest.

It seems difficult to perceive what more resulted from all this blockading than the protraction of decisive issues. It was generally believed that Buonaparte hoped, by keeping his fleets quiet in harbour, to weaken ours by a process of rotting in aimless blockadings. He might also conjecture the hatred of our sailors to this sort of service, and count upon a spirit of insubordination as a consequence. Captain Brenton, in commenting upon that letter of Collingwood from which I have just quoted, says: "Every one knows that the ruler of France had the earliest and most correct intelligence of whatever was passing in the British fleet; and if he had thought that by continuing the war a little longer he could fan the flame of discontent in our ships, and produce thereby an open display of insubordination, the result to England might have been most disastrous."[2]

It must be admitted, however, that a certain degree of slackness had come about under Lord Bridport's command.

---

[1] *Life of Howe*, p. 217.
[2] *Life of the Earl of St. Vincent*, vol. i. p. 437.

Nelson, writing to St. Vincent from Plymouth, January 28th, 1801, says : "I did not wish to begin a scene here; I should perhaps have been thought impertinent and troublesome, for, except in two or three captains, I see such slackness that in the Mediterranean I have not been used to; and it requires a man of our friend Collingwood's firmness to keep some of them to their duty."[1] St. Vincent's methods, however, were not successful. "Our friend Collingwood" recognized the need of a policy the efficacy of which demanded a humaner theory of discipline than the old Earl was capable of devising. In this same letter to Lord St. Vincent, Nelson has this postscript: "Collingwood's wife and child arrived at seven o'clock last evening, 2 p.m."

To this meeting Collingwood had been looking forward with passionate anxiety. The prospect of embracing his Sarah—his "jewel," as he calls her to Sir Edward Blackett —and one at least of his little girls, "has cured me," he writes to his father-in-law, "of all my complaints; indeed, I believe the cause of them was vexation and sorrow at being, as it were, entirely lost to my family." Nelson had asked Collingwood to dine with him, and as they were about to sit down a message came from Mrs. Collingwood, announcing her arrival at Plymouth. Collingwood flew to the inn, " and found her and little Sarah as well after their journey as if it had lasted only for the day. No greater happiness is human nature capable of than was mine that evening." And afterwards he wrote to his old friend, Mrs. Moutray: "How surprised you would have been to have popped into the Fountain Inn and seen Lord Nelson, my wife, and myself sitting by the fireside cosing, and little Sarah teaching Phillis, her dog, to dance."

This picture takes an extraordinary tenderness from

1 Nelson's *Dispatches and Letters*, p. 7 ; *Addenda*, ccxxviii.

H

contrast with the grim realities of Collingwood's life at
that time, and it is rendered the more impressive to the
imagination because of Lord Nelson having been a
spectator of his friend's felicity.   There is something
remarkable in Nelson and Collingwood having been
together at such a moment as this, in such a scene of
affecting domestic happiness as Collingwood paints.   Only
a few days before, namely, on the 13th of January, Nelson
had parted from his wife for ever—divorced himself from
her for Lady Hamilton.   Amongst his last words to
her were, " I call God to witness there is nothing in you or
your conduct I wish otherwise."   But all the same, in
uttering these strange words of approval, he was turning
his back upon her for ever.   " My dear Fanny," he wrote
from Southampton on the day of his quitting her, " we
are arrived and heartily tired ; and with kindest regards
to my father and all the family; believe me, your
affectionate Nelson."   And this was the end of it all !—of
years of devotion between them, of admiration on her
part, of her affectionate cherishing of him when he came
home after Teneriffe with one arm gone, of her more than
daughter-like care of his old father !   Yet never did a
tenderer heart beat in the human breast than in Nelson's,
and it might not be hard, I think, to figure with some
degree of accuracy the thoughts which visited him, the
memories which arose in him, as he sat watching Collingwood and his wife, or directing his gaze at their little girl
playing with the dog.

Collingwood and his wife and child were together
for a few hours only.   " At dawn," he writes to his father-
in-law, " we parted and I went to sea."   It is hard to read
his letters about this brief meeting without emotion.   To
my mind they represent the character of Collingwood as
the finest compliment ever paid to the profession of the

sea. "She gloried in being a sailor's wife," wrote Jane
Austen of her heroine Anne,[1] "but she must pay the tax
of quick alarm for belonging to that profession which is, if
possible, more distinguished in its domestic virtues than in
its national importance." Collingwood cannot break away
from the subject of this brief meeting. He and his wife
were together in January, and in March he is writing
from off Ushant: "You will have heard from Sarah what
a meeting we had, how short our interview, and how
suddenly we parted. It is grief to me to think of it now;
it almost broke my heart then. After such a journey[2] to
see me but for a few hours, with scarce time for her to
relate the incidents of her journey, and no time for me to
tell her half what my heart felt at such a proof of her
affection! but I am thankful that I did see her and my
sweet child." And again, off Brest, April 20th: "I can
still talk to you of nothing but the delight I experienced
in the little I have had of the company of my beloved
wife and of my little Sarah. What comfort is promised to
me in the affections of that child, if it should please God
that we ever again return to the quiet domestic cares of
peace!"[3]

In a letter from Mrs. Collingwood to Sir Edward
Blackett, bearing the address of 38, George Street, Plymouth Dock, and dated February 15th, 1801, we catch a
glimpse of her life ashore—of the life of a sailor's devoted
wife—and there were many like her in those days who took
up their abode in lodgings and little cottages, as near to
where the ships came in for shelter or to replenish, as the
long-shore accommodation permitted: "The weather here
is very severe. I never suffered so much from cold, and

[1] In *Persuasion.*
[2] From Newcastle to Plymouth—a long journey indeed in those days.
[3] *Correspondence and Memoir,* pp. 85-6.

have been confined to the house some days with rheumatism, but hope soon to get out again. I wish I could give you any account of Admiral Collingwood. I have only heard once since they sailed, and that was from Torbay, where they were blown in for a few hours; but as the *Barfleur* is in the course of pay this month, I hope it will not be very long before they return into Cawsand Bay. In the meantime, I have the satisfaction of knowing how much my husband is respected here by the very great kindness and attention that everybody shows me. I might, if I pleased, be engaged out every day; but as I have my little girl with me, that would not answer at all, as it would be leaving her too much, so I shall now stay more at home. Pray tell Uncle Harry[1] that Mrs. and Miss Turon have called on me, and I went to the Citadel the next day to return their visit, and saw poor Governor Campbell, who is in a melancholy state, having had a paralytic stroke that has altered him much. . . . They gave us a very kind reception, and said they hoped to see us to a family dinner soon. I feel very much obliged to you, my dear sir, for your kind invitation to Thorpe Lea, which I shall be very happy to accept of when I leave this part of the country; but at present I fancy I am to remain here, or in the neighbourhood of Torbay, for some time, as it is the only chance I can have of seeing my husband. . . . I have received great kindness and attention from Sir Thos. Pasley, the Port-Admiral here; he has two public days in the week, and I was to have dined there yesterday, but was obliged to send an excuse, being so poorly, and this morning he has sent me some books to amuse me. I am indeed most grateful for the kind attention I have received here." [2]

[1] The Rev. H. Blackett, vicar of Boldon, Durham.
[2] Letters in possession of J. C. Blackett, Esq.

We hear of her again, this time at Paington, August 10th, 1801. She writes to Mrs. Blackett: "I have been at this place some time waiting the *Barfleur's* coming into port, and as the fleet have been at sea five months, I hope it will not be much longer before I have the pleasure of seeing Admiral Collingwood."[1] Five months! And waiting for a husband, who is not off Cádiz, nor in the West Indies, nor in distant seas, but just over the way; the royals of his ship—if ever he sets them—sunk but a little distance below the rim of the horizon of the water that washes to the cliffs, on which this tender loving wife stands gazing oceanwards. I am perfectly well aware that by every canon of the nautical profession we are prohibited from witnessing any sentiment in the career of the gentlemen of the jacket; nevertheless, sentiment will creep into that career, and make it engaging and touching and beautiful, sanctifying it by the pathos it must otherwise lack. It may be that only a sailor's wife in these days will know how to sympathize to the very heart with the wife of the sailor in those red and thunderous times of war. She will be in spirit with Mrs. Collingwood, with the scores of other wives of admirals, captains, officers; she will know the meaning of the hurricane note of the gale in the black night roaring in the chimney, and furiously rattling the rain-lashed window casements; she will know the meaning of the storming noises of colliding waters running in hills, whitening out into fields of foam under the ink of the Channel sky; she will know the meaning of the news of wrecks—of the reports of dismasted ships—of the sinister rumours subtly penetrating from one knows not what source, of vessels ashore, of loss of life! Something of all this may happen again; there will be anxiety, grief, spells of bitter suspense; but never can it all happen

[1] Letters in possession of J. C. Blackett, Esq.

again as it then did, for science has extinguished two-thirds of those elements and conditions, which, in their combined form in the days of Collingwood—and with the days of Collingwood we are dealing—rendered the life of the sailor the most desperately perilous of all callings, and the expectations, the hopes and the fears of the sailor's wife the most poignant and affecting of emotions.

On the 21st of February, 1801, Admiral Cornwallis was appointed to command the Channel fleet in the room of Earl St. Vincent, who was now First Lord of the Admiralty. In the preceding month Collingwood had been promoted Rear-Admiral of the Red, in a promotion of flag-officers on the occasion of the establishment, by Act of Parliament, of the union between Great Britain and Ireland. It will be seen by the following letter that the severities of St. Vincent's discipline had not been of very much use as an influence over the minds of the seamen. Writing on board the *Barfleur* at Spithead, January 1st, 1801, to Sir Edward Blackett, Collingwood says:

"I hope the rest of my New Year's days may be on shore in peace and comfort with my family, for in truth my domestic comfort has been very much interrupted. We are rather under disagreeable circumstances at present. When it was known that the French were about to send a great armament to the West Indies, four of our ships, viz. *Temeraire, Formidable, Vengeance,* and *Majestic,* were fitted for foreign service, and ordered to sail—to open their further orders in a certain latitude. It was pretty well understood among the sailors that they were to go to the West Indies, and they peremptorily refused to weigh anchor except to England. Having, in this instance, thrown off their obedience to the officers (as is ever the case), they proceeded to other irregularities, in which they were opposed by the officers in the *Temeraire,* and several

of the most active taken into custody. As there was a
strong suspicion, and in some ships evident proof, that the
determination not to go abroad was too general, the whole
squadron was ordered to this port, and the men in
confinement are to be tried very soon. Except in the
Temeraire, the general deportment of the men has been
very orderly, but I doubt whether it would have been so
in any vessel that was ordered to sail. It is a melancholy
consideration that under whatever circumstances the
country may be, there should be a doubt whether its active
force can be applied in the prompt manner that may be
necessary. I hope, however, that Peace, established on a
firm basis, will soon put an end to our anxieties on this
subject. . . .

"From what I understand, Lord St. Vincent's illness
renders him quite incapable of attending to public business.
On all despatches arriving at the Admiralty lately, Mr.
Addington has been immediately sent to, and in one
instance, Lords Grenville and Spencer were sent to, and
they were long in consultation before it was settled that
the fleet should return to England. The state of the
West Indies is at this time very critical indeed. The
French principles of equality, which have loosened all the
ties of government in Europe, have (doubtless by their
emissaries) found their way to the negroes, and what will
be the consequence is dreadful to look forward to; for the
number of Europeans there is trifling to that of the
blacks. A West Indian estate is at present a very pre-
carious hold of a fortune; but after the revolutions and
changes made by such a war as we have worked through,
it hardly appears to be the same world we were born to." [1]

In the marine chronicles of this period one follows the
movements of Collingwood until sent to Cadiz, as though

[1] Letters in possession of J. C. Blackett, Esq.

they were current and of the moment. Nothing brings the
past so close to us as the old newspaper paragraph. We
seem to read it with the eyes of a contemporary, respire the
atmosphere of the age, see what is passing, and hear what
is said. For instance : " Portsmouth report—September
5th. Sailed the *Barfleur* of 98 guns, Rear-Admiral
Collingwood, Captain Ommaney, to join the Channel
Fleet." " Plymouth report—March 4th, wind N.N.E.,
fair. This day was paid the *Barfleur*, 98 guns, Rear-
Admiral Collingwood.—March 8th, wind N.N.E., fair. In
the forenoon great fog. Sailed for Torbay the *Barfleur* of
98 guns, Rear-Admiral Collingwood; and the *London* of
98 guns, Captain G. Murray; they are victualled and
stored for five months." " Portsmouth report—June 4th.
Admiral Collingwood arrived here on Thursday and hoisted
his flag on board the *Diamond* frigate, Captain Elphinstone,
and will sail to-morrow to join the Channel fleet. Captain
G. Reynolds also goes to take the command of the *Venerable*, of 74 guns, which is to be the Admiral's flag-ship."
And so on.

These are the touches which give to the historic portrait
the bloom and movement of life itself. We taste the salt
wind; we see the great fog lifting; Portsmouth Water—
Plymouth Sound—are before us crowded with the craft of
that day : the line-of-battle ship lifts the gleaming buttons
of her trucks on high, the blood-red cross of St. George
proudly waves at a score of gaff ends, the small armed
sloop is beating out, and some saucy brig is bowling in
with a flowing sheet in company with three or four prizes,
black, sulky-looking French luggers, and Dutch hoys with
bows of the shape of an apple ; and we watch the *Diamond*
frigate getting under way, flashing into white canvas to
the merry strains of the boatswain's pipe, and leaning from
the breeze as her yards are braced to it, with Collingwood

pacing the quarter-deck, sending many a lingering glance ashore whilst he thinks of his wife and his little girls, and of his home up at old Morpeth, and of the months of salt beef and Channel surge, and ceaseless vigilance which lie before him.

Shortly after Collingwood's death there appeared in the *Courier*, a newspaper of that period, a very graphic account of our hero, obviously written by some one who knew him personally. Portions of this description are so applicable to his experiences whilst blockading Brest, that I cannot do better than quote them here: "He was of middle stature, but extremely thin and temperate in his general habits; ate always with an appetite, drank moderately after dinner, but never indulged afterwards in spirits or in wine; while his personal attention to the lowest guest at his table was always universally observed. It was his general rule in tempestuous weather, and upon any hostile emergency that occurred, to sleep upon his sofa in a flannel gown, taking off only his epauletted coat. The writer has seen him up on deck without his hat, and his grey hair floating to the wind, whilst torrents of rain poured down through the shrouds, and his eye, like the eagle's, on the watch. Personal exposure, colds, rheumatisms, ague, all—nothing seemed to him when his duty called. His judgment was sound and firm, his mind acute and penetrating, his wit so very lively it led him constantly to pun; and though in general punsters must be frequently insipid, he seldom failed to produce the playful equivoque he wished.

"To his religious duties he constantly attended; his religion like himself was without terror, pure without fanaticism, and gentle without levity. He was always perfectly dignified in his deportment, without that execrable pride which we often see assumed as a cloak to conceal a want of worth. Unprejudiced he was not; one prejudice he had which was singular as his mind was liberal. He deemed it the bounden duty of every Englishman to hate a Frenchman as his natural foe, and no man ever hated the national character and the nation more cordially than he. As he sometimes expressed a respectful pity for the Spaniards, and as the love of his country was the leading feature of his noble soul, this probably arose from a concealed opinion he entertained, 'that universal dominion would be the fate of France.' " [1]

[1] Abridged from the extract in the *Naval Chronicle*, vol. xxiii. p. 351.

CHAPTER VI.

N the 1st of October, 1801, preliminary articles of peace between France and Great Britain were signed by Lord Hawkesbury and Citizen Otto. The definitive treaty, however, known as the Peace of Amiens, was not concluded until the 25th of March, 1802. This peace, brief as it was, enabled Collingwood to return to Morpeth. We may conceive that his long spell of salt water rendered his home and the shore-going occupations he made for himself infinitely delightful to him. His amusements were wholly domestic; he read extensively, particularly in history; he studiously exercised himself in composition by making abstracts from books, and closely observing the style and turns of the best authors; he gave several hours a day to the education of his daughters. He drew with taste; [1] he was also very fond of gardening, and passed much of his time in the cultivation of his garden on the bank of the pretty river Wansbeck. This, indeed, seems to have been his favourite employment; and it is told that on one occasion a brother Admiral, who had been hunting about the grounds for him in vain, discovered him with his gardener, an old man named Scott, in the bottom of a deep trench which they were busily occupied in digging. We also obtain a sight of Collingwood at home from a letter written by J. E. Blackett to his brother, Sir Edward, dated April 21st, 1803:

"I went to Morpeth soon after I wrote to you, and spent a week there very agreeably with the Admiral and my daughter. The weather was very fine: too much so for the season. We were out most of the day till drove into the house by the heat: the Admiral busy with his axe and spade, and all of us employed. There was a great change in the weather on Saturday. . . . My granddaughters have not received that improvement from the school at this place that their parents expected. So they are taken away from it, and are at present at home under the instruction of their father and mother. . . . A fortnight ago Thomas Bates, your tenant, being at the Morpeth market, dined at Admiral Collingwood's, and produced a gold ring which was found on removing some stones near

---

[1] A story is told of his skill as an artist. Nelson and he were often together, when at Antigua, at the house of Commissioner Moutray. Nelson had lost his hair from fever, and its place was supplied by a wig of the most grotesque character. Collingwood said to him one day, "Nelson, I must draw you in that wig." This he did, and produced a coloured drawing which is said to have been a very good likeness. After the picture had been looked at and laughed over, Nelson said, "Now, Collingwood, in revenge I will draw you in that queue of yours," and made a pencil sketch of his friend. These two portraits were long in the possession of Mrs. Moutray.

Old Admiral, hunting for Collingwood, finds him digging with his gardener—
Old Scott.—p. 110.

the Roman encampment, which (as the Admiral at that time daily expected to be called to town) Bates requested that he would take with him to be delivered to you. . . . But at present it is not likely that Admiral Collingwood will have a call." [1]

A very patriotic habit of Collingwood was to plant acorns with a view to oak trees and ships of the line in the future. He was constantly lamenting the prospect of a decay of timber in this country; and indeed, when one considers the enormous quantity of wood that went to the construction of a single ship of the line, and when one reflects that, despite one or two small experiments, there was no hint to be found in that age of the probability of iron replacing timber, one cannot but sympathize with Collingwood's forebodings. "If," says he, "the country gentlemen do not make it a point to plant oaks wherever they will grow, the time will not be very distant when to keep our navy we must depend entirely on captures from the enemy. . . . I wish everybody thought on this subject as I do; they would not walk through their farms without a pocketful of acorns to drop in the hedge-sides, and then let them take their chance." It was computed that the construction of a 74-gun ship consumed about 3,000 loads of timber, each load containing 50 cubic feet. Two thousand large well-grown trees, averaging two tons each, were needed. Allowing a space of 33 feet between each tree— 30 feet being the usual planting distance—then a statute acre would contain 40 trees; and the building of a 74-gun therefore absorbed the timber of 50 acres! Even so recently as 1844—thirty-four years after the death of Collingwood—a writer was declaring that "the man who plants 500 acres of land with 20,000 oak trees, which in 90 or 100 years will be available in the construction of

_____
[1] Letters in possession of J. C. Blackett, Esq.

ten sail of the line, is a true patriot; whilst by such an act his posterity will reap an ample fortune." [1]

This was the last time that Collingwood was at home; he was to live for another seven years; but never again was he to revisit the scenes which he loved, which held all that was dearest to him in this world. So wonderfully human is the character of this fine sailor and good and great man, so present to our sympathies—long ago as it is—is all that concerns his life, that though knowing how it is to be with him—that he is about to go forth to earn renown for himself—to play so distinguished a part as to become one of the most striking of the historic figures of a great historic age—though knowing this, still do we seem to attend his departure from his home with reluctance, and linger in fancy with him on the threshold of his house at Morpeth with such emotion of personal concern at the eternal separation he is unconsciously entering upon as makes one wonder at the magic of the character that could produce a sentiment of the kind eighty years after his death.

Never for a moment had there been hope in this country of a continuance of peace between Great Britain and France. Whilst all seemed at rest, the French ports were full of the business of warlike preparations. Gun-vessels and flat-bottomed boats were being built; a number of powerful liners were in the docks at Brest, repairing and nearly ready; there were ships of great force on the stocks at Lorient, at St. Malo, at Nantes, at Bordeaux, at Rochefort, at Toulon, at Marseilles, and elsewhere. Buonaparte's intentions were clearly defined in his instructions to General Decaen. On the 8th of March, 1803, the King of England sent a message to Parliament that was accepted by the public as virtually a declaration

[1] *Nautical Magazine*, 1844, p. 226.

of war against France. War was declared on the 16th of May; letters of marque were issued and general reprisals ordered, and an embargo was laid upon ships belonging to Holland, which was regarded as a province of France.

On the 17th of May, Admiral the Hon. William Cornwallis sailed from Cawsand Bay with a fleet of ten ships of the line to cruise off Ushant and watch the harbour of Brest. Collingwood's flag was aboard the *Venerable*, and it is said that when Admiral Cornwallis saw the ship he exclaimed, "Here comes Collingwood; the last to leave and the first to join me." Once again he had resumed the wretched, monotonous business of blockading. His days and nights were to be dedicated to watching the motions of the French fleet. He bids adieu, he says, to snug beds and comfortable naps at night; there is no more "turning-in" with him unless it be "all standing"; whenever he lies down he has all his clothes on. His interpretation of the obligation of alertness must speedily have destroyed a man of a weaker constitution than his. He would pass whole nights on the quarter-deck, pacing to and fro with many a pause between to direct a falcon glance seawards. His lieutenant (Clavell) sometimes endeavoured to persuade him that so much vigilance on his part was unnecessary, that a good look-out was kept, and that he must be almost exhausted with fatigue. "I fear *you* are," Collingwood would reply; "you have need of rest; so go to bed, Clavell, and I will watch by myself." Often they would doze together on a gun, from which Collingwood repeatedly started to sweep the horizon with his night-glass.[1]

To the misery of experiences of this sort was to be added the horror of unseaworthy ships. In the beginning of 1803 the *Venerable* was sent to Cawsand Bay that her

[1] *Correspondence and Memoir*, p. 9?.

sailors might be refreshed. Their "refreshment" consisted in being worked almost to death. First of all some slight defects appeared in the ship; they invited a closer scrutiny, and at last it was discovered that the *Venerable* was so utterly rotten as to be unfit for sea. "We have been sailing," he wrote, "for the last six months with only a sheet of copper between us and eternity."[1] The sailor in those days had enemies of a deadlier sort to contend with than ever the French or the Spaniards were—I mean the rogues of the English shipbuilding yards. The copper bolts used as fastenings, instead of being employed for holding the ship together, were sold to the marine-store dealers. It was the duty of the master-builder and his assistants to see that these bolts were driven effectually into their proper places, and that this vigilance might be eluded, the villains contrived what was called a "devil-bolt," composed of the head and tail of a copper bolt affixed to a common wooden plug, so that to the eye the ship appeared properly copper-fastened. Captain Brenton[2] attributes the loss of two line-of-battle ships to these sham fastenings, and speaks of others which in a sea-way "worked" to such a degree as to oblige them to be docked, when on inspection they were found to be held together by "devil-bolts."

Assuredly Collingwood did not leave the *Venerable* too soon. He shifted his flag to the *Culloden*, and in November 1804, in a black night, and during a heavy gale of wind, the *Venerable*, then lying with the fleet at anchor in Torbay, went ashore near Paington, and a number of her people perished. She was a vessel of historic interest, having carried Admiral Duncan's flag at the battle of Camperdown. It was this ship that singled out the *Vryheid*, with

---

[1] *Correspondence and Memoir*, p. 95.
[2] *Life of the Earl of St. Vincent*, vol. ii. p. 160.

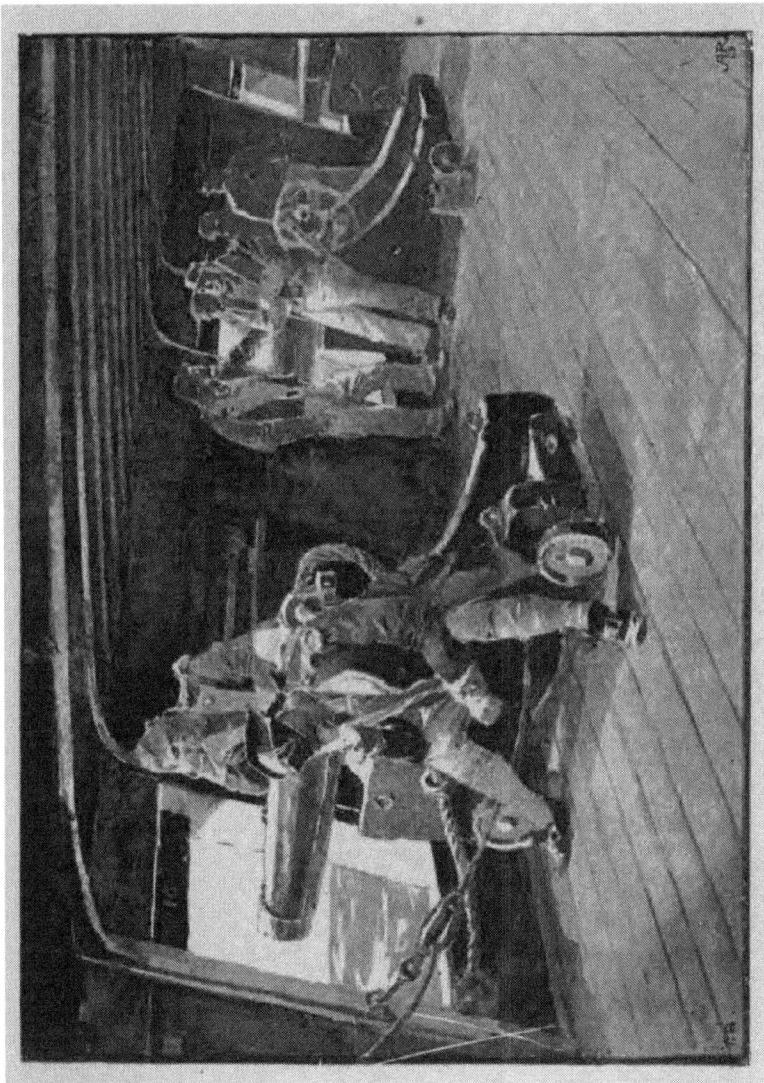

the gallant Admiral de Winter on board, and fought her until Duncan was obliged to haul off and wear round on the starboard tack; on which the *Triumph* approached to give the Dutchman the *coup de grâce*, when, after sustaining the united fire of four British vessels with magnificent spirit, De Winter, with his three masts gone and his stout craft the sheerest of hulks, struck his colours.

On the promotion of Admirals on the 23rd of April, 1804, Collingwood was made Vice-Admiral of the Blue. The character of the blockade maintained by Cornwallis obliged our hero to shift his flag from ship to ship, so that he might always be on the station in a vessel fit for instant service. Of this he complains a good deal. He writes, for instance, that he has been at sea for eighteen weeks at a stretch, and that though he has not a sick man in his ship, the severity of the cold is making all hands feel the want of warm clothing. "When I sailed," says he, "I had not time to make a coat, and I have only two, one of which is very old; but I did not suspect I should have been so long without the means of getting one." He is to be believed indeed when he asserts that, "nothing but a sense of its being necessary for the safety of the country could make us support such a deprivation of everything which is pleasurable."

The grim reality of the life is brought home to us by his writing in August 1804, that he had not seen a green leaf on a tree since he left Portsmouth in June 1803. He curiously justifies Lord Howe's opinion on blockading when, in writing on board the *Dreadnought* in February 1805, he says that the public seem content so long as they know that the fleet is at sea, little imagining that every gale of wind encountered by the ships diminishes the security of the country. "The last cruise," he says, "disabled five large ships, and two more lately; several of them must be docked."

Meanwhile his thoughts are for ever with his home; he seems unable to turn his eyes away from contemplation of his daughters. "I am delighted," he writes to his father-in-law, "with your account of my children's improvement, for it is a subject of the greatest anxiety to me. Above all things keep novels out of their reach. They are the corrupters of tender minds, they exercise the imagination instead of the judgment; make them all desire to become the Julias and Cecilias of romance; and turn their heads before they are enabled to distinguish truth from fictions devised merely for entertainment. When they have passed their climacteric it will be time enough to begin novels."[1]

A month later than the date of the letter in which this passage occurs, Collingwood was detached from the Channel fleet with a squadron with orders to go in pursuit of the enemy's fleet, which, having sailed from Toulon, were at this time being chased across the Atlantic by Lord Nelson. His power in this command, however, was largely discretionary. Nelson sailed from Antigua on June 13th, and on the 18th of July, whilst on his way to Gibraltar to victual the ships, he fell in with Collingwood in the *Dreadnought*, and two other sail of the line. Nelson wrote to his old friend to tell him how miserable he was through not having met the enemy's fleet. "But for false information," he says, "the battle would have been fought where Rodney fought his on June 6th." He is in doubt now whether Villeneuve has not tricked him and gone to Jamaica. He adds that the moment the fleet is watered he will pay Collingwood a visit—"not, my dear friend, to

[1] *Correspondence and Memoir*, p. 102. But at this time Scott and Jane Austen were not. The novel of Collingwood's day was indeed miserable stuff; and he certainly would not advise his wife to put the earlier novelists—Fielding, Smollett, Richardson—into the hands of his daughters.

take your command from you (for I may probably add
mine to you), but to consult how we can best serve our
country by detaching a part of this large force." Collingwood's sagacity penetrated the real motive of the movement
of the combined fleets. In answer to Nelson's letter he
writes, dating July the 21st: "I have considered the invasion of Ireland as the real mark and butt of all their
operations. Their flight to the West Indies was to take
off the naval force which proved the great impediment of
their undertaking. This summer is big with events."

His hope of shaking Nelson by the hand, and of enjoying a long talk with his old friend, was disappointed. "We
are in a fresh levanter," wrote Nelson to him, "you have
a westerly wind—therefore I must forego the pleasure of
taking you by the hand until October next, when, if I am
well enough, I shall (if the Admiralty please) resume the
command." Collingwood seems to have been much vexed
by Nelson's failure to visit him. His clear, wise mind
could not but have been helpful to Nelson in suggestion
at this time. He might have felt, too, that he had earned
the compliment of a conference. James, in referring to
Nelson's falling in with Collingwood, says that the latter
had no information concerning the enemy to impart "beyond what his own sagacity—and that was of no common
kind—suggested." [1] But Nelson, weary of the sea, and
unwell, was anxious to get home for the few weeks' rest
he was looking forward to.

Nothing of interest happened until August 20th, when
at ten o'clock in the morning the combined fleet of 29
ships of the line, exclusive of frigates and corvettes, hove
into sight. Collingwood, on board the *Dreadnought*, had
for his consorts the *Colossus* and *Achille*, 74's. Here were
these three ships alone, with the horizon in the north-

---

[1] *James*, vol. iii. p. 354.

west whitened with the crowded canvas of the Franco-Spanish fleets! Collingwood relates the incident to his wife thus: "I have very little time to write to you, but must tell you what a squeeze we had like to have got yesterday. While we were cruising off the town down came the combined fleet of 36 sail of men-of-war; we were only three poor things with a frigate and a bomb, and drew off towards the Straits, not very ambitious, as you may suppose, to try our strength against such odds. They followed us as we retired with 16 large ships, but on our approaching the Straits they left us, and joined their friends in Cadiz, where they are fitting and replenishing their provisions. We in our turn followed them back, and to-day have been looking in Cadiz, where their fleet is now as thick as a wood. I hope I shall have somebody come to me soon, and in the meantime I must take the best care of myself I can."

The modesty in this relation is as remarkable as the gallant spirit and fine seamanship the incident illustrates. A writer, referring to this experience of Collingwood, says: "In the memorable autumn of 1805, when he with difficulty got the *Dreadnought* into the stream of the Gut of Gibraltar, he stood upon the poop smiling at 35 sail of the enemy with only five ships under his command; and when they wore back he wore himself in their face, and actually blockaded the Bay of Cadiz, they within."[1] Mr. Newnham Collingwood is correct in saying that the skill the Admiral exhibited in these manœuvres excited great admiration at the time.[2] The *Dreadnought* was a very slow sailer; Collingwood nevertheless contrived to keep his ships just

[1] *Naval Chronicle*, vol. xxiii. p. 351. I rely upon James, the naval historian, for the number of ships given.
[2] Nelson wrote to him, Oct. 10th, 1805—"Everybody in England admired your adroitness in not being forced unnecessarily into the Straits."

out of gunshot, saying, "I am determined they shall not drive me through the Straits unless they follow me." The pursuers, perceiving his object, shifted their helm; the English ships immediately did the same and followed them. This occurred two or three times; eventually the enemy abandoned the chase, and headed for Cadiz, Collingwood sticking to their skirts and resuming the blockade with his four vessels—he had been joined at midnight by the *Mars*, 74, Captain George Duff—before half of the French and Spanish ships had entered the harbour.

Captain, after Sir Edward, Codrington, who certainly did not love Collingwood, refers to this experience in one of his letters. After Trafalgar he had occasion to visit Collingwood, whom he describes as very good-humoured, chatty, and communicative. "He says the French could not have come up with him without passing the Gut of Gibraltar, which they wished to avoid, and that as soon as he got between the Capes he shortened sail; but they would not follow. He seems to do everything himself, with great attention to the minutiæ."[1] It is indeed declared of Collingwood, that the professional judgment he showed at this time in blocking up the port of Cadiz with only four ships of the line, and confining the enemy's fleet in their own harbour, "is an instance of genius and address that is scarcely to be paralleled in the pages of our naval history."[2] His method was to divide his little force so as to deceive the enemy, incredible as the success of such a stratagem may appear. Two of his vessels lay close in where the signals they made to the other two could be observed by the Franco-Spanish, and these signals of the inshore ships being repeated by the other two at a distance, led to the belief that they in their turn were signalling to

[1] *Memoir of Sir Edward Codrington*, p. 44.
[2] *Naval Chronicle*, vol. xv. p. 369.

a force out of sight behind the horizon. But this was not all. As Napoleon had never contemplated the diversion of his fleet to the southward and to Cadiz,[1] no provision in the shape of stores had been made at that port for the supply of the thousands who filled the ships which lay in it. Neutral vessels were therefore employed in transporting biscuits and meat and the like from Nantes to the small ports of the neighbourhood, and the stoppage of these supplies by Collingwood undoubtedly ended in forcing the hand of the enemy's admirals, and compelling them to put to sea.

On the 22nd of August, Rear-Admiral Sir Richard Bickerton reinforced Collingwood off Cadiz with four sail of the line. Sir Richard's health, however, obliged him shortly afterwards to shift his flag and proceed to England. On the 30th Sir Robert Calder joined with 18 line-of-battle ships. The Admiralty, according to Collingwood's own showing, appeared to have abandoned him to his own devices. He says that it will be a happy day that relieves him from this perpetual cruising which is wearing him to a lath. His chief difficulty lay in maintaining the health of his men. The procuring beef from the Moors demanded a number of ships which he could ill spare; yet 200 bullocks scarcely sufficed for a week, and a transport laden with wine about a month. " How happy," he exclaims, in a letter to his father-in-law, dated September 21st, " should I be could I but hear from home and know how my dear girls are going on ! Bounce is my only pet now, and he is indeed a good fellow; he sleeps by the side of my cot, whenever I lie in one, until near the time of tacking, and

---

[1] Effected by Sir Robert Calder, in an action rendered memorable by the scandalous treatment to which he was subjected. But Nelson, . as the Duke of Wellington said, had taught the nation not to be satisfied with half measures.

then marches off to be out of hearing of the guns, for he is not reconciled to them yet." [1]

Bounce was his dog, but of what breed I am unable to state; yet a humorist, to judge from Collingwood's references to it. The loneliness he complains of illustrates a favourite saying of Nelson: "Every man becomes a bachelor after he passes the Rock of Gibraltar." In some letters, written by Captain Duff of the *Mars*, between May 1804 and the 21st of October, 1805, on which glorious day he was killed by a cannon-ball taking off his head, Collingwood is occasionally mentioned; and as examples of the opinion in which our hero was held by those serving under him, I introduce them in this place. On May 6th, 1804, Duff writes: "I have been paying my respects to-day to Admiral Collingwood. He is the senior officer ordered to be ready for foreign service, and a fine, steady, good officer he is. I do not know one I would so soon go on service with." On August 26th, he says that Collingwood has " taken him close " to himself, and adds, " He is a very fine fellow, and stuck very close to the combined fleet with his little squadron." Again, on October 10th, he gives an instance of Lord Collingwood's kindness : "I am sorry the rain has begun to-night, as it will spoil my fine work, having been employed for this week past to paint the ship *à la* Nelson, which most of the fleet are doing.[2] He (Nelson) is so good and pleasant a man that we all wish to do what he likes without any kind of orders. I have been myself very lucky with most of my Admirals, but I really think the present the pleasantest I have met with ; even this little detachment is a kind thing to me, there being so many

---

[1] *Correspondence and Memoirs*, p. 112.
[2] Nelson, I believe, was the first to paint his ships with broad bands chequered with the black gun-ports. These bands were then yellow; they were afterwards white.

senior officers to me in the fleet, as it shows his attention and wish to bring me forward ; but I believe I have
to thank my old friend Collingwood for it, as he was on
board the *Victory* when I was sent for." [1]

References, which in any way characterize a man as these
do, are valuable, as helping us to a true knowledge of his
heart and qualities. Another who knew Collingwood, the
late Admiral Hercules Robinson, in a lively little volume
of memoirs, entitled *Seadrift,* has much to say of • him :
" Collingwood's dry, caustic mind lives before me in the
recollection of his calling across the deck to his fat, stupid
captain [2]—long since dead—when he had seen him commit
some monstrous blunder. After the usual bowing and
formality, which the excellent old chief never omitted, he
said, ' Captain ——, I have been thinking whilst I looked
at you how strange it is that a man should *grow* so big and
know so little. That's all, sir, that's all.' Hats off, low
bows." Again, " Nelson and Collingwood, who were about
as yielding as their respective anchor-stocks, and who regarded a shower of shot as much as a shower of snowflakes,
were as tender-hearted as two school-girls. When Collingwood promoted me from his own ship to be lieutenant of
the *Glory,* he sent a commendation with me which, when
my new Captain (Otway) read it to me, made my cheek
tingle, knowing how undeserved it was, and feeling that
my having been discovered playing with and petting
Bounce, the Admiral's dog—' *Poor Bouncie, good dog, dear
Bouncie, &c.'*—and feeding *Nanny,* his goat, with biscuit
when she butted her head at me, had effected more than I
cared to acknowledge in my promotion." " Pr—tt was
officer of the watch when the hammocks were piped down
(a man who neglects his hammock has it locked up in the
store-room, compelling him to prick for the softest plank

[1] *Naval Chronicle,* 15, pp. 276—292.   [2] Certainly not Rotheram.

instead of a comfortable bed whereon to repose, and to endure also a term on the black list). The master-at-arms reported that he had found Thomas Jones' hammock on the deck, and had locked it up in the store-room. 'Well,' said Pr—tt, 'don't mind it for once.' After this compassionate order he turned round, and there was the Admiral twiddling his thumbs, and not affecting to have heard anything; but certainly Pr—tt was promoted very soon after. He was a clever man and an excellent officer, and it was quite right; but I think that Tom Jones stepped him up the ladder, and that the transaction was considered by Collingwood a straw in the air which showed how the wind blew." [1]

Admiral Robinson repeats what was proverbial in the service—that Collingwood's economy of the King's stores was "conscientious to scrupulosity, to a passion." It was minute even to the ordering of stray rope-yarns to be picked up and saved, instead of being thrown overboard. This useful quality in him was of old standing. Shortly before the Battle of St. Vincent a new fore-topsail had been bent in the *Excellent*. In the hottest moment of the engagement with the *St. Ysidro*, Collingwood called out to his boatswain: "Bless me, Mr. Peffers, how came we to forget to bend our old topsail? They will quite ruin that new one. It will never be worth a farthing again." At the Battle of Trafalgar a top-gallant studding-sail was seen to be hanging over the top-gallant hammocks, the halliards having been shot away. Collingwood called to Lieutenant Clavell to help him to take it in, observing that they should want it again some other day; and the pair went to work to roll it carefully up, and place it in the boat. Collingwood's son-in-law tells us that during the five years in which the Admiral held the command in the Mediterranean the

---

[1] *Seadrift*, by Admiral Hercules Robinson, 1858, pp. 59—66.

whole amount of his demand for extraordinary disbursements was only £54, in which were included the expense of a mission to Morocco, the postage of letters, and other matters.

By certain of the wags of his fleet, when he held command after the death of Nelson, he was called "Salt Junk and Sixpenny." This I have on the authority of a writer whose name is little heard of now, though his published writings are full of interest, and exhibit high literary skill and great and varied experience of life. I refer to Charles Reece Pemberton, a noted Chartist. He was impressed, and served under Collingwood off Cadiz, and in a passage referring to the Admiral, he says, "*Salt Junk and Sixpenny,*—a sobriquet which his penurious hospitality won. With salt junk and a wine which he was proud of saying 'cost him sixpence per gallon,' he regaled his dinner guests. Of course 'this was occasioned by his ardour for the service which kept him so long at sea, away from ports where supplies could be obtained.' There were, however, many worse men in the service than old Collingwood."[1] This is the sarcasm of a forecastle hand, of a man who catches up whispers from the quarter-deck, credits them, and garnishes them. In truth, there was nothing niggardly in Collingwood's hospitality. He was by nature very reserved, and when he took command of the Mediterranean, and business of the utmost importance crowded upon his time, he saw very few visitors, and indeed little or nothing of his own officers save in the way of shipboard routine; but whenever he had leisure to entertain, he took care that the company were as liberally and elegantly served as the resources of an ocean larder permitted.

[1] *The Life and Literary Remains of Charles Reece Pemberton*, p. 161.

At the same time it must be remembered that at the period when Pemberton was grinning over the nickname of "Salt Junk and Sixpenny," Collingwood's income, including his full pay, barely amounted to £1100 a year, "as appears from several of his letters respecting the Income Tax, to which he was peculiarly solicitous that the most correct return should be made."[1] The obligation of economy is therefore very apparent. Mr. J. E. Blackett was a rich man, and Sir Edward Blackett, his brother, a man of very large fortune; but though Collingwood was grateful for his father-in-law's liberal help during the harder part of his professional career, neither self-dignity, nor honour, would suffer him to tax Mr. Blackett's bounty by unnecessary expenditure on his own part, in directions, at all events, which might have rescued him from the sobriquet that Pemberton speaks of.[2]

Nelson, in a letter dated September 7th, writes to Collingwood from the Admiralty, London : " I shall be with you in a very few days, and I hope you will remain second in command. You will change the *Dreadnought* for the *Royal Sovereign*, which I hope you will like."

[1] *Correspondence and Memoir*, p. 167.

[2] The poor pay and the social and domestic obligations of the naval officer of eighty years ago form the subject of a communication full of protest and indignation, in a naval publication of the period. The post-captain's lowest full pay, after the Income Tax had been deducted, was about £270. One half he might draw in quarterly instalments, but the remainder was withheld till his own and the accounts of the warrant-officers had been passed. This was the pay of the captain of a small frigate. He had to furnish a cabin and provide himself with plate, linen, wine, stores, telescopes, sextants, charts, timepiece, and the like. His dress was expensive, and there was the cost of society when in port. The pay increased gradually, till the captains of two or three of our largest ships received about £720 a year ; but these were like plums in a sailor's duff—quite out of hail of one another.

K

This ship, however, did not join the fleet until rather more than a month later. Nelson sailed from Portsmouth in the *Victory* on the morning of the 15th September, and despatched (on the 26th) the *Eurylaus* frigate in advance to let Collingwood know that he was coming, and to request, if the fleet were in sight of Cadiz, not only that no salute should be fired, but that no colours should be hoisted, "for," he added, "it is as well not to proclaim to the enemy every ship which may join the fleet." The reception Nelson met with delighted him. He wrote to Lady Hamilton that he believed his arrival was most welcome, not only to Collingwood, but to every individual in the fleet. "When," says he, "I came to explain to them the '*Nelson touch*,' it was like an electric shock. Some shed tears, all approved. 'It was new—it was singular—it was simple!' and from admirals downwards it was repeated, 'It must succeed if ever they will allow us to get at them! You are, my lord, surrounded by friends whom you inspire with confidence.' Some may be Judases, but the majority are certainly much pleased at my commanding them." [1]

That there were Judases amongst the captains of that fleet, Nelson's sensitiveness, rather than his conviction, might cause him to fear; but assuredly he would not suppose that Collingwood was one of them. The relations of these two great men before the famous battle—down to Nelson's dying hour, in short—were never more cordial.

[1] The theatrical side of Nelson's character shows strongly in his letters to Lady Hamilton—if indeed he wrote half that was printed in the work that contains them. The sentiment of that age was not opposed to tears even in the nautical calling; at the same time it is difficult to imagine such men as Collingwood, Duff, Rotheram, and others of the seasoned lobscousers, *weeping* over the "Nelson touch." If tears fell they must have been of the iron sort that Pluto, by the poet, was deemed capable of shedding.

"Telegraph upon all occasions without ceremony," writes
Nelson to Collingwood; "we are one, and I hope we shall
be." "I send you my plan of attack," he says, October
9th, "as far as a man dare venture to guess at the very
uncertain position the enemy may be found in; but, my
dear friend, it is to place you perfectly at ease respecting
my intentions, and to give full scope to your judgment
for carrying them into effect. We can, my dear Coll.,
have no little jealousies: we have only one great object
in view — that of annihilating our enemies and getting
a glorious peace for our country. No man has more
confidence in another than I have in you; and no man
will render your services more justice than your very old
friend, Nelson and Brontë."[1]

Codrington, who seldom loses an opportunity to sneer
at Collingwood, says: "On the Sunday morning Lord
Nelson, as a compliment to Collingwood, called him on
board by signal to consult with him, saying to Hardy
jocosely that he should not be guided by his opinion
unless it agreed with his own; and upon asking him,
Collingwood gave his opinion in favour of attacking the
fleet immediately. Lord Nelson, however, kept to his own
plan of waiting till he could get them further off."[2] One
is reluctant to question the testimony of such a witness
as Sir Edward Codrington, who holds a foremost place in
the ranks of British seamen and commanders; but the
word of a Collingwood must stand high, very high, above
the assertion of a Codrington.

> Whatever record leap to light
> *He* never shall be shamed!

And Collingwood is himself clear on the point. "In this
affair," he wrote November 2nd, 1805, referring to Nelson

[1] Nelson's *Dispatches and Letters*, vol. vii. p. 95.
[2] *Memoir of Sir Edward Codrington*, p. 54.

and to the battle " he did nothing without my counsel. We made our line of battle together, and concerted the mode of attack, which was put in execution in the most admirable style." [1] The character of Collingwood speaks for itself. We find him the soul of honour throughout his career, dignified, upright, of spotless integrity, animated by a sense of dutifulness unparalleled in its acts of self-devotion. *He* was not the man to lay claim to merits to which he had no title. Nelson's opinion of Collingwood's professional genius was too sincere to suffer him to be in earnest in the language which Codrington put into his mouth. He consulted Collingwood, and Collingwood approved, and his words, which I have quoted, admit of no further interpretation than that of cordial endorsement of Nelson's pre-arranged tactics.

It is interesting to observe the part allotted to Collingwood in Nelson's memorable General Order, October 18th. The fleet is to be kept in that position of sailing (with the exception of the first and second in command) that the order of sailing is to be the order of battle. If the enemy is seen to windward in line of battle, and the two lines and advanced squadron of British ships can "fetch" them —that is to say, arrive at them by a single board or by beating—it is assumed that they may be so extended as to prohibit their van from succouring their rear. "I should, therefore," says Nelson, " probably make the second in command a signal to lead through about the twelfth ship from their rear (or wherever he could fetch if not able to get so far advanced)." The second in command— that is to say, Collingwood—"will in all possible things direct the movement of his line by keeping them as compact as the nature of the circumstances will admit." Should the enemy's fleet be discovered in line of battle to

[1] *Correspondence and Memoir,* p. 136.

leeward, the divisions of the British will be brought nearly within gun-shot of the enemy's centre; the signal will then most probably be made for the lee-line (Collingwood's) to bear up together, "and to crowd sail so as to arrive as quickly as possible at the enemy, cutting through him at the twelfth ship from the rear." Finally, the entire direction of the line (after the intentions of the Commander-in-Chief are signified) is intended—with a reservation that implies merely anticipation of the unexpected—to be left to Collingwood. The whole spirit of this General Order breathes the foregone conclusion of the enemy's annihilation. There must be no loss of time—this is the true genius of the Nelson "touch." The business must be decisive; the second in command having dealt his blow, must follow it up until the assaulted ships are captured or destroyed. The essential point is to throw the whole weight of the British fleet some two or three ships ahead of the enemy's commander-in-chief, who is supposed to be in the centre. The object, of course, is to deal with the windward vessels before those to leeward could work up to their assistance. In effect, it is a repetition of Nelson's tactics at the Nile, saving that here the ships were in motion, whilst in Aboukir Bay the French were at anchor.

Interest, however, in these old battle manœuvres cannot but be languid nowadays. They are as obsolete to the mariner as the methods of warfare in the times of the sling and the arrow, the cross-bow, and the complete suit of mail. One may study such an order as this of Nelson without discovering a single hint likely to prove applicable to our steam and metal era. The lee and weather divisions of the future can signify only the quarter from which the wind blows. What other significance is to be attached to these words beyond their meaning as mere sea terms when your propeller can put your ship into any position you choose her to occupy? Moreover, it is conceivable that before the naval officer ventures to offer an opinion upon the character of the tactics likely to be employed in future marine conflicts, he will first want to know what kind of a ship he is going to be put in command of. Everything is uncertain to positive vagueness. Of nothing can we be sure saving that the science of ocean warfare, brought to its height by Nelson in the days of tacks and sheets, is now for all purposes of suggestion as absolutely useless as in this age would be the ships which he commanded.

The Battle of Trafalgar was fought on the 21st of October, 1805. At dawn on this day the combined fleet of French and Spaniards were descried at a distance of some ten or twelve miles. The morning was somewhat misty, but the risen sun clarified the atmosphere, and his light flashed upon a spectacle of splendour, colour, and beauty. There was a light wind, but a swell with some weight was rolling in from the Atlantic. The eastern sea-line looked full of ships, and towering among them was the colossal *Santissima Trinidad*, the huge fabric which Nelson, in a letter written some time earlier, had hoped to see his old friend "Coll." alongside of—remembering the Battle of St. Vincent.

CHAPTER VII.

IT is not proposed to attempt a description of the Battle of Trafalgar. The tale is hoary with its burden of eighty-five years, and every bookshelf has a volume containing it at large. Our business is with Collingwood and with his ship the *Royal Sovereign,* and we will follow the fine old craft as best we can as she slides over the wide heave of the Atlantic swell to the light impulse of her outstretched wings of studding-sail, slowly widening the distance betwixt herself and the ships astern of her as she goes, so that, as we all know, she was in action a quarter of an hour or twenty minutes, amidst a furious fire, which she was returning with tragic and tremendous effect, before the nearest of the British ships was within gunshot. "See," cried Nelson, viewing this magnificent exhibition of British pluck with the generous enthusiam that was one of the finest qualities of his grand character; "See," he cried to Captain Blackwood, "how that noble fellow Collingwood takes his ship into action!" and it is believed that Collingwood, much about the time when this speech was uttered, exclaimed, "What would Nelson give to be here!" Let the late Admiral Hercules Robinson, who was an eye-witness, here spin us a Trafalgar yarn:

"There is now before me the beautiful misty sunshiny morning of the 21st October; the sea like a mill-pond, but with an ominous ground swell rolling in from the Atlantic. The noble fleet with royals and studding-sails on both sides, bands playing, officers in full-dress, and the ships covered with ensigns hanging in various places! How well I remember the ports of our great ships hauled up, the guns run out; and as from the sublime to the ridiculous is but a step, the *Pickle* schooner close to our ship with the boarding nettings up and her tompions out of her four guns—about as large and as formidable as two pairs of Wellington boots. How I see at this moment glorious old Collingwood a quarter of a mile ahead of his second astern, and opening the battle with the magnificent black *Santa Anna*, cutting the tacks and sheets and halliards of his studding-sails as he reached her, and letting them drop into the water (grieving, I have no doubt, at the loss of so much beautiful canvas), and as his main-yard caught the mizzen-vangs of his opponent, discharging his double-shotted broadside into her stern, and extinguishing one ship of the thirty-three we had to deal with. Don Ignatio Maria d'Alava, whose flag she bore, told me five years afterwards at the Havannah, that one

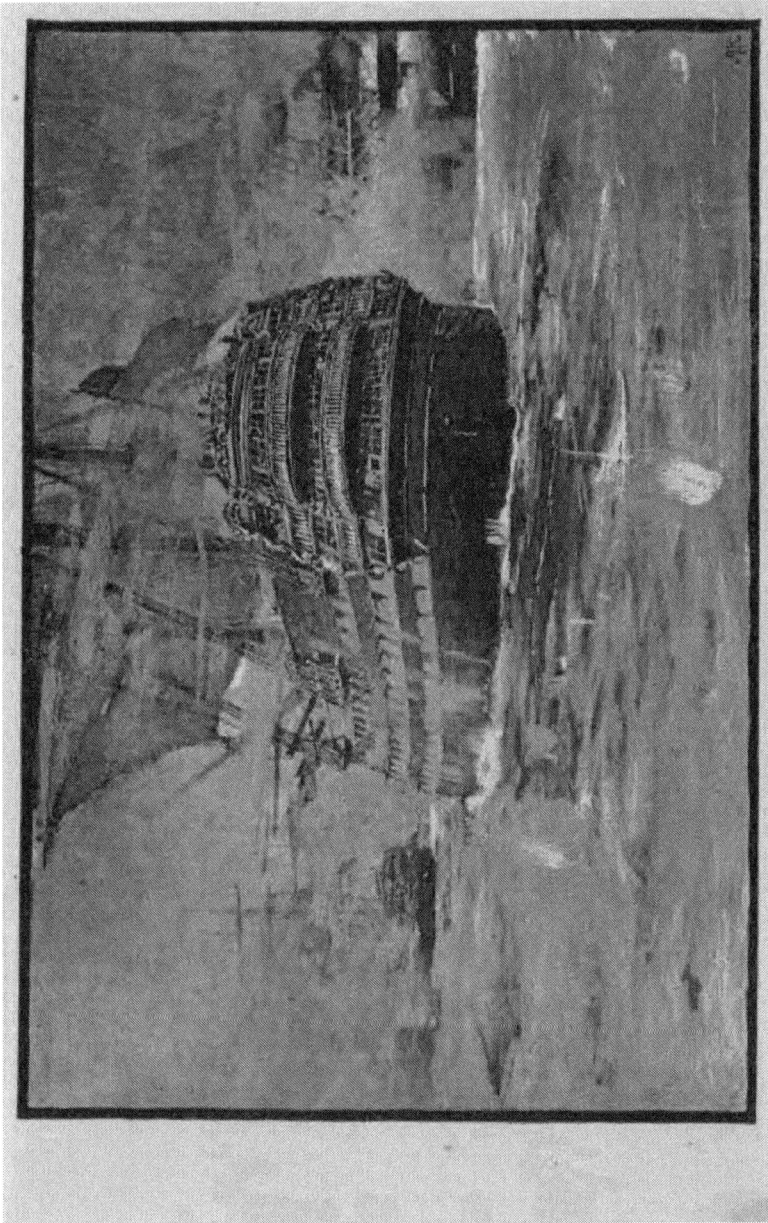

broadside killed 350 men, and he added, ' *Il rompait todos ;* '
and though he fought on afterwards for a couple of hours
like 'a man of honour and a cavalier,' the first broadside
did his business, and there was an end of him.

"I see before me at the end of half a century dear
old Cuddie (as we called Collingwood), walking the break
of the poop with his little triangular gold-laced cocked
hat, tights, silk stockings and buckles, musing over the
progress of the fight and munching an apple." [1]

It was about ten minutes past noon when, having sailed
to within pistol-shot of the *Santa Anna,* the *Royal Sovereign*
discharged a smashing broadside into her which, so the
Spanish officers afterwards declared, killed and wounded
some four hundred of her crew, and disabled fourteen of
her guns. With her starboard artillery similarly charged,
the *Royal Sovereign* let fly at the *Fougueux,* but the distance
was too great for the projectiles, and not much mischief
resulted. Collingwood's next manœuvre was to range close
alongside his huge opponent, the *Santa Anna;* the two
ships rubbed channels together; the very muzzles of the
guns seemed to touch. A furious cannonading followed;
so close and thick was the storm of balls that the
sailors saw the iron missiles strike one another as they
were discharged, and fall flattened into the water.
Whilst the *Royal Sovereign* was contending with the
Santa Anna, she was raked by the *Fougueux* and
the *San Leandro;* while, within 300 yards of her, upon
her starboard bow and quarter, were the *San Justo* and
Indomptable. It was like being in the heart of a volcano
in full blaze. Five ships to one ! It is amazing that the
Royal Sovereign was not cannonaded into staves before a
single ship could come to her relief. Undoubtedly this particular bit of conflict was working strong in Collingwood's

[1] *Seadrift,* p. 252.

memory when, long after, he issued the Order of Battle,
to which reference will be made in its place.

The *Royal Sovereign* was fighting single-handed for a
quarter of an hour or twenty minutes—flaming away at
her five opponents whilst the rest of the British fleet were
swarming slowly down into action and viewing the noble,
heroic sight with admiration and delight. Could the
sailors demand a more inspiriting example than the
spectacle of Collingwood's line-of-battle ship alone in the
thick of the enemy? Happily four of his five opponents
in a little while discovered that they were injuring themselves seriously by their own cross fire; by this time also
three or four British ships were at hand; and the four
two-deckers shifting their helms, made off, leaving the
Santa Anna to fight the *Royal Sovereign* alone. At the
expiration of some twenty minutes, the *Belleisle* hauling
up, fired a broadside into the lee quarter of the *Santa
Anna*, and then headed for the *Indomptable;* but the
combat still raged between Collingwood's ship and the
Santa Anna, on board which was the flag of the Spanish
Vice-Admiral Alava, nor did it terminate until at the end
of about an hour and a quarter, when, her three masts
having gone over the side, the Spaniard, that had most
nobly sustained the contest, struck to the *Royal Sovereign.*
Scarcely had this happened when the *Royal Sovereign's*
mizzenmast came down; she was so ploughed-up and
shattered indeed that whilst manœuvring to get ahead of
her prize, her mainmast went over the side, leaving nothing
but the tottering foremast standing.

James justly comments on the wonderful modesty with
which Collingwood refers in his dispatch, after the Battle
of Trafalgar, to the part taken by his own ship. The
passage in that dispatch says no more than this: "The
Commander-in-Chief, in the *Victory*, led the weather column,

and the *Royal Sovereign*, which bore my flag, the lee. The action began at twelve o'clock by the leading ships of the columns breaking through the enemy's line, the Commander-in-Chief about the tenth ship from the van, the second in command about the twelfth from the rear." That is all. Had he been a spectator viewing the engagement from the deck of a distant frigate, as Colonel Drink- . water viewed the Battle of St. Vincent, his language could not be more unsuggestive of the magnificent part he himself played.

Several characteristic anecdotes of Collingwood, whilst approaching the enemy and whilst in the thick of him, are preserved. At dawn, on the morning of the 21st, his servant, Smith, entered his cabin and found him already risen and dressing. He asked Smith if he had seen the French fleet; the man replied he had not, on which Collingwood told him to look at them, adding that in a very short time he would see a great many more vessels. "I then," says Smith, "observed a crowd of ships to leeward; but I could not help looking with still greater interest at the Admiral, who during all this time was shaving himself with a composure that quite astonished me." [1] Collingwood dressed himself that morning with unusual care. One notices this attention to personal appearance on the eve of conflict in many others besides Collingwood. Meeting Lieutenant Clavell, he advised him to pull off his boots. "You had better," he said, "put on silk stockings as I have; for if one should get a shot in the leg they would be so much more manageable for the surgeon." He then visited the decks to encourage the men, and addressing the officers, exclaimed: "Now, gentlemen, let us do something to-day which the world may talk of hereafter."

[1] *Correspondence and Memoir*, p. 124.

It is said that Collingwood's crew were drawn principally from the district of Newcastle-on-Tyne.[1] This circumstance would account for a strong *esprit de corps.* His Captain (Rotherham), born at Hexham, was a Newcastle man by virtue of residence. A story of his coolness during the action is related. A heavy shower of the enemy's musketry swept the quarter-deck of the *Royal Sovereign,* and left Rotherham almost alone. He wore a gold-laced cocked-hat, described as "rather a remarkable one," and gold epaulets. On being asked his reason for thus defiantly exposing himself to the enemy's small-arms' men, he replied, "I have always fought in a cocked-hat, and I always will."[2] Rotherham was a man after Collingwood's own heart: of a dryness of humour that gained largely in point and effect from the Northumberland burr in his articulation. His father had been for many years senior physician of the Newcastle Infirmary. Rotherham was early grounded in mathematics by the celebrated Dr. Hutton, then of Newcastle, and went to sea as Cook did, in a collier, whence he entered the navy and served under Admiral Barrington, whose officers enjoyed great reputation for skilfulness in naval tactics. On the 1st of June, Rotherham was first lieu-

---

[1] *Newcastle Chronicle,* November 4th, 1876. That a large proportion of Collingwood's crew on board the *Royal Sovereign* in the action at Trafalgar were men belonging to the district in which he was born seems confirmed by a picture in possession of Earl Nelson. His Lordship has been good enough to send me the following description: "There is the *Royal Sovereign* on one side with a medallion of Collingwood; on the other a medallion of Nelson and a picture of the *Victory.* Around the Admiral's (viz., Nelson's) medallion is the great signal. Around Collingwood 'Tars of the Tyne,' as if that had been a last word given to his own sailors before going into the Battle. I think the flag of the *Victory* is half-mast high, betokening the Admiral's death, whilst Fame is blowing her trumpet and pointing to Collingwood as the surviving hero."

[2] *Naval Chronicle,* vol. xv. p. 110.

tenant of the *Culloden*, and it was he who commanded the
French ship *Le Vengeur* so long as she could be kept afloat.
He was made post-captain in 1800, and in the Battle of
Trafalgar exhibited a degree of intrepidity and judgment
that abundantly justified Collingwood's high opinion and
esteem.

Whilst the *Royal Sovereign* was sailing into the combined
fleet, the memorable signal was made aboard the *Victory*:
"England expects that every man will do his duty." On
Collingwood observing it before learning its signification,
he said that he wished Nelson would make no more
signals, for they all knew what they were to do; but on
the purport of it being communicated to him, he expressed
great delight and admiration, and at once desired that it
should be made known to the officers and ship's company.
It is said that a universal shout arose from the British
fleet on this signal being flown. Admiral Hercules Robinson contradicts this. He says, "Lord Nelson's 'England
expects, &c.,' was sublime; but then there is the historical
lie, 'It was received throughout the fleet with shouts of
acclamation, and excited an unbounded enthusiasm.' Why,
it was noted in the signal-books and the logs, and that was
all about it; we certainly never heard one word about it
in our ship till we heard of our transports on our return to
England!"[1] One by one our traditions are pricked, and
leave behind them nothing but thin air. Is not our belief
in the uproarious shout of the Jacks of the fleet on
"England expects, &c.," being hoisted one of the most
sacred of our articles of patriotic faith? Yet it is to be
feared that Admiral Hercules Robinson is quite right.
Here and there a shout might have arisen; but the crews
were at quarters; nor could the signal by any possibility
have been simultaneously interpreted aboard the various

[1] *Seadrift*, p. 250.

ships. I fear then we must abandon this old inspiriting incident of the battle, and let something that might have happened take its place.

The editor of Collingwood's letters tells us that when the *Royal Sovereign* had floated some distance in advance of the line of ships in her wake, Lieutenant Clavell observed that the *Victory* was setting studding-sails, and that officer asked permission to imitate her example, influenced by a very intelligible spirit of emulation. "The ships of our line," answered Collingwood, "are not yet sufficiently up for us to do so now; but you may be getting ready." The halliards were accordingly manned, and in about ten minutes Collingwood, seeing Clavell's gaze fixed upon him, gave him a nod. Clavell instantly went to Captain Rotherham and told him that the Admiral desired him to make all sail. This story I consider fit only for the marines. If it is to be received it must dim something, nay, dim much of Collingwood's glory on this occasion—his eagerness to be first in the fray, his delight at the comparatively rapid pace of his ship over the long swell. The noble spirit of rivalry was everywhere manifest; every ship was in as great a hurry as the soft air that was breathing would permit. Collingwood led; it was pre-arranged that he should lead; to be first must be everything with him. Are we to suppose that he "kept all fast," as though the ships astern were a convoy, and it was his business to await the convenience of the laggers?

Some of Newnham Collingwood's anecdotes, however, are credible, and must properly find a place here. He claims that the nearest of the English ships was distant about a mile from the *Royal Sovereign* when Collingwood discharged his first gun, that his vessel might in some degree be hidden by the smoke. It may be inferred from contemporary testimony that the speed of the vessels as they approached the combined fleet did not exceed a mile in the hour. Indeed, we know that the wind failed wholly as the *Victory* floated into the foe, that the impulse barely gave her steerage way, and that her momentum was almost wholly owing to the swell. If Newnham Collingwood be right in his time and distance, then those who contend that Collingwood was a quarter of an hour or twenty minutes in action alone must be right also. In the heat of the engagement with the *Santa Anna*, Rotherham stepped up to Collingwood, and shaking him by the hand, said, " I congratulate you, sir; she is slacking her fire and must soon strike." It needed but the hauling down of the *Santa Anna's* colours to round off and make perfect this most nobly heroic, single-handed affair. " It was indeed expected on board the *Royal Sovereign* that they would have had the gratification of capturing the Spanish Admiral in the midst of a fleet of thirty-three sail before the arrival of another English ship."[1] Yet the *Santa Anna's* business was as good as completed before the arrival of the *Belleisle.*

Collingwood throughout the action was everywhere on board his ship; he visited the men, he enjoined them not to fire a shot in waste he himself sighted several of the guns, warmly commending the groups of hearties the while, particularly a coloured sailor, who, whilst the Admiral stood beside him, fired ten times directly into the porthole of the *Santa Anna.* " Lord Collingwood," wrote Codrington, " certainly went into action in the finest style possible, and is as brave a man as ever stepped on board a ship; I can also believe him to be a very good man in his way, but he has none of the dignity an Admiral should have, and seems to lose all the great outline of a chief command in his attention to the *minutiæ.*"[2] Codrington's theory of dignity is

---

[1] *Correspondence and Memoir,* p. 128.
[2] *Memoir of Sir Edward Codrington,* p. 66.

L

perhaps scarcely worth inquiring into. Most of us will doubtless think that the figure of Collingwood in that field of Trafalgar exhibits, not only all the dignity, but all the rest of the heroic and sublime qualities one looks for in a great commander, a great seaman, and a great man at such a time. " He fought like an angel," wrote the lion-hearted Blackwood, of Collingwood, and there was no man in that fleet but would have agreed with him.

Great events are often best realized by observing points of them which seem of trifling importance. The imploring cry of a Frenchman struggling for his life in the water at the Battle of the Nile ; the defiant crow of a cock in the pause of a furious cannonade ; such a view as Admiral Robinson gives us of the figure of Collingwood quietly pacing the deck and gravely munching an apple as he enters the scene of battle ; these things are like a flashing of little lights upon a canvas so wide that much of it lies in gloom. The flame is small, yet it will disclose, though dimly perhaps at the extremities, a considerable area of the picture, and what we thus see is often a revelation that enables us to compass much that would otherwise show darkly to the gaze. I like, and for this reason reprint, a touching letter written by young Aikenhead, who was midshipman in the *Royal Sovereign* at Trafalgar. He was killed four hours after the letter was written : " We have just piped to breakfast," says he ; " thirty-five sail, besides smaller vessels, are now on our beam about three miles off. Should I, my dear parents, fall in defence of my king, let that thought console you. I feel not the least dread on my spirits. Oh, my parents, sisters, brothers, dear grandfather, grandmother, and aunt, believe me ever yours ! Accept perhaps for the last time your brother's love, be assured I feel for my friends should I die in this glorious action—glorious, no doubt, it will be. Every British heart pants for glory. Our old Admiral (Collingwood) is quite young with the thoughts of it. If I survive, nothing will give me greater pleasure than embracing my dearest relations. Do not, in case I fall, grieve—it will be to no purpose. Many brave fellows will no doubt fall with me, on both sides." [1]

It is an old-fashioned letter, but all the same there is the throb of a brave human heart in it. It brings the scene before one—and more especially that moment of solemn pause which comes upon the heroic spirit on the eve of contest. We see Nelson kneeling in his cabin writing down his touching and beautiful prayer. Throughout the fleet there were scores of men snatching the last opportunity they might ever have in this world to send a God's blessing to those they loved, to assure them that they meant to do their duty, to promise their dear ones that nothing but their death should ever cause them a sigh. "What think you, my own dearest love?" writes Blackwood on board the *Euryalus* to his wife. "At this moment the enemy are coming out, and as if determined to have a fair fight. . . . You see, dearest, I have time to write to you and to assure you that, at the latest moment of my breath, I shall be as much attached to you as a man can be." [2]

When Nelson was wounded Captain Hardy sent a message to that effect to Collingwood. Hardy had learnt from Dr. Beatty, the *Victory's* surgeon, that the wound was mortal; but knowing the love that Collingwood bore the hero, he hoped to spare his feelings by cautiously breaking the news. Collingwood appears to have thought that Lieutenant Hills, the officer sent to inform him that the Commander-in-Chief was wounded, had arrived at the request of Nelson. "When my dear friend received his wound," Collingwood wrote to

[1] *Naval Chronicle*, vol. xv. p. 119.
[2] *Blackwood's Magazine*, vol. xxxiv. p. 10.

J. E. Blackett, November 2nd, " he immediately sent an
officer to me to tell me of it, and give his love to me.
Though the officer was directed to say the wound was not
dangerous, I read in his countenance what I had to fear,
and before the action was over, Captain Hardy came to inform me of his death. I cannot tell you how deeply I was
affected; my friendship for him was unlike anything that
I have left in the navy—a brotherhood of more than thirty
years."[1] Beatty is, however, express on this point. He
says in a note appended to his narrative of the death of
Nelson, that Hardy considered it his duty to advise Collingwood of Nelson being wounded, as soon as the fate of the
day was decided; but fearing that Nelson might object, he
directed that Lieutenant Hills should be detained on deck
till he (Hardy) came up from the cockpit. The matter,
however, is of no importance.

Remembering the affection that subsisted between
Nelson and Collingwood, there is something singularly
touching in the few lines which our hero addressed to the
Duke of Clarence on the death of his friend : "He had,"
he says, "all the qualities that adorn the human heart,
and a head which, by its quickness of perception and depth
of penetration, qualified him for the highest offices of his
profession. But why am I making these observations to
your Royal Highness, who knew him ? Because I cannot
speak of him but to do him honour. Your Royal Highness
desires to know the particular circumstances of his death.
I have seen Captain Hardy but for a few minutes since,
and understood from him that at the time the *Victory* was
very closely engaged in rather a crowd of ships, and that
Lord Nelson was commending some ship that was conducted much to his satisfaction, when a musket-ball struck
him on the left breast. Captain Hardy took hold of him

[1] *Correspondence and Memoir*, p. 136.

to support him, when he smiled and said, 'Hardy, I believe they have done it at last.' He was carried below; and when the ship was disengaged from the crowd, he sent an officer to inform me that he was wounded. I asked the officer if his wound was dangerous. He hesitated; then said he hoped it was not, but I saw the fate of my friend in his eye; for his look told what his tongue could not utter. About an hour after, when the action was over, Captain Hardy brought me the melancholy account of his death. He inquired frequently how the battle went, and expressed joy when the enemy was striking; in his last moments showing an anxiety for the glory of his country, though regardless of what related to his own person."[1]

In this action Collingwood escaped with his life by a miracle. In describing the scene to his wife, he tells her that all were killed or wounded on the quarter-deck and poop saving himself, Rotherham, and Cosway, his secretary. He was himself injured—oddly enough in the leg, as though in justification of his use of silk stockings; he was struck by a splinter, and he writes, "It was a pretty severe blow. I had a great many thumps, one way or the other; one in the back, which I think was the wind of a great shot, for I never saw anything that did it." He tells an affecting story of the death of one of his officers, Mr. Chalmers. Collingwood was standing close to the poor fellow when a ball almost divided his body. "He laid his head upon my shoulder, and told me he was slain. I supported him till two men carried him off. He could say nothing to me but to bless me; but as they carried him down he wished he could but live to read the account of the action in a newspaper. He lay in the cock-pit amongst the wounded until the *Santa Anna* struck;

[1] *Correspondence and Memoir*, p. 163.

and joining in the cheer which they gave her, expired with it on his lips." [1]

The *Royal Sovereign* having been reduced to the condition of a sheer hulk, Collingwood hoisted his flag aboard the frigate *Euryalus*. In many of the British ships the death of Nelson was not known until, on the evening drawing around, the sailors noticed that there were no lights aboard the *Victory*, and that the *Euryalus* bore the lights of the Commander-in-Chief. [2]

The result of the Battle of Trafalgar may thus be summed up: of 18 sail of the line the French lost nine, and of 15 sail of the line the Spaniards preserved six only. Collingwood claimed that the Vice-Admiral Alava had delivered his sword to him; Alava thought otherwise, and some interesting correspondence was the result. Collingwood at first imagined that Alava was dead of his wounds; on learning to the contrary, he wrote, on October 30th, he had heard with pleasure that he was in a hopeful way of recovery. "But, sir," he added, " you surrendered yourself to me, and it was in consideration only of the state of your wound that you were not removed into my ship. I could not disturb the repose of a man supposed to be in his last moments; but your sword, the emblem of your service, was delivered to me by your captain, and I expect that you consider yourself a prisoner of war until you shall be regularly exchanged by cartel." Alava's reply has the grave and courteous tone that Robinson Crusoe commends in the Spaniard; but he equivocated, and though Collingwood dissembled his disgust, further interchange of civilities with Admiral Alava was wanting in cordiality. The Spaniard's excuse was that he had fallen senseless in the action, that he did not know what

---

[1] *Correspondence and Memoir*, p. 204.
[2] Nelson's *Dispatches and Letters*, vol. vii. p. 172.

happened afterwards; that on receipt of Collingwood's letter he made inquiries, and learnt that the sword which had been delivered belonged to Don Francisco Riguelme, who had taken command of the *Santa Anna*, and retained it till she struck. He added, by way of confirming his statement, that the sabre which he used in the battle, together with the swords which he was generally in the habit of wearing, was still in his possession.

There were other difficulties, however, in connection with the swords of the vanquished Admirals. The *Conqueror* in the action was commanded by Israel Pellew, brother of the famous Sir Edward Pellew, afterwards Lord Exmouth. She fought the *Bucentaure,* on board of which was Admiral Villeneuve; when the Frenchman's foremast fell a white handkerchief was waved from her in token of submission. Pellew, unwilling to weaken his ship by securing the *Bucentaure,* sent Captain Atcherly of the Marines to bring Villeneuve on board. The valiant but unfortunate French Admiral received Atcherly on the quarter-deck, and inquired in English to whom he had surrendered. He was told to Captain Pellew. Believing him to be Sir Edward Pellew, Villeneuve appeared to find consolation in discovering that he had struck to so celebrated an officer. Atcherly, with Villeneuve and other prisoners of distinction, entered the boat to seek the *Conqueror*, but she was not to be found; Atcherly thereupon took his charge on board the *Mars*. The gallant Duff of that ship was dead; his amiable and heroic first lieutenant [1] had succeeded to the command, and he claimed

---

[1] William Hennah. I know nothing more characteristic of the tenderness of the "hearts of oak" of that grand old age of the British sailor than Hennah's letter to Mrs. Duff on the death of her husband—

H.M.S. Mars, off Cadiz, Oct. 27th, 1805.

"MADAM,
     "I believe that a more unpleasant task than what is now

Villeneuve and the others as *his* prisoners. Atcherly lost no time in communicating this extraordinary pretension to Pellew; but nothing could be done till next day, when the *Conqueror* was far inshore, and some time passed before she communicated with the fleet. Meanwhile Collingwood had taken Villeneuve on board the *Euryalus* and retained his sword. This, it is contended, was done

---

imposed upon me, can scarcely fall to the lot of a person whose feelings are not connected by the nearer ties of kindred ; but from a sense of duty (as first lieutenant of the *Mars*), as being myself the husband of a beloved partner, and the father of children ; out of the pure respect and esteem to the memory of our late gallant Captain, I should consider myself guilty of a base neglect should you only be informed of the melancholy circumstances attending the late glorious though unfortunate victory to many, by a public gazette. The consequences of such an event, while it may occasion the rejoicings of the nation, will in every instance be attended with the deepest regrets of a few. Alas! madam, how unfortunate shall I think myself should this be the first intimation you may have of the irreparable loss you have met with ! What apology can I make for entering upon a subject so tender and so fraught with sorrow, but to recommend an humble reliance on this great truth, that the ways of Providence, though sometimes inscrutable, are always for the best !

"By this, Madam, you are in all probability acquainted with the purport of my letter. Amongst the number of heroes who fell on the ever-memorable 21st in the defence of their King and country, after gloriously discharging his duty to both, our meritorious and much-respected Commander, Captain George Duff, is honourably classed ; his fate was instantaneous, and he resigned his soul into the hands of the Almighty without a moment's pain.

"Poor Norwich [Captain Duff's son] is very well. Captain Blackwood has taken him on board the *Euryalus* with the other young gentleman that came with him, and their schoolmaster.

"The whole of the Captain's papers and effects are sealed up, and will be kept in a place of security until proper persons are appointed to examine them. Meanwhile, Madam, I beg leave to assure you of my readiness to give you any information, or render you any service in my power.

"And am, Madam, with the greatest respect,
  "Your most obedient and most humble servant,
                                    "WILLIAM HENNAH."

—*Naval Chronicle*, vol. xv. p. 274.

without Pellew's permission. Osler, who tells the story, adds that "Captain Pellew, who was modest and retiring to a fault, would never claim what ought not to have been withheld, and what indeed was distinctly admitted by the Admiral to be his right."[1]

Everything I have consulted is silent on this incident. It is not stated in Osler's narrative that Collingwood, who admitted Pellew's claim to the sword, delivered the weapon to him. Might it not be a mere conjecture on the part of Osler that Collingwood granted the sword to be Pellew's? If Pellew was too modest to claim it, how could Collingwood imagine his claim? I find nothing in Collingwood's correspondence referring to this matter; but in the face of his letter to Alava, and bearing in mind also his high and noble sense of professional honour, one cannot but believe that had Pellew explained his right to the sword, it would have been instantly and ungrudgingly delivered to him.

"How well," exclaims Admiral Robinson, "I remember our receiving Villeneuve on board the *Euryalus*, and the Captain of the Fleet, Majendie, to convey them to England. I could include both of them in my *tableau* were I the artist I wish. Villeneuve was a tallish, thin man, a very tranquil, placid, English-looking Frenchman; he wore a long-tailed uniform coat, high and flat collar, corduroy pantaloons of a greenish colour, with stripes two inches wide, half-boots with sharp toes, and a watch-chain with long gold links. Majendie was a short, fat, jocund sailor, who found a cure for all ills in the Frenchman's philosophy—'*Fortune de la guerre*' (though this was the third time the goddess had brought him to England as a prisoner), and he used to tell our officers very tough stories of the 'Mysteries of Paris.'"[2]

---

[1] *Memoir of Admiral Sir Israel Pellew, K.C.B.*, appended to the *Life of Lord Exmouth*, p. 381.   [2] *Seadrift*, p. 253.

It is universally admitted that the unfortunate and unhappy Villeneuve exhibited the utmost bravery at Trafalgar, fighting as one worthy to cross swords with a Nelson. The French pretended that the instructions he gave his officers were unintelligible to them. There must always be a reason for defeat. In truth, Villeneuve's plan of battle was admirable. Brenton rightly says that the French Admiral's " *Celui qui ne serait pas dans le feu ne serait pas à son poste,*" [1] was almost equivalent to "England expects every man will do his duty," and nearly a literal translation of the words of Nelson that "no captain can do wrong who lays his ship alongside of an enemy." [2] The condition of the *Bucentaure* when taken possession of illustrates the desperation of the valour with which her people had fought her. Besides the full crew of a flag-ship, she carried a large number of troops commanded by General Contamin. The soldiers, ignorant of shipboard manœuvring, increased the confusion, and the slaughter amongst them swelled their disorder into panic. The dead littered the decks in mounds, and still the shot had gone on ploughing through those heaps of corpses, hideously mangling the remains. The fearful task of counting the slain was attempted, and it was discovered that more than 400 had been killed and wounded, of whom an extra-ordinary proportion had lost their heads.[3]

The dispatch in which Collingwood communicated the particulars of the battle is the most masterly composition of the kind in the language. I have already referred to the exquisite modesty of his reference to the part he himself played. Equally noble in language and senti-

---

- [1] "He who will not be in the fire will not be at his post"— literally ; but the *point* goes further.
  [2] *Naval History,* vol. ii. p. 73.
  [3] *Life of Lord Exmouth,* appendix, p. 377.

ment is his General Order, in which he thanks the officers and seamen and others of the fleet for their conduct. The language rises to the occasion. How lofty are the opening lines, how organ-like the rolling music of these words : " The ever-to-be-lamented death of Lord Viscount Nelson, Duke of Brontë, the Commander-in-Chief, who fell in the action of the 21st, in the arms of Victory, covered with glory—whose memory will be ever dear to the British Navy and the British Nation, whose zeal for the honour of his King and the interests of his country will be ever held up as a shining example for a British seaman—leaves to me a duty to return my thanks," &c. Equally noble is this, similarly dated the day following the battle : " The Almighty God, whose arm is strength, having with His great mercy been pleased to crown the exertions of his Majesty's fleet with success, in giving them a complete victory over their enemies on the 21st of this month ; and that all praise and thanksgiving may be offered up to the Throne of Grace for the great benefit to the country and to mankind, I have thought proper that a day should be appointed of general humiliation before God, and thanksgiving for His merciful goodness, imploring forgiveness of sins, a continuation of His Divine mercy, and His constant aid to us in defence of our countries, liberties, and laws, without which the utmost efforts of man are naught." [1]

[1] Of Collingwood's dispatch, Lord Eldon wrote as follows to Moises, Collingwood's old master at the Newcastle Grammar School—

" DEAR SIR,

" I cannot forbear congratulating you, whilst we are all congratulating our country, upon the services which your former scholar and my old schoolfellow, Lord Collingwood, has done the country, and the honour he has done himself. I can sincerely assure you that my satisfactions upon the late events have been materially increased by a notion I entertained that you would receive some

The Battle of Trafalgar was ended, but a new conflict was now to be entered upon—a struggle with old ocean ; such a contest as was to tax the consummate skill of Collingwood as a seaman to the uttermost degree. As the night approached it came on to blow strong and stronger yet, from the south-south-east—an inshore wind, that speedily raised a sea, ugly, hollow, troubled and broken, as the surge always is when it sweeps into shoaling water. It would be difficult to imagine a scene of wilder confusion than this that followed on that night of the ever memorable 21st. In all directions ships, dismasted and utterly helpless, were rolling their tall sides deep in the foaming brine. Some of them were in a sinking state. The soundings gave but 13 fathoms of water, and the Trafalgar shoals were to leeward. A few only of the ships were in a position to bring up. The cables of most of them had been cut by shot; the machinery of the ground-tackle had been damaged, and a number of them, chiefly the prizes, had not a stick standing upon which to spread a rag of cloth. Yet unless everything that could not claw off or hold its own against the dead inshore sweep of the gale was not to take the ground and go to pieces, the signal to anchor must be made to whatever had an anchor to let go with a hawser bent to it.

Fortunately, towards midnight the wind shifted, blowing

---

pleasure in recollecting that he had been educated under you. My gracious master the King observing the other day that Collingwood's was an excellent letter, added immediately, ' He was, however, bred at the same school as the Chancellor.' I told him that I was confident the Admiral would refer to you all the merit he had, either in expressing himself so well as to his language, or in expressing sentiments which do him so much honour as a virtuous and pious man. God bless you, my dear sir, and believe me, with the most sincere and affectionate regard and respect,

"Your faithful friend and servant,
"ELDON."

with redoubled violence from the south-south-west, on
which Collingwood signalled for the ships to wear with
their heads to the westward. More space than I have
at command would be required to follow in detail the
adventures of the British ships and prizes. Nelson's dying
injunctions were that the fleet should anchor. James
is of opinion that had Collingwood attended to Nelson's
directions many of the prizes would have been preserved,
and he quotes the case of the *Defence* and her prize, the
San Ildefonso, both which ships, having anchored on the
evening of the action, weathered the gale in safety. He
also names the *Swiftsure* and *Bahama,* which, having
anchored, were saved with the help of the *Donegal* and
Phoebe.

But then the difference between James and Collingwood
is this: James arrived at his conclusions seated at his
desk; Collingwood happened to be in the gale. Collingwood was a sailor; James was a man of letters, an insipid,
acid, accurate man of letters, who had probably never
been out in a stiff breeze of wind in his life, who knew
sea-terms as a parrot might know them, and whose
opinion, therefore, on the merits of Collingwood's behaviour
in so tremendous a crisis as he was called upon to deal with,
would hardly be worth more than a parrot's. And it will
perhaps be allowed that Lord St. Vincent knew more about
the sea and the obligations which the sea suddenly and
too often fiercely and terribly imposes than James the
historian. In the *Anecdote Book,* Lord Eldon says: "I
heard Lord St. Vincent say that Collingwood's conduct
after the Battle of Trafalgar in destroying, under difficult
circumstances, the defeated fleet, was above all praise." [1]
It must surely be clear to everybody that Collingwood's
desire to preserve the prizes would be as great as that of

[1] Twiss's *Life of Eldon,* vol. ii. p. 119.

any other man in the fleet. Greater, for obvious reasons, it undoubtedly was; 'but we will suppose him at all events as anxious as Codrington, who is very unsparing in his denunciations on this occasion. " Could you witness the grief and anxiety of Admiral Collingwood (who has done all that an Admiral could do), you would be very deeply affected," [1] wrote Captain Blackwood to his wife. Had the Bay of Cadiz been the Downs, and Cadiz, Deal, with fleets of hovellers ready to put off with anchors and cables, then indeed Collingwood might have seen his way to anchor those vessels which had been rendered by the battle unable to anchor. But would he have done so? Would any sailor have anchored a crowd of mutilated craft in water that shoaled rapidly, in a time of the year when violent weather was to be expected, with a certainty of destruction should the wind come out of the south and west and the ships drag? As to destroying the prizes— even Codrington, who grumbles in his gizzard against Collingwood in most of the letters he sent home after Trafalgar—even Codrington, I say, gives us to see by implication that there was nothing else for it but the measures adopted by Collingwood. " I towed a prize," says he, " belonging to *Bellerophon* from close to Trafalgar in safety for three days, but having my topsails blown out of the bolt-ropes and one bumpkin carried away, with the foremast wounded, and only six miles from the lee-shore, near St. Mary's, in the worst hurricane I ever saw, I was obliged to quit her to save my own ship, which I had little hopes of." [2]

[1] *Blackwood's Magazine*, 1833, p. 13.
[2] *Memoir of Sir Edward Codrington*, p. 57.

CHAPTER VIII.

Fresh Attempt—Rewards—Parliamentary Votes—Newnham Collingwood—Letters to Lady Collingwood—A Nelson Memorial—
Young Sea-Officers—Codrington on Collingwood—Fresh Commission—Dumanoir's Squadron—Familiar Letters—Novelists'
Sailors—Position of Commander-in-Chief in Mediterranean—
Letter from the Queen of Naples—Sir John Duckworth—Action
off San Domingo—Enemy's Force.

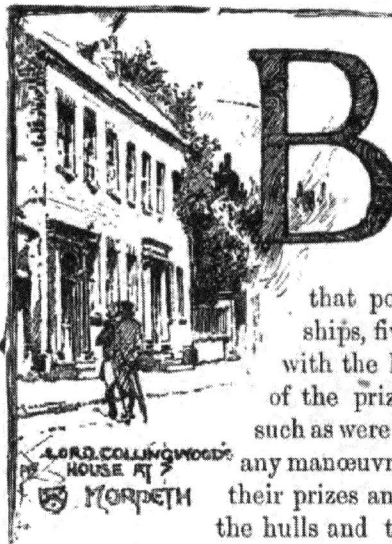

BUT the weather and the condition of the prizes were not Collingwood's only anxiety. On the morning of the 23rd, the senior French officer at Cadiz weighed from that port with five line-of-battle ships, five frigates, and two brigs, with the hope of recapturing some of the prizes. The British ships— such as were capable of taking part in any manœuvres, ten sail in all—cast off their prizes and formed in line between the hulls and the enemy. The French commander did not come within gunshot, but his frigates managed to recapture the *Santa Anna* and *Neptuno*, both which ships they conveyed into port. Writing on this day, and even at this time indeed, Blackwood says : "The remains of the French and Spanish fleet have rallied,

M

and are at this moment but a few miles from us. . . . The Admiral (Collingwood) is still on board of my ship ; and we are leading the fleet, which, you will believe, suits my taste. . . . Lord C. appeared delighted with *Euryalus*, and will not, I hope, leave her if another action takes place, where he will see so much better what is to do than if engaged himself."[1]

But, in truth, Collingwood's own official letter to the Admiralty, dated off Cadiz, October 24th, is the most intelligible and convincing explanation that could be given of his reasons for destroying the prizes: "On the 22nd, in the morning, a strong southerly wind blew with squally weather, which, however, did not prevent the activity of the officers and seamen of such ships as were manageable from getting hold of many of the prizes (thirteen or fourteen), and towing them off to the westward, where I ordered them to rendezvous round the *Royal Sovereign* in tow by the *Neptune*. But, on the 23rd, the gale increased, and the sea ran so high that many of them broke the tow-rope and drifted far to leeward before they were got hold of again, and some of them, taking advantage of the dark and boisterous night, got before the wind and have perhaps drifted upon the shore and sunk. On the afternoon of that day, the remnant of the combined fleet, ten sail of ships, which had not been much engaged, stood up to leeward of my shattered and staggering charge,[2] as if meaning to attack them, which obliged me to collect a force out of the least injured ships and form to leeward for their defence. All this retarded the progress of the hulks; and the bad weather continuing, determined me to

[1] *Blackwood's Magazine*, 1833, p. 13.
[2] I would call the reader's attention to the wonderfully vivid lingwood's language communicates to dispatches, which others are commonly rendered as dry and disgusting the log-book.

destroy all the leewardmost that could be cleared of the men, considering that keeping possession of the ships was a matter of little consequence compared with the chance of their falling again into the hands of the enemy; but even this was an arduous task in the high sea which was running. . . . I hope their Lordships will approve of what I (having only in consideration the destruction of the enemy's fleet) have thought a measure of absolute necessity."

Collingwood was rewarded for his services by a peerage. The title was Baron Collingwood of Caldburne and Hethpoole, in the county of Northumberland. His arms were augmented by the introduction in chief of one of the lions of England navally crowned, and surmounted with the word Trafalgar; an additional crest was granted representing the stern of the *Royal Sovereign*. Parliament voted him a pension of £2000 per annum for his own life, and in the event of his death, £1000 per annum to Lady Collingwood, and £500 per annum to each of his two daughters. He was presented with the freedom of the City of London and a sword valued at two hundred guineas; by the Common Council of Newcastle a silver kettle valued at one hundred and fifty guineas; by the Newcastle Trinity House the freedom of that Corporation in a gold box; by the Newcastle Volunteer Infantry a piece of plate valued at a hundred and twenty-five guineas. He wrote to his wife that he had received congratulatory letters and freedoms from the London Goldsmiths' and Drapers' Companies, from Bath, Bristol, Exeter, Cork, Portsmouth, Southampton, and other places. In the House of Commons little more was said about Collingwood than was to be conveyed in a formal motion of thanks to him and to those with him; but in the House of Lords more feeling was expressed and more

appreciation exhibited. The Duke of Clarence proposed
to add to Lord Hawkesbury's resolution the thanks of the
House to Lord Collingwood for "his decision in destroying
the ships which had been captured." Lord Hawkesbury
willingly adopted the spirit of that part of the amendment
which recognized the services performed by Lord Collingwood after the Battle of Trafalgar. The gallant veteran,
Lord Hood, said: "I cannot refrain from troubling your
Lordships with a few words from the very high opinion I
have long entertained of that truly meritorious officer,
Lord Collingwood . . . and I will venture to presage that
the noble lord, now in the command of his Majesty's fleet
in the Mediterranean, wants only an opportunity to prove
himself another Nelson in judgment as well as valour." [1]

One figures a dry smile disturbing the austere tran-
quillity of Collingwood's countenance as he reads Lord
Hood's well-intentioned but infelicitous compliment.
Collingwood's mind was of an order of greatness—in
the sense of the word that was in Ben Jonson's thoughts
when he applied it to Francis Bacon—that would not find
much to please it in comparative criticism. What he
relished far more highly than such assurances as this of
Hood was the praise of his King, and the handsome
testimony of the King's son, the Duke of Clarence.
There was certainly no stint in the King's expression of
approval. What could prove more animating to the loyal
heart of Collingwood than such words as these:

"His Majesty considers it very fortunate that the
command under circumstances so critical should have
devolved upon an officer of such consummate valour, judgment and skill as Admiral Collingwood has proved himself
to be, every part of whose conduct he considers deserving
his approbation and entire admiration. The feeling

[1] Nelson's *Dispatches and Letters*, vol. vii. pp. 319—21.

manner in which he has described the events of that
great day, and those subsequent, and the modesty with
which he speaks of himself, whilst he does justice in terms
so elegant and so ample to the meritorious exertions of the
gallant officers and men under his command, have also
proved extremely satisfactory to the King." The Duke of
Clarence sent him a letter full of compliments and kindness. "Earl St. Vincent and Lord Nelson," wrote the
Prince, "both, in the hour of victory, accepted from me a
sword, and I hope you will now confer on me the same
pleasure;" and he ends his letter, "Yours unalterably."

There is something singularly engaging in the character
of this Prince—in his relations, at all events, with men of
the calling he had been himself bred to. The ocean
seems to have flavoured his nature. There is a cordiality, a
large-heartedness, an absence of affectation that expresses
him a sailor by nature. One need not read much about
him to guess that here was a man who had wrested more
than one theory of conduct, more than one inspiration of
action, out of the heart of old ocean; whose spirit was
made princelier than ever mere birth could have created it
by the magnanimity that had visited it, like an impulse, from
the wide and shoreless reaches of the deep. He was seen
to weep at St. Paul's when Nelson was buried, and I dare
say no sincerer tear was shed in that time of mourning.

Collingwood, having no son, was desirous that his richly-
deserved honours should be perpetuated in his daughters'
successors. He wrote to Lord Barham to that effect; told
him that though his family had for several ages been of
considerable distinction in the North, yet now that it had
been raised to a high degree of eminence he was ambitious
to perpetuate its elevation to posterity. "I have not
a son," he said; "but if the honours which have been
conferred on me could be continued in the heirs of my

daughters, I should be made very happy." In a second letter relating to this desire of his, dated five months later, he says drily: "I believe your lordship will allow that I have a sort of claim to be indulged when I tell you that but for my constant service at sea since the year 1793, I should probably ere now have had half a dozen sons to succeed me. I left my family then, and have seen little of them since."[1]

Collingwood's wish was not gratified. The peerage therefore became extinct at his death. His son-in-law, George Newnham, who took the name of Collingwood, lived in the hope that on the accession of the Duke of Clarence as William IV., the King would raise him to the peerage as Baron Collingwood. "On the death of William IV.," says Mr. John Clayton, "without having thus gratified the ambition of Mr. Newnham Collingwood, the latter soon sunk and died."[2]

One of the most charming of the many delightful letters written by Lord Collingwood is addressed to his

---

[1] *Correspondence and Memoir*, pp. 161—209.

[2] *Archæologia Æliana.* Mr. Clayton gives further particulars of Newnham Collingwood. He was a young barrister when he married Collingwood's elder daughter Sarah, and was employed by the British Government in the investigation of claims of British subjects on the French. The Honourable Mrs. Newnham Collingwood joined her husband in Paris, and before their return a son was born, who died in infancy. Mr. Newnham now assumed the name of Collingwood, and retired with his wife to the village of Hawkhurst, where he wrote and edited the *Memoir and Correspondence* of his father-in-law, to which everybody who deals with the life of the Admiral must owe a large proportion of the information it is now possible to obtain. He left a widow and two daughters. One of the daughters died under age ; the other married first a Mr. Hall, and next a Mr. Howell, by neither of which marriages was there any surviving issue. Here, perhaps, it may be as well to add that the younger Miss Collingwood, the Honourable Mary Patience, married Mr. Anthony Denny, and Mr. Clayton informs us that there is issue by this marriage still in existence. Some time before her death Mrs. Newnham Collingwood became very eccentric.

wife, dated on board the *Queen*, off Carthagena, December
16th, a little less than two months later than the date of
the Battle of Trafalgar. "It would be hard," he says, "if
I could not find one hour to write a letter to my dearest
Sarah, to congratulate her on the high rank to which she
has been advanced by my success. Blessed may you be,
my dearest love, and may you long live the happy wife of
your happy husband. I do not know how you bear your
honours, but I have so much business on my hands from
dawn till midnight that I have hardly time to think of
mine except it be in gratitude to my King, who has so
graciously conferred them upon me.

"But there are so many things of which I might so
justly be a little proud—for extreme pride is folly—that
I must share my gratification with you. The first is the
letter from Colonel Taylor, his Majesty's Private Secretary
to the Admiralty, to be communicated to me. I enclose
you a copy of it. It is considered the highest compliment
the King can pay; and as the King's personal compliment
I value it above everything. I am told that when my letter
was carried to him he could not read it for tears: joy and
gratitude to Heaven for our success so entirely overcame
him. I have such congratulations both in prose and verse
as would turn the head of one a little more vain than I
am. The adding a red flag at the main to the navy on
this occasion is a proud thing:[1] but I will tell you what I
feel nearest to my heart after the honour which his
Majesty has done me, and that is the praise of every
officer of the fleet. . . . What does Admiral Roddam say
of our fight? It would have done his heart good to have
seen it. There is a thing which has made a considerable
impression upon me. A week before the war, at Morpeth,

[1] On the 9th of the previous month of November, Collingwood
was advanced from the Blue to the rank of Vice-Admiral of the Red.

I dreamed distinctly many of the circumstances of our late battle off the enemy's port, and I believe I told you of it at the time; but I never dreamed that I was to be a Peer of the Realm. How are my darlings? I hope they will take pains to make themselves wise and good, and fit for the station to which they are raised."

A little more than a week after the great battle had been fought, namely, on the 2nd of November, Collingwood sent a memorandum to the captains serving under him, in which he expressed his assent to the erection, at the general expense of the Squadron, of a monument on Post Down Hill to the memory of Nelson. He proposed that a sum of £2000 should be deducted out of the prize-money arising from the action off Cape Trafalgar.[1] This was entered in the respective logs, and it is characteristic of Codrington that he should have written in the log-book of the *Orion* (the ship he commanded): "The people thought it too little." If one were to assume Collingwood's character from what Codrington wrote of him, the inference must be that he was the most unpopular man in the service. Undoubtedly he lacked the magic of the influence that Nelson exercised over everybody that was associated with him. He was reserved and even cold in his bearing, not very easy of access, stern and unbending in his theories of professional discipline and in his resolution to exact from those serving with him everything that they had it in their power to contribute to the well-being of the service and to the cause of the country. His own wonderful life of self-devotion had rendered him insensible to, or impatient of, any sort of grievance in others that did not rise to the dignity of a great trouble, or wrong, or misfortune that merited remedying. Above all, he was a north-countryman of a deliberative habit, capable indeed

---

[1] Nelson's *Dispatches and Letters*, vol. vii. p. 218.

of as much chivalrous, heroic, patriotic enthusiasm as could swell the heart of a Nelson, but without Nelson's ability to communicate it. Then, again, at this time he was growing advanced in years; he had never wanted the philosophic mind, but time had fully confirmed and completed the impulse and the animation of it in him. He was indeed fifty-eight years old, and at fifty-eight the sympathies and sentiments of a man who has spent the greater part of his life at sea, whose best years have been expended in the dryest, stubbornest, dullest, least satisfactory walks of the vocation, must doubtless seem to want all necessary briskness and acuteness in the eyes of younger men serving under him—men whose spirits are fresh and whose hopes are green, unsicklied as yet by the yellow of disappointment.

There were several such men under Collingwood, and the best they can find to say of him is poor enough. " The Admiral," says Hoste, writing on board the *Amphion* at Gibraltar, November 15th, " is a very different man from Lord Nelson, but as brave an old boy as ever stood."[1] According to Blackwood, Collingwood "is a reserved, but a pleasing good man." He had not Nelson's sociable qualities. Codrington, for instance, writes shortly after Nelson had joined the fleet off Cadiz: " The signal has been made this morning for all of us who did not dine on board *Victory* yesterday to go there to-day. What our late chief would think of this I don't know; but I well know what the fleet think of the difference, and even you, our good wives, who have some causes of disapprobation, will allow the superiority of Lord Nelson in all these social arrangements which bind us captains to their Admiral."[2]

No purpose can be served by looking about for an apology for a behaviour that could provoke this sort of

[1] *Memoir and Letters of Captain Sir W. Hoste*, vol. i. 253.
[2] *Correspondence and Memoir*, p. 45.

criticism. Collingwood had formed a clear theory of his duties and responsibilities; and his theory did not meet with the approval of Codrington and some few others whom Nelson would probably style Judases. It is history repeating itself. Collingwood was a younger man by seven or eight years when he was writing to Mr. Blackett off this same Cadiz, where we find him again, that "All that intercourse of friendship which was the only thing like comfort which was left us is forbidden; for the admirals and captains are desired not to entertain, even at dinner, any who do not belong to their ships."[1] There seems, however, to have been a prejudice in Codrington that should make us very cautious in judging of the Admiral by what this (then) Captain says of him. The *Orion* has scarcely arrived off Cadiz when we find Codrington writing: "We have got into the clutches of another stay-on-board Admiral (Collingwood), who never communicates with anybody but upon service; and so, unless Buonaparte orders his fleet out, we stand a very good chance of forgetting that anything like society is known amongst men."[2] But then, to be sure, Codrington was born to grumble. When the Trafalgar medals arrived, we seem to see him picking up his and turning it about with a face of disgust. "They are exactly similar to the others," says he—referring to the medals of the 1st of June, St. Vincent and the Nile—"well designed but badly executed. They seem to come in a most ungracious way from the Ministry, and were received by us in a most unwelcome manner, I must say." Collingwood, however, was fortunate enough to please our friend on this occasion: "Our Admiral delivered them to us in a pleasing strain, and it was only afterwards that we made our comments on the whole."[3]

[1] *Correspondence and Memoir*, p. 70.
[2] *Life of Sir E. Codrington*, p. 43.   [3] *Ibid.* p. 100.

· Codrington, like the rest of the captains, and for that matter like Collingwood himself, wanted to get home, and apparently half his quarrel with Collingwood lies in the Admiral's detention of him—which was really due to his own representations of the state of his ship. That a man should be devoured with anxiety to return home after such a battle as that of Trafalgar, whilst his honours were still blushing upon him, is certainly the most natural thing in the world, especially in such a nature as that of Codrington, who combined with a very great deal of heroism a very large quality of vanity. He was annoyed on believing that the ships were to be sent home in "driblets," and told his wife that such a proceeding must deprive the victory of all *éclat!* "Here are several officers with me," writes Collingwood to his lady, "very much in distress that they cannot get home; but what can I do? The Admiralty will not say a word to me about the prizes, the promotion of officers, or any subject. I never did, nor ever will I do, anything but what I think conducive to the public good. I am not ambitious of power or wealth more than I have, nor have I connections of any kind to sway me from the strict line of my duty to the country. I have neither sons nor cousins to promote by any of those tricks which I have ever held in contempt, so that when I err it will be from my head, and not my heart."[1] Codrington might not have known what was passing in Collingwood's mind, yet here are sentiments which, had they been communicated, must surely have corrected his opinion of his Admiral.

But Codrington wanted to get home: "Hope has been fourteen months at home in these eight years," he writes; "and Captain Rutherford told us yesterday, declaring that it was d—d foolish for a sailor to marry, that he had been in that happy state for nine years, one only of which he

[1] *Correspondence and Memoir*, p. 200.

had been with his wife!"[1] Daylight at last dawned for Codrington. The *Queen* and the *Royal George* having rejoined the fleet, Codrington went on board the Admiral's ship to know what arrangements he had made about the *Orion*. Collingwood "offered some of his professions of good intention," and then dismissed the Captain with the information that he should send his ship to England whenever he thought it best for the service to do so. Then follows what resembles a small quarter-deck dispute. "You never told me," says Collingwood, "your ship was in such bad condition before." "Because, my lord," answers Codrington, "whenever I touched upon the subject you showed a suspicion of my veracity; and my heart disdaining the imputation, I told you the ship should speak for herself." To this Collingwood answers, in his "petulant" manner, "that he had more complaints from the *Orion* than from any other ship." "Does your Lordship mean to say," cries Codrington, "I have done more than my duty in reporting my want of sails to follow the enemy if he came out, or the sickliness of my ship's company for want of vegetable diet?" "No," says Collingwood, curtly, "I do not mean to say it was." This conversation occurred on November the 10th; on the morning of the 11th, to the astonishment of Codrington, Collingwood sent him a very polite letter, bidding him go to England with the *Orion* that evening, and go alone. "I could not allow myself to believe it," writes Codrington, "until I positively got my orders; . . . . such was my anxiety to be out of reach of his signals on the next morning that I *forced* the ship all night at the rate of nine miles an hour against a very heavy head sea."[2]

And so Captain Codrington disappears from this scene, thrashing his way out of sight behind the horizon, and

---

[1] *Correspondence and Memoir*, p. 47. [2] *Ibid.* p. 113.

leaving behind him the great, the stout-hearted, the noble-minded, the dutiful Collingwood to stick to his post—away from his wife and daughters, away from all the happiness and applause, the comfort and the pleasures, that awaited him in England—for another long four years, dying at it !

Shortly after the news of the Battle of Trafalgar had been received at the Admiralty, Lord Barham, the First Lord, sent Collingwood a commission of the same extent as that which Nelson had held. In a letter to Lord Barham, dated December 4th, there appears a characteristic touch, worthy of Collingwood and of the noble service he adorned. " I had another view," he says, "in keeping the sea at that time (which had a little of pride in it), and that was to show the enemy that it was not a battle nor a storm which could remove a British squadron from the station which they were directed to hold; and I have heard that our keeping the sea after what had passed was a matter of the greatest astonishment to them." At Cadiz, after the battle, there were lying at anchor ten or eleven of the enemy's ships in a more or less shattered condition. Collingwood, throughout the greater portion of the year, continued to watch the port. How effectually the work had been done at Trafalgar may be gathered from the incident of the French Admiral Rosily arriving at Cadiz, direct from Paris, to supersede Villeneuve, and finding not eighteen fine French ships, but four disabled ones, and a fifth barely in a condition to enable him to hoist his flag and put to sea.

Four liners, under the command of Rear-Admiral Dumanoir, had escaped from Trafalgar when the fate of the battle was decided. They were fallen in with on the 2nd of November, by a squadron under the command of Sir Richard Strachan, who at the close of October had been detached from the Channel fleet in search of the Rochefort squadron under Rear-Admiral Allemand. A long chase ensued; but on the 4th, Dumanoir, finding an action unavoidable, hauled on the starboard tack and awaited the British. The Frenchmen were captured, and the four prizes carried to Plymouth, and added to the British Navy. It is said that when the news of this defeat reached Napoleon, he exclaimed, alluding to Byng's fate, that "he would teach French Admirals how to conquer." He tranquillized his mind, however, by believing, or feigning to believe, that the lies he had caused to be published about the French reverses were credited by the world at large, England perhaps omitted.

Collingwood's familiar letters at this time provide some wonderfully choice and interesting reading. He writes to his wife, December 20th: "Until we have peace I shall never be happy; and yet how we are to make it out in peace I know not with high rank and no fortune. At all events we can do as we did before. It is true I have the chief command, but there are neither French nor Spaniards on the sea, and our cruisers find nothing but neutrals, who carry on all the trade of the enemy. Our prizes, you see, are lost; but was there ever so complete a break-up of an enemy's fleet? If we have not saved them to ourselves, we have at least put them out of the power of doing further mischief. Villeneuve's ship had a great deal of money in her; but it all went to the bottom. I am afraid the fees for this patent will be large and pinch me, but never mind; let others solicit pensions. I am an Englishman, and will never ask for money as a favour. How do my darlings go on? I wish you would make them write to me by turns, and give me the whole history of their proceedings. Oh! how I shall rejoice when I come home to find them as much improved in knowledge as I have

advanced them in station in the world; but take care
they do not give themselves foolish airs. Their excellence
should be in knowledge, in virtue, and benevolence to all;
but most to those who are humble and require their aid.
I am out of all patience with Bounce. The consequential
airs he gives himself since he became a right honourable
dog are insufferable. He considers it beneath his dignity
to play with commoners' dogs, and truly thinks that he
does them grace when he condescends to lift up his leg
against them. This, I think, is carrying the insolence of
rank to the extreme, but he is a dog that does it." [1]

It is impossible to read literature of this sort without
understanding why it is that the name of Collingwood is
held in admiration and veneration throughout the navy,
and I may add amongst all educated men in the British
Merchant Service. It is not only his genius as a sea
chieftain, his ardour and patriotism as an ocean warrior;
it is also because his life, his character, his culture, are the
noblest and most effectual protest in the world against the
scurrilities which have been heaped upon the head of the
sailor since the days of Smollett. We can go on laughing
at Trunnion, and at Pipes, and at Hatchway; at their
foul mouths, their grotesque appearance, their swinish
manners. But Collingwood gives the lie direct to such
representations as we find not only in Smollett, but in
other naval novelists and in the illustrations which accom-
pany their works. I yield to no man in admiration for
Marryatt, but I protest if I had to depend for notions of
shipboard life on his diverting stories, I should assume
that the moment a man stepped on to the quarter-deck of
a ship of the State he became irreclaimably and immov-
ably a coarse, swearing, grog-loving son-of-a-gun, full of
fight and liquor, with literature enough to enable him to

[1] *Correspondence and Memoir*, p. 168.

write up a log-book and no more. Yet, despite Colling-wood, the typical sailor of the pig-tailed period holds his own. Yes; we believe in him to this day, because of Smollett, and Marryatt, and Chamier, and Fenimore Cooper, and Michael Scott, and Douglas Jerrold, and the like—because, in a word, we go for our ideas of the sea to novels, instead of to memoirs and biographies of sailors and to their letters.[1]

In January 1806, Collingwood is calling himself advanced in years; and so, as a sailor, he was; for no vocation ages a man so rapidly as that of the sea. Salt-beef eats into the soul; hard weather dries up the skin; the constant wet penetrates the marrow; and there is scarcely a young sailor that escapes without a kink in his back. The intellect is made harsh and dry by the absence of softening home and domestic influences. It was so in those times, when a man had to keep the sea for months and years at a stretch. Collingwood, on New Year's Day, 1806, feeling himself growing an old man, tells his father-in-law that he had made up his mind to retire from sea service, when in the following May his three years shall have expired; "but I am afraid," says he with a sigh in the note of his written rhetoric, "that is now quite out of the question, and as long as I have health I must go on."

And still is he puzzled to know how he is to support the dignity to which he has been raised. He will not plead for pensions; he can be rich without money, "by endeavouring to be superior to everything poor." He adds nobly: "I would have my services to my country unstained by any interested motive; and old Scott and I

---

[1] *Singleton Fontenoy* was probably written by James Hannay as a protest against the world's acceptance of the novelist's sailor. Hannay sprinkles his pages with rose-water and sweet-smelling essences—he goes perhaps to the other extreme, yet "Welwyn" is much truer of his day than "Trunnion" was of his.

can go on in our cabbage-garden without much greater expense than formerly."

The position of Commander-in-Chief in the Mediterranean was one of such extraordinary responsibility, the duties of it growing every week, one might say, more and more burthensome, by reason of the ceaseless and ever-varying twistings, warpings, intricacies, and complexities of European politics, that, failing Collingwood, it is hard on looking round at the naval men of that period to know which of them would have been fit for the position.   It is said by Osler, in his *Life of Admiral Viscount Exmouth,*[1] that there was no Ambassador on whom a weightier diplomatic responsibility was imposed than the Admiral in command of the Mediterranean fleet.   " It formed by much the largest and most anxious portion of Collingwood's duties; and the greatness of the trust, the impossibility of transferring it to another than the Commander on the station, and the uncommon ability with which Collingwood sustained it, gave the British Government much uneasiness when the state of that officer's health threatened to deprive them of his services."   It would occupy too much space to attempt even a brief recital of the condition of Europe when the Mediterranean command was given to Collingwood. Austria had been subdued at Austerlitz; the policy of Prussia was one of treachery and of contradiction; a treaty was about to be entered into between England and Russia for the purpose of rescuing the Continent from the domination of Napoleon; there was in existence a convention between Frederick William and the Emperor Alexander, in which the Court of Berlin engaged to make common cause against France; and at the same time there was a treaty in which the King of Prussia agreed with Napoleon to cede Anspach, Neuchatel, and Cleves, and indemnify

[1] p. 278.

N

himself by the seizure of the territories of his ally, the Elector of Hanover.

Collingwood's principal concern was the kingdom of Naples. It was required of him that by every means in his power he should defend the dominions of the Sicilian king. This was the gist of the instructions he gave to Sir Sidney Smith, when that gallant officer joined him for a few hours off Cadiz. Amongst the earliest of the letters he received was one from the unhappy Queen of Naples:

"Though I have not the pleasure, Milord, to know you, the last glorious battle, your friendship for the immortal and to me always dear and regretted Lord Nelson, and the command of the Mediterranean confided to your care, are so many motives to make me desire your acquaintance, at least for the moment by correspondence. The assurances which the Chevalier Elliott[1] has given us in your name have greatly touched me; we are just now in a very, very painful and critical situation. I count that you will do for us that which was done by the respectable Milord Nelson, our friend, protector, and defender. The King and all my dear family share my sentiments, and hope for everything from your brave nation and from your active co-operation. Count upon my sincere esteem and eternal gratitude, with which I am, and always shall be, your affectionate Charlotte."

When Captain, afterwards Admiral, Markham was in the Mediterranean in 1784, he was with the King of Naples on several occasions, and thus he wrote of the royal couple: "His pleasures are very innocent—hunting, shooting, and sailing about the Bay of Naples. He is more liked, though less courted, than the Queen, in whom, in fact, the whole authority is vested. I was disgusted in observing that she does not attempt to conceal the contemptuous

[1] British Ambassador at Naples.

opinion she entertains of the King's abilities." [1] Collingwood's dislike and distrust of this Queen was lively. His
aversion was not to be moderated by his recollection of
Nelson's devotion to the Sicilian cause—for Nelson's was
a sentiment Collingwood would justly deem in excess of all
patriotic and professional demands, and he would correctly
attribute its inspiration to Lady Hamilton. Collingwood
met the Queen later on, and expressed himself very freely
about her; we shall presently see what he says. Tory as he
was, and hating the French, with all Nelson's sincerity of
detestation, he must yet find something very repugnant in
the dedication of British blood and treasure to the bolstering
up of certainly the most hateful government of the day—
a court of rogues and courtesans, of treacherous cowards,
and slavering impostors. He writes, nevertheless, in
courtier-like language to the Queen : "I beg your Majesty
to consider me as an officer devoted to the service of his
country. The Allies of my Sovereign, and the patrons of
my friend Lord Nelson, whose noble character obtained
for him the regard of your Majesty, will be ever dear to
me; and if my humble service shall aid in giving tran-
quillity to your kingdom and happiness to your Majesty,
the pleasure I shall receive from it will be amongst the
blessings of my life."

He had, however, no hope of the result. He knew
that for some time their Sicilian Majesties had been pursuing a despicable policy of cunning which could only result
in their overthrow; that whilst apparently submitting to
Napoleon, they were secretly working for the protection of
Great Britain, Russia, and Austria; that whilst with one
hand they were ratifying a convention with France, with
the other they were delivering a secret counter declaration
to the Russian Minister. The wretched King of Naples

---

[1] *A Naval Career during the Old War*, p. 78.

writes to Collingwood on the 18th of February, that his
position is *affreuse*, that the Russians have abandoned
him, that the British troops have been withdrawn, that his
measures to accommodate matters with the French have
proved fruitless, that Joseph Buonaparte is in the kingdom
of Naples at the head of a powerful army. His son is
fighting—or, at all events, his son is with his troops;
but he himself, this squireen king, is at Palermo, with
his queen. His whole hope, he says, is in the brave and
loyal British nation. His situation is horrible, and equally
horrible, the poor creature believes, is the situation of his
subjects. He begs that the defence of Sicily may be provided for by a powerful division of British ships of war.
" Veuillez, Milord," he concludes, " accourir à mon secours
par les moyens et choix de forces que vous jugerez pou-
voir assurer mon existence, et encourager mes efforts. Sur
ce je prie Dieu qu'il vous ait en sa sainte et digne
garde."

To this piteous letter Collingwood replied as reassuringly
as his hopes or misgivings would permit him. He told the
King that he had already sent reinforcements of ships to the
coast of Sicily, that he was now sending others; so that the
whole force provided promised to be superior to anything
that the enemy could collect. He pointed out that his one
object was to hinder the French squadrons cruising in the
ocean from passing through the Strait of Gibraltar into the
Mediterranean; but writing on the same date, March 6th,
to his father-in-law, he says that the arrangements he has
made for protecting the coast of Sicily will, he hopes, give
the King all the security he requires; " but for Naples he
must wait until events on the Continent are more favourable." Indeed, before the end of the month in which
Collingwood dated his letter to the King, the French were

¹ *Correspondence and Memoir*, p. 185.

in possession of the whole kingdom of Naples, except Gaeta and Civitella del Tranto.

Meanwhile, that is to say, early in February, Collingwood learnt that four of the five frigates which were lying at Cadiz, where they had been at anchor since the Battle of Trafalgar, were ready for sea, and waiting for an opportunity to sail. With a view of coaxing them out of their nest, Collingwood with his ships took up his station about thirty miles away from Cadiz, and lay there out of sight, leaving behind him two vessels, the *Hydra* frigate, and the brig-sloop *Moselle*, to keep an eye upon the port. A strong easterly breeze of wind that came on to blow on the 23rd drove Collingwood's squadron so far to the westward that the French commander, La Marre, who had been informed of Collingwood's situation by the telegraph posts erected along the shore, weighed with four frigates and a brig, provisioned for six months, with a number · of troops on board. They were descried and chased by the *Hydra* and *Moselle*, afterwards by the *Hydra* alone, the *Moselle* having been sent to communicate with Collingwood; and on the 27th the frigate captured the French brig *Furet* and carried her off as a prize, M. La Marre apparently taking no notice of the conflict, but proceeding on his voyage to the westward as though nothing was wrong.

Collingwood was cheered in the spring of this year by news of the success of the squadron under command of Sir John Duckworth. "It is a victory," he says in a letter to the Right Honourable C. Grey, dated April 1st, "worthy the zeal and perseverance of the distinguished officer who achieved it." In the previous November, Rear-Admiral Louis, by orders of Collingwood (who was at Gibraltar), was blockading the surviving French and Spanish ships in the port of Cadiz, when Sir John Duckworth, in the *Superb*, joined and took the command. A few days afterwards there arrived news of a French squadron of five sail of the line and some small craft having dispersed a convoy of six sail off the Salvages, between Madeira and Teneriffe. Sir John Duckworth at once raised the blockade, conjecturing that the Frenchmen were the notorious Rochefort squadron under Allemand.

On the 25th of December nine strange sail were made out. Sir John packed on canvas in chase. The squadron proved six sail of the line, with other vessels, under the command of Rear-Admiral Willaumez, on their way to St. Helena. The unequal sailing powers of the British ships rendered the pursuit unavailing, and Sir John hoisted a signal annulling the chase. James deals harshly with Sir John Duckworth for not making a dash at the enemy with the *Superb*, when most of his ships were miles astern; but surely the subsequent victory justifies the British Admiral's decision not to invite the capture of his ship by an over-whelming force before any assistance could reach him. Sir John stretched away for the Leeward Islands to obtain a supply of fresh water, and on the 19th of January anchored in Bass-Terre Road, St. Christophers, where, on the 1st of February, he received intelligence of a French squadron having been seen steering towards the city of San Domingo. The British ships arrived off that port on the 6th, and found nine sail at anchor. Five of them were line-of-battle ships, and a sixth the remaining frigate of the squadron of Rear-Admiral Leissegues. The result of the action was the capture of three of the French ships, and the stranding or driving on shore of the rest. Sir John joined Collingwood off Cadiz on April 29th, after an absence of five months, during which he had certainly made the best use of his time. "Lord Collingwood, who took no rest himself, but was always mindful of the repose of others, ordered Duckworth to England."[1]

n's *Naval History*, vol. ii. 109.

During the course of this year the five French two-deckers that had escaped from the Battle of Trafalgar into Cadiz were repaired and rendered fit for sea. Further, the Spaniards had got ready several ships lying in that port, raising the Franco-Spanish force there to a total of eleven or twelve sail of the line. There were also eight Spanish liners in Carthagena, and three French two-deckers and some frigates in Toulon.

CHAPTER IX.

Letters to his Wife—Property bequeathed—Pension—Life on Board
Ship—Purity of Collingwood's Character—Resolutions of Con-
quest—Education of his Children—Lady Collingwood—Loneli-
ness—Morpeth—Portugal—Sir Sidney Smith—Battle of Maida
—Fall of Gaeta—Admiral Louis dispatched to the Dardanelles
—Expedition under Sir Thomas Duckworth.

AN interval now occurs that cannot be better filled than by drawing upon some of Collingwood's letters, written in 1806. Those to his wife and father-in-law exhibit his character to a degree that no mere enumeration of his qualities could approach. He writes thus to his wife, March 21st:

"I have at present no prospect of sending a letter, but I begin this because I love to write to you ; and I know that were it only to tell you that I am well, it would be gladly received. If some of those French who are flying about do not come hither soon, I shall get horribly tired of sauntering here, with the thousand causes of care and anxiety in other quarters. I have many in search of their squadrons, and shall ever hope—for could we but once meet them again I doubt not that we should make as complete a business as the last was. At least you may depend upon it your husband will leave nothing in his power undone to make you a Countess; not that I am ambitious of rank, but I am to be thought a leader in my country's glory, and to contribute to its security in peace.

"I wish some parts of Hethpoole could be selected for plantations of larch, oak, and beech, where the ground could be best spared. Even the sides of a bleak hill would grow larch and fir. You will say that I have now mounted my hobby; but I consider it as enriching and fertilizing that which would otherwise be barren. It is drawing soil from the very air. I cannot, at this distance, advise you on the education of our darlings, except that it should not stop for a moment. They are just at that period of their lives when knowledge should be acquired; and great regard should be had to the selection of the books which they read, not throwing away their precious time on novels and nonsense, most of which might be more fitly used in singeing a capon for table than in preparing a young lady for the world. How glad I should be just now to have half an hour's conversation with you on these important subjects!"

In March Collingwood received news of the death of his cousin, Edward Collingwood, of Dissington and Chirton, who bequeathed to him the estate of Chirton. This property belonged in the early part of the eighteenth century to the family of the Milburns, from whom it came by marriage to the Roddams, of whom the last daughter, Mary, married Edward Collingwood of Byker and Dissington, who died in 1783, aged 81, and was succeeded by his eldest son Edward, who departed this life aged 72, bequeathing the Chirton property, as we have seen, to

Collingwood.[1] On receipt of the news, our hero, dating his letter on board the *Ocean*, May 1st, writes to Mr. J. E. Blackett:

"I am much obliged for the information you give me about Chirton, and I wish that the very letter of the will of my deceased friend should be observed. Whatever establishment may be found there for the comfort of the poor, or the education and improvement of their children, I would have continued and increased. I want to make no great accession of wealth from it, nor will I have anybody put to the smallest inconvenience for me. I shall never live there; nor were it as many thousands as it is hundreds would I quit my present situation to regulate it."

He was much vexed about this time on reading the report of the speeches made in the House of Commons referring to the settlement of a pension upon his daughters. He was spoken of as being poor; but the statement did not seem to vex him so much as the idea it suggested— that the representation of his slender finances was made with his concurrence. "The pension," he says, "was most honourable to me, as it flowed voluntarily from his Majesty's bounty, and as a testimony of his approbation; but if I had a favour to ask, money would be the last thing I should beg from an impoverished country. I am not a Jew whose god is gold; nor a Swiss whose services are to be counted against so much money. I have motives for my conduct which I would not give in exchange for a hundred pensions." He felt, as he told his wife, as though he had been held up in the House of Commons as an object for compassion. Indeed, one might suppose that at this time Collingwood would consider himself fairly well off, with income enough to provide for the dignity of his wife and two daughters at home; his own personal ex-

---

[1] *Newcastle Chronicle*, December 5th, 1885.

penses, as we have seen, being insignificant.   There was
his pay as Commander-in-Chief; there was his pension of
£2000 a year; there was the estate at Chirton; and there
was also Mr. J. E. Blackett to back him—Mr. Blackett,
who, I am informed by a representative of the family, was
a considerable ship-owner and a very prosperous man,
whose house in Charlotte Square, Newcastle-upon-Tyne,
was as much the home of Lady Collingwood and her
children as their residence at Morpeth.

 Of the discomfort and, indeed, the frugality of Collingwood's life on board ship, we find several hints in his correspondence. Still keeping to this same year of 1806, we find
him, on April 27th, telling his wife that his man Smith
provides him with his dinner, but he says that, owing to his
losses and removals and breakages, he has scarcely a knife or
fork left, and is indeed very badly off for everything.   His
wants were supplied by his wife by June, and he thanks
her for sending him knives, forks, and a teapot.   " Here I
get nothing," he says, " but then my expenses are nothing,
and I do not want it."   His thoughts are hourly with his
home.   With a hand almost paralyzed with the fatigue of
writing letters to Kings and Ministers, to Ambassadors, to
the Admiralty, to Generals, to Admirals, and to Governors,
he can yet send a blessing to his wife, a line to his girls.
" My darlings, little Sarah and Mary," he writes, " I was
delighted with your last letters, my blessings, and desire
you to write to me very often and tell me all the news of
the city of Newcastle and town of Morpeth.   I hope we
shall have many happy days and many a good laugh
together yet.   Be kind to old Scott; and when you see
him weeding my oaks give the old man a shilling.   May
God Almighty bless you! "   He is ceaseless in his en-
treaties to his wife to watch over the education of these
dear ones.   " I beseech you, dearest Sarah," he says, " I

beseech you keep them constantly employed; make them
read to you, not trifles, but history, in the manner we used
to do in the winter evenings: blessed evenings indeed!
The human mind will improve itself if it be kept in
action; but grows dull and torpid when left to slumber.
I believe even stupidity itself may be cultivated."

It was said of Samuel Johnson that the proof of the
goodness and greatness of his character lay in his reputation being supported and heightened by the publication of
his most familiar thoughts, of his dinner-table chat, of his
club arguments over a bowl of punch, of every scrap of
correspondence that Boswell and that Boswell's successors
could lay hands on. One thinks the same of Collingwood.
Those who served with him recognized in him the admirable sea-officer, the long-headed diplomatist, an ocean
warrior who embodied all Nelson's fighting qualities, but
unemotionally, without the least taint of the theatric
expression one finds amongst the ardent combatants of
that day, amongst men such as Lord Cochrane, Sidney
Smith, Jahleel Brenton, in whom the spirit of war had
been worked up into a glorified spirit of murder by the
magnificent headlong example of the hero of the Nile.
But the associates who lived closest to Collingwood—
whose reserve had something of austerity—never, I will
venture to say, suspected that his cold professional exterior
concealed a heart as soft as a woman's, animated by an
exquisite sensibility; a heart overflowing with goodness,
with thanksgiving, with love, and gratitude. This one
sees in his letters, when he talks with his pen, as it
were, grasping the hand of those of his correspondents
whom he loved and honoured. He little suspected as he
wrote that a day must come when his engaging prattle,
lightful epistolary chats, would be collected in a
d given to the world. Sub-edited to a certain

degree, I do not doubt these letters were; certain of them
may have been suppressed; here and there a phrase may
have been erased; but enough is given to persuade us
that had all Collingwood ever written been printed, the
whole could but have more convincingly expressed the
sweetness, the gentleness, purity, chivalry, patriotism,
the ever-governing influence of high moods we find in
this great man's character as it stands exhibited in his
published correspondence.   To be sure such qualities may
seem irreconcilable with all inherited notions of what
is termed the "Sea-Dog"; but it will be found that the
more closely the "Sea-Dog's" character is inspected, the
more conspicuously will there show in him precisely those
very virtues and merits which our traditions should assure
us he must be the least likely of all persons to possess.

   And all the same Collingwood can go on thinking, in
his quiet way, of what Nelson loved to call "glory," with
as fixed and obstinate a resolution to achieve everything
as ever prompted the spirit of his friend.   "I have a
letter," he writes to his wife on the 1st of May, "from a
kinsman of mine (for I have several new kindred lately)
who derives our descent from Lancaster (Talebois) who
came with William the Conqueror, and tells me of many
great people to whom we are allied, and that I am of much
more noble ancestry than I was at all aware of.   I do not
know much of what we were formerly, but I can tell him
that if I can get hold of the Frenchmen again, I will be a
Viscount or nothing."   Referring to his desire that his title
should be perpetuated in his daughters, he writes to Lord
Radstock, July 5th : "I must look for the means of calling
his Majesty's attention to me, and with God's blessing, I
will before the year is out; I am in the field for it and
hope for everything."   "I have written a long letter to
Admiral Roddam," he says, addressing his father-in-law,

September 25th, "informing him of the state of the fleets here, which I think will make his mouth water to have a touch at the Dons. They are getting so strong that I have little doubt of their coming out, and a blessed day it will be; but they must not run too fast; for many of my ships are bad sailers, nor can my feeble limbs carry me about for two or three days and nights as they used to do. I dare say I have more of the decrepitude of age than the Admiral would have had but for his accident."[1] The spirit that we find under Bowyer's flag on the Glorious First, in the *Excellent* on the great St. Valentine's day, aboard the *Royal Sovereign* on the 21st of October, shows as strongly, burns as brightly, in these and scores of similar passages, as ever it did, spite of the burden of years that is now upon him, spite of his legs, as he tells his wife, "growing lady-like," spite of distress from an internal complaint, whose cause was perhaps as yet unsuspected, though in a few short years it was to destroy him.

Some of the happiest passages in his correspondence are those which relate to the education of his children. He devoted himself with delight to the task of instructing them when at home, and it is touching to find him continuing these efforts amidst the worries, the distractions, the enormous obligations of his position. The following is a good example of his theories of education, of his patience in imparting them, of his impassioned interest in the well-being of his children. "How do the dear girls go on?" he writes, on June the 16th, to his wife. "I would have them taught geometry, which is of all sciences in the world the most entertaining: it expands the mind more to the knowledge of all things in nature, and better teaches to distinguish between truths and such things as have the appearance of being truths, yet are not, than any other.

---

[1] *Correspondence and Memoir*, p. 243.

Their education and the proper cultivation of the sense which God has given them are the objects on which my happiness most depends. To inspire them with a love of everything that is honourable and virtuous, though in rags, and with contempt for vanity in embroidery, is the way to make them the darlings of my heart. They should not only read, but they require a careful selection of books; nor should they ever have access to two at the same time; but when a subject is begun it should be finished before anything else is undertaken. How would it enlarge their minds if they could acquire sufficient knowledge of mathematics and astronomy to give them an idea of the beauties and wonders of the creation? I am persuaded that the generality of people, and particularly fine ladies, only adore God because they are told it is proper and the fashion to go to church; but I would have my girls gain such knowledge of the works of the creation that they may have a fixed idea of the nature of that Being who could be the author of such a world. Whenever they have that, nothing on this side the moon will give them much uneasiness of mind."

There is before me a letter written by Lady Collingwood to Miss Woodman, dated November 22nd, 1806, in which I seem to find something that brings before me the realities of Collingwood's life—of the life of this great soul, sundered from his home and his love—with an accentuation that I might miss in a direct description. It runs thus:

" MY DEAR MARY,

    " . . . I must begin the account of the Ball with the three ladies' dresses from this house. Mrs. Trevelyan wore white sarsnet with lace let in round the breast, and a silver gauze pinned upon her head. Miss Brown was

o

plain and elegant—a white thin muslin dress, short, and a white satin waist over it, with a gold band on her head. My dress was my black velvet gown with my gold trimming down the front and round the breast and sleeves. It looked, I must say, very handsome. My black-and-gold handkerchief on my head, gold lace band and my diamonds and topazes—so much for my Ladyship. We went at nine o'clock, and found the dining-room very full. Mr. Mayor asked me if I intended dancing, as he requested the honour for the two first dances; which of course I declined, and Mrs. Brandling began with the Mayor.

"The ball-room was beautiful, and proved sufficiently light, but the heat was beyond everything, from the number of lamps—fifteen behind each transparency. The company looked brilliant and everybody well-dressed. The Ridleys, Brandlings, Ellisons (Hebburn), Mrs. Lisle and her young ladies, the Riddells, Bewicks, Blacketts, about an hundred and seventy odd, sat down to supper, and at the next ball they expect two hundred. I am invited to that also, but I have excused myself. The Reays are to be at that, and they dine here and take a bed; and we have invited to dinner on that day the Askews, Prossers, and Linskills, who are all to be at the Mansion House that evening. The supper was very handsome; soups and game of all kinds hot, and everything else cold. We did not go to supper till near half after two o'clock; there was no dancing after. We moved the first, and it was near four when we got home. . . .

"But to return to the Ball. Nothing could be more pleasant nor better conducted. It is said that there are to be *six* more balls, in which case you will come in for your *share*. The parties have begun very early this winter. We have had two great dinners, and on Saturday next we are to have seventeen at dinner, the Mansion House

family, &c. . . . So much for our gaieties. My father is
certainly very much better. He continues to use the
warm bath every other night; and I fancy I must soon
come to that myself, for I have been much teased with
rheumatics in my hip, and I have it now in my knees very
bad, and last night got no sleep. Sarah has had a bad
cold, but is well again; they [1] go to Mrs. Wilson's three
times a week to dance and draw, and Mr. Kinlock comes
to them at home once a week, and with Mr. Bruce and Mr.
Thompson, they are kept very busy. I have not heard
from my Lord since I left Morpeth, and am now getting
very anxious. . . . I hope your sister, Fenwick, is better,
as you did not mention her particularly. My father joins
me and my girls in kindest regards and good wishes to you
and Mrs. Woodman and your sister, and pray remember
me to all your family.

    " I remain, my dear Mary,
       " Most truly your affectionate friend,
             " S. COLLINGWOOD." [2]

This letter attaches in an uncommon degree the idea
of isolation to the figure of Collingwood. We may freely
suppose that he would not have given twopence for the
ball, for the six to follow, for the great dinners and the
rest of the round of diversions; the society of his old
gardener, Scott, a bed of potatoes to dig, a tree to plant,
his daughters to instruct—these were entertainments to
amply fill the measure of the wants of this great and
simple heart. But to us who are capable of sending a ·
glance, first at Newcastle-on-Tyne and at her Ladyship
in her black velvet gown with gold trimming down the

---

[1] Lady Collingwood's two daughters.
[2] The original of this letter was in possession of the late Mr. John Clayton.

breast, and then at the cold November sea off Cadiz, with the tall shadow of *H.M.S. Ocean*, swaying from side to side upon the restless Atlantic heave, the contrast is so strong as to produce the impression of a vivid picture.

"Should we decide to change the place of our dwelling," he writes to his wife, "our route will of course be to the southward of Morpeth : but then I should be for ever regretting those beautiful views which are nowhere to be exceeded ; and even the rattling of that old wagon that used to pass our door at six o'clock on a winter's morning had its charms. The fact is, whenever I think how I am to be happy again, my thoughts carry me back to Morpeth, where, out of the fuss and parade of the world, surrounded by those I love most dearly, and who love me, I enjoyed as much happiness as my nature is capable of." Thus he thinks and thus he writes of his home. I know not where else to look for so much of tenderness and loyalty of affection, of simple, touching sincerity of home-yearning, that yet leaves unweakened all professional resolves and iron-hard theories of duty and conduct, as I find in Collingwood's letters. You discover no dwindling of emotion and passion through absence—through a separation that was protracted to the grave itself—through a divorce so long, persistent, inexorable, that the most deep-rooted of human sentiments might be pardoned for languishing and even for withering in the frost and gloom of the atmosphere of the ordeal.

In September, Lord St. Vincent was at Lisbon, endeavouring, to employ the language of Collingwood, to "inspire a decayed Government with vigour and to give strength to a nerveless arm." The condition of Portugal will be inferred from the letter St. Vincent addressed to Lord Howick shortly after his arrival in the Tagus, in August : "The army," he says, "is very much diminished in numbers since I was last in Portugal. Thirteen thousand ill-armed infantry are the utmost that can be counted upon; and the cavalry beggars all description, both as to officers and men. The magazines and all the woodwork of the interior of the barracks in and about Lisbon have been torn away and consumed in cooking the soldiers' dinners. One 74-gun ship and a few frigates are cruising in the Strait's mouth, and they are now making every effort to equip a 64, and a frigate to go out after an Algerine of twenty guns." [1]

Portugal had indeed sounded the very depths of political and social degradation. The Prince Regent was unequal to forming a resolution; should he welcome General Junot as his deliverer, or should he fly with his family to the Brazils? The object of St. Vincent's visit was to furnish him with the protection of a British squadron; this the Prince hesitated to accept; he sulkily, indeed, for some time declined to admit St. Vincent's ships to pratique. On the 18th October the Earl returned to Ushant, to renew the blockade of Brest, by which period his mission had not been without some degree of efficacy, since he writes of a complete change in the sentiments of the people touching his motives, of much kindness shown to himself and to his officers by all ranks and orders, particularly the clergy, from the Pope's Nuncio downwards.

Meanwhile Collingwood's pressing anxiety lay in the direction of Sicily, and in the affairs of the King and Queen of Naples. The hope of the Queen of regaining possession of the kingdom he regarded as the vainest dream that ever entered the imagination of a woman. "When they possessed it," he wrote to Mr. Elliott, the British Ambassador, "with all the resources of the country

---

[1] Brenton's *Life of Lord St. Vincent*, vol. ii. 304.

at their command, with the (professed, at least,) loyalty of
an armed people, and the army of the Allies at their head,
it was abandoned as untenable ; and now that the country
is disarmed, every person supposed to be yet attached to
their Prince removed from it, and the enemy possessing
every place of strength, on what foundation can the hope
of success be built ?   Let her beware of counsels which I
suspect are of French origin," he adds with intuitive perception of the desperate and dishonourable game the
unfortunate Queen was presently to play, "and of the
people from whom they come.   Whatever can diffuse the
limited force and scanty resources of Sicily, or distract
her counsellors, is favourable to the enemy and may be
suspected to come from them." [1]

It had been represented to him that the Queen of
Naples, in expectation of being reseated on her throne,
had engaged to show her gratitude to Sir Sidney Smith
by creating him a Sicilian Duke, and giving him an estate.
"If," says Collingwood, addressing his wife, September 13th,
with an involuntary recurrence perhaps to the memory of
Nelson as he writes—"If they offer me a Dukedom, I
tell you beforehand how I will show them what my estimation of it is.   I shall reply, after returning my thanks
for the intended honour, that I am the servant of my
Sovereign alone, and can receive no rewards from a foreign
prince. If, in obeying the commands of the King, I render
benefit to his allies, the acknowledgment of it must be
highly gratifying to me ; but that is all the reward I
can accept from any prince but my own. They have
not revenue to defend their country, and are perpetually
craving to me for money ; instead of which I give them
good advice, and show them how to enrich their country
and make their people happy." In short, he hated their

---

[1] *Correspondence and Memoir,* p. 240.

Sicilian Majesties and abhorred the obligation of serving them.

Sir Sidney Smith, as we have seen, had joined Collingwood off Cadiz in April, but the immediate defence of Sicily was so imperative that he was detained for a few hours only by the Admiral. On his arrival at Palermo on the 21st April, he found that Collingwood had already sent there three sail of the line, with which, and his own ship, the *Pompeé*, and a fifth ship, the *Eagle*, which afterwards joined him, he proceeded to execute Collingwood's orders. The instructions upon which these orders were grounded originated in a minute which Nelson had placed in the hands of Pitt, and the plan of operations comprised the recovery of Naples and its territories in Calabria from the French by disembarking forces to co-operate with the loyal subjects of the King of Sicily for the expulsion of "King" Joseph. To follow Sir Sidney Smith would be to carry us entirely away from Collingwood. On his command ceasing in Sicily and Calabria, he wrote to Collingwood from Malta, February 3rd, 1807: "I thus take my leave of this service with a conscious certainty that I have acted from the purest motives for the common cause against the cruel and rapacious foe we have had to do with, on the general principle of 'pursuing a beaten and flying enemy, and to assist a known friend in view.' I have given every support to the British army in my power, paying every deference to his Majesty's Minister Plenipotentiary and the Commander-in-Chief, although they did not agree with me in the application of the general principle which is, and I trust will remain, that on which his Majesty's naval service habitually acts. In so doing I am happy to have met your Lordship's approbation."[1]

[1] Barrow's *Life and Correspondence of Admiral Sir William Sidney Smith*, vol. ii. 185.

The difference of opinion, or perhaps the difficulties, to which Sir Sidney refers, concerned Mr. Elliott's disapproval of the measure of conveying ordnance stores from Palermo for the defence of Gaeta, because that measure had obtained the sanction of the Queen of Naples and of the Prince Royal; and the unwillingness of Sir John Stuart, who was in command of the British army, to acquiesce in Sir Sidney's proposal of the invasion of Calabria, because that scheme happened to be the wish of Ferdinand. Yet the memorable and remarkable battle of Maida was the issue of Sir Sidney's advice, and the moral and triumph of his persuasion. I must not omit a brief description of this swift and wonderful conflict. The French general, Regnier, on hearing of the disembarkation of the British forces, rapidly marched from Reggio. He encamped near the village of Maida with some 4,000 infantry and 300 cavalry, and here he meant to wait for two or three days, expecting to be reinforced by 3,000 troops. The British general's total rank and file, including the Royal Artillery, numbered 4,795. Regnier quitted his position, which, in the opinion of the British general, was impregnable, and crossing the river, entered the open plain with his whole force. The two corps fired a few rounds; the distance between them was about a hundred yards; "when," says General Stuart, "as if by mutual agreement, the firing was suspended, and in close compact order and awful silence they advanced towards each other until their bayonets began to cross." There was something so terrible in the aspect of the British, something so tremendous in the grim and solemn stillness of their approach, that the French took flight—they broke, appalled, and fled; but the British bayonets penetrated them as they ran, and this little field of battle became as bloody a shamble as was ever contrived by the genius and machinery of murder. Seven hundred of the enemy were slain ; a thousand were wounded and taken prisoners ; another thousand, left at the various posts, offered to surrender to preserve themselves from the fury of the people. The total loss was estimated at four thousand men. On the British side one officer, three sergeants, forty-one rank and file were killed ; and eleven officers, eight sergeants, two drummers, and two hundred and sixty-one rank and file wounded.

Shortly after this both Calabrias were evacuated by the French ; but the fortress of Gaeta was not to be preserved ; it surrendered by capitulation on the 12th of July, and before the end of the year the French had recovered nearly every important post.

Collingwood, still off Cadiz, writes to Sir Sidney Smith, October 7th : " The fall of Gaeta did not surprise me. I consider it as a thing of course to happen upon any reverse of fortune ; its defence, in fact, depended solely upon the preservation of the Prince of Hesse, and its surrender was the natural consequence of the anarchy which took place on his being wounded. All subordination appears to have ceased ; and it was not easy to discover with whom the command rested until the Sicilians determined that question." It was a loss, however, that he viewed lightly. Waiving consideration of the point of honour in defending the fortress, he held that the cost of its protection exceeded its value. It drew ships from employment of importance ; it exhausted in Sicily the munitions of war, and it reduced the British naval strength by involving the landing of guns and men, "so that altogether," he adds, "if it could be held only by such means perhaps there was a profit in its fall."

Sicily, however, was to be but a single detail in the long catalogue of Collingwood's responsibilities at this time.

The resignation or the deposition of the Sultan Selim in favour of his nephew Mustapha had created a struggle between the Russian and the French Governments as to which of them should become the favourite nation at the Porte. On the 10th of August the French Ambassador, General Sebastiani, arrived at Constantinople, and in a few days his intrigues had resulted in causing the Porte to recall the reigning Hospadars from Moldavia and Wallachia. He further demanded that the Canal of Constantinople should be shut against Russian ships, and he threatened the vengeance of the French nation in case of refusal. The effect of this is shown in some sentences in a letter from the British Ambassador at Constantinople, Mr. Charles Arbuthnot, to Sir Sidney Smith, dated September 27th, 1806. "France has produced such a panic that the Porte is wholly alienated from us, and the most vigorous measures alone can now preserve our interests in this part of the world."[1]

It is said by James that the British Admiralty directed Collingwood, on the 22nd of October, to detach three sail of the line to reconnoitre the situation of the forts of the Dardanelles as a precautionary and provisionary measure.[2] A letter from Mr. Grenville, however, written, on his appointment as First Lord of the Admiralty, to Collingwood, would seem to give all the merit of this prompt detachment for surveillant purposes to Collingwood himself: "The detaching," Mr. Grenville says, "of the squadron under Sir Thomas Louis had in a great measure anticipated the wishes of the King's Government, and the promptitude and judgment with which that step had been taken could not but be highly satisfactory to his Majesty."[3] This might appear as confirmed by Colling-

[1] *Life and Correspondence of Sir Sidney Smith*, vol. ii. 210.
[2] *James*, vol. iv. 214.   [3] *Correspondence and Memoir*, p. 264.

wood, who wrote to his wife on December 20th, 1806: " I
have lately had a most anxious time about the Turks.
The accounts I received from the Ambassador stated war
with them to be inevitable, and I dispatched that instant
a squadron under Sir T. Louis to present himself before
the Seraglio. A squadron of English men-of-war must
have a fine effect in a Seraglio !" It is strange, in the
face of the foregoing, to read of the Honourable Thomas
Grenville complaining in the House of Commons, so long
after as February 1808, that Collingwood had suffered six
weeks to elapse before executing the orders he had
received. "This shows," says James, "how requisite it is
to attend to dates." If dates were all !

Sir Thomas Louis was dispatched by Collingwood, on
November 2nd, in the 80-gun ship *Canopus*, and with
him went the *Thunderer* (74) and the *Standard* (64), with a
frigate and a sloop. One month after the arrival of this
squadron in the Dardanelles, the Admiral was joined by
the *Endymion*, with the British Ambassador and suite on
board, together with the whole of the British merchants
resident at Constantinople. It had been reported that in
case a British force commenced hostilities the Turkish
Government would seize the *Endymion* and detain the
Ambassador, his suite, and all the British residents as
hostages, and there was talk of death by torture to follow.
Sir Thomas Louis received all these people, and on
the 1st of February, 1807, the squadron proceeded to the
Island of Tenedos.

In the preceding month of November, Collingwood had
been directed to detach a force to the Dardanelles, and the
orders stated that as the required service demanded much
ability and firmness in the officer in command, the execution of it was to be entrusted to Vice-Admiral Sir John
Thomas Duckworth. Collingwood appears to have found

something unusual in this positive nomination of a junior officer. It is to be regretted that he did not himself carry out the resolution he appears to have formed to command this expedition.[1] The port of Cadiz, however, still demanded his anxious attention. Determined to contribute by all the means in his power to the success of Duckworth's expedition, he increased the force appointed by the Admiralty by two additional ships.[2] As Collingwood was not present, there is no occasion for more than a brief reference to the proceedings of the squadron under Sir John Duckworth. There can be little doubt that the choice of this officer was a mistake, for which, however, Collingwood was in no sense responsible. Sir Sidney Smith was the man who should have been selected. Unhappily Sir Sidney was never very popular with the authorities at home. He had made himself obnoxious to Lord St. Vincent and to Lord Nelson in the Mediterranean, and the Earl, if Sir Sidney's own testimony is to be credited, hated him to the day of his death. "In the Mediterranean," says De Quincey, "he made many enemies, especially amongst those of his own profession, who used to speak of him as far too fine a gentleman, and above his calling. Certain it is that he liked better to be doing business on shore, as at Acre, although he commanded a

---

[1] *Correspondence and Memoir*, p. 265.

[2] Captain Brenton has the following: "I remember a very remarkable trait in the character of the late Lord Collingwood. . . . When he sent Sir John Duckworth to the Dardanelles the orders he gave to that Admiral were so clear and distinct that it was thought impossible to misconstrue them. Duckworth, after looking over them, returned into the cabin and asked the Commander-in-Chief what he was to do in the event of certain contingencies. 'Read your orders,' said the plain-dealing, upright Admiral, 'and then if you don't understand them, come to me and I will explain them.' Duckworth read his orders again with attention, and told his chief that he was perfectly satisfied. This is the way in which orders should be given."
—*Naval History*, vol. ii. p. 641.

fine 80-gun ship, the *Tigre*. But, however that may have been, his services, whether classed as military or naval, were memorably splendid; and at that time his connection of whatsoever nature with the late Queen Caroline had not occurred, so that altogether to me his case is, inexplicable." [1]

Having arrived at the mouth of the Dardanelles, Duckworth's ships let go their anchors off Cape Janizary. This was on the 11th of December; and now Duckworth exhibited a degree of hesitation that was ominous of the future. In February he wrote to Collingwood that in consequence of the batteries which flanked every turn of the passage through the Dardanelles—the handiwork of French engineers—he conceived the service pointed out in his instructions as completely altered; "and," he adds, "viewed in whatever light it may be, has become the most arduous and doubtful that ever has been under-

---

[1] *Autobiographic Sketches,* p. 159. Sir Sidney used himself to tell this story of Lord St. Vincent: " At the breaking out of the war in 1803 with the Consular Government of France, Sir Sidney Smith was appointed to the *Antelope*, and given the command of a squadron for the protection of the entrance of the Thames. Upon this occasion he was sent for by Lord St. Vincent, who, on presenting him with his commission, requested him to leave town that very evening. Sir Sidney Smith had been sent for most unexpectedly, and had left his papers, &c. at the house of Sir John Douglas, at Blackheath, where he was in the habit of leaving them carelessly in his table-drawer. His being hurried off so unexpectedly must have convinced him that it proceeded from some other object besides the mere service in question, the ship being known not to be by any means in a state of forwardness. Sir Sidney, however, in the evening got also a most friendly note from Sir Evan Nepean, entreating him to be particular in attending to the injunction of Lord St. Vincent, and on no account to omit leaving London that very evening. Sir Sidney contrived with great exertion to get into his carriage before daylight next morning; and on stepping out of his lodging, he observed the servant of Lord St. Vincent, in livery, close to the door. Was this a watch set by the old gallant Admiral on his former friend the Captain Plenipotentiary ?"—*Life of Sir Sidney Smith,* vol. ii. p. 470.

taken." He puts a sturdy resolution, however, into tl tail of his communication, which in justice ought not 1 be omitted : "I entreat your Lordship to believe that as am aware of the difficulties we have to encounter, so I a resolved that nothing on my part shall be left undone th; can secure the means of surmounting them."

It is generally admitted that the force placed under h control was inadequate to the work it was expected 1 perform. Collingwood, in his instructions to him, state that the number of the ships was greater than had origi ally been intended, as at the time this service was plann(it was not known that the Russian squadron would be : a situation to co-operate; he had, however, by lett requested the Russian Vice-Admiral Siniavin, who w: then cruising in the Archipelago with nine or ten sail the line, to detach four of his ships to serve with tl British force.

CHAPTER X.

UCKWORTH'S squadron was weakened by the loss of the *Ajax*, a fine 74-gun ship, commanded by Captain the Hon. Henry Blackwood. This reduced it to eight ships of the line. The Russians, moreover, did not co-operate. It was generally asserted by naval men that the expedition should have consisted of twice the force of line-of-battle ships under Duckworth, with ten frigates, many bombs, brigs and fire-ships, 20,000 troops, and a train of artillery and store-ships. The loss of the *Ajax* must be referred to, as it occasioned some correspondence between Collingwood, Blackwood, and the Admiralty. She took fire on the night of the 14th of February at nine o'clock, and burnt with inconceivable swiftness. Captain Blackwood himself says that "from the moment of alarm, exactly at nine o'clock, when all (sentinels and those on watch excepted) were in bed, till she was in flames from the main to the mizzen-rigging, sails and all, did not exceed twenty minutes." Her nett complement of men and boys was about 633, of whom it is believed 250 perished. "To-morrow," continues Blackwood in the same letter from which I have just quoted, "if the present wind holds, the squadron in which my poor fellows are divided proceed up to Constantinople; and when we see what can be effected there, we are to proceed on our way to Lord Collingwood, off Cadiz, to be tried. The opinion of the Court of Inquiry, which I inclose, will show you from whence the fire issued; and had it not been for a cruel restriction of Lord Collingwood's to Sir J. Duckworth, and which all feel as most hard and oppressive from the highest to the lowest, it would have sat yesterday." [1]

Collingwood, on receiving the news of the fate of the *Ajax*, sent to Blackwood a letter remarkable for its tone of grave and dignified apology. He admits in himself an

---

[1] *Blackwood's Magazine*, vol. xxxiv. p. 16. Admiral Hercules Robinson, who was midshipman aboard the *Euryalus* under Blackwood at Trafalgar, relates the following incident in connection with the loss of the *Ajax:* "Sir Henry Blackwood was a man of wonderful vigour and courage, and after swimming through the cold dark sea of a stormy night for nearly an hour, was picked up by a boat sent from the *Tonnant* to assist in saving the men. Blackwood never forgot his dignity and his position; and on being dragged into the boat, he said, 'I am quite cool and collected, sir; I am quite cool and collected.' Poor George Macpherson, now no more, and whose child Blackwood (who never forgot a friend) took care of, was midshipman of the boat, and replied to the assurance made to him, 'I don't know, my boy, whether you are collected or not, but I should think you are pretty cool.' Several drowning men cried out, 'Pick me up: I am captain of the *Ajax!*'"—*Seadrift*, p. 237.

error of judgment, and explains it thus, dating his communication Cadiz, April 5th, 1807 : "This event is more
calamitous if possible to me by the sensations it has
awakened in you at the delay in holding the court-
martial. I beg, sir, you will believe that nothing is more
repugnant to me than giving uneasiness or cause of
remonstrance to any person; and I am sorry that in your
address to the Court of Inquiry, which Sir John Duckworth ordered, you had occasion to make any complaint.
I believe I ought not to have required court-martials to
be held here; and that, as you have explained at large
to the Board of Inquiry in your address, the Act of Parliament requires that there should be as little delay as
possible. It was my error, to which I was really led by a
desire to establish officers and men, who had been unfortunate, in ships where there were vacancies for them. It
did not occur to me at the time that it was either con-
travening the law (which I have ever revered), or likely
to be attended with those disadvantages which I am sorry
to find have given you cause of complaint." He added
that he had now directed Sir John Duckworth, or the
officer remaining in command of the squadron, to hold
court-martials, and he handsomely concludes : "I hope the
delay which has occurred will not be attended with any
other consequence than that of keeping a mournful subject
longer on your mind than I wish it to be." He wrote to
the same effect to the Right Honourable Thomas Grenville, deploring that any act of his should have increased
the misfortune of the survivors of such a disaster as that
of the destruction of the *Ajax*. "I have," he says, "too
much reverence for the law to violate it intentionally. I
have ever to the best of my understanding made it my
guide, and the temperate administration of it my study.
So far from distorting it to aggrieve any person, I have

P

constantly sought the means of softening its rigour, when it could be done in justice to the service; and if I have in this instance exceeded the power prescribed by it, I am anxious to establish in your mind, sir, that my motive was rather lenient than harsh." [1]

Blackwood went on board the flag-ship the *Royal George* as a volunteer. The squadron passed the forts of Abydos and Sestos, and though fired upon by the batteries and a number of ships, got through with trifling loss. Duckworth temporized; the Turks, full of craft, excited hopes merely to baffle them; their object was to gain time to put themselves in such a posture as would enable them to set the British at defiance. Duckworth was deceived; so, too, was the astute Sir Sidney Smith. Collingwood's instructions had been precise and surely intelligible, although James speaks of contingencies tacked to them "which rendered them complicated and obscure." [2]   Duckworth was to be advised by the British Ambassador as to when hostilities should begin, and on Mr. Arbuthnot giving the word, the "British Admiral was to make the peremptory demand of the surrender of the Turkish fleet." But, continued Collingwood—and the whole gist of the instructions lies in this—should it appear that the Turkish Government were endeavouring to gain time for preparing their resistance or securing their ships, "I would recommend that no negotiation should continue more than half an hour, and in the event of an absolute refusal you are either to cannonade the town or attack the fleet wherever it may be, holding it in mind that the getting into possession, and next to that the destruction of the Turkish fleet, is the object of the first consideration." This seems clear enough; but Duckworth transformed a taut order into an elastic one. He continued

<hr/>

[1] *Memoir and Correspondence*, pp. 278—80.
[2] *Naval History*, vol. iv. p. 216.

to consult the Ambassador *after* hostilities had commenced, and eventually, on the 3rd of March, conceiving the situation of the squadron to be one of extreme danger, he weighed and proceeded down the Channel, under a storm of shot, one of which, of marble or stone, weighed 800 pounds, and by noon anchored off Cape Janizary, with no better result than a total loss, taking the expedition from start to finish, of 42 killed, 4 drowned, and 235 wounded.

Here he was joined by the Russian Admiral with eight sail of the line. According to Brenton, Siniavin requested Sir John to return with him and renew the attack or the negotiations; but this was declined on the ground that "where a British squadron had failed, no other was likely to succeed." Let the issue of Duckworth's expedition have proved what it might, Collingwood had all along witnessed the impolicy of the British identifying themselves at Constantinople with the Russians, and manifesting a friendship which, he perceived, they were not in the least degree disposed to reciprocate. "I may," he writes to Sir Alexander Ball in March of this year, "be thought to hold the Russian friendship light: indeed I do not; but I believe that if Buonaparte can convince Russia that her interest goes another way than ours her friendship will soon follow." He was put out of temper and sunk in his spirits by Duckworth's report. The Turkish business, he wrote to his wife, ought to have succeeded. "There was nothing in the state of the enemy to prevent it; but the day is completely gone by, for the defences which were neglected and nought are now impregnable." His health, too, at this time was giving him trouble. He complains of physical weakness, yet without any corresponding sensation of illness, and he wrote as though apprehensive that his ailing condition would impair his intellect. He says that his eyes are weak, his body swollen, and his legs shrunk to tapers; "but they serve my turn," he adds, "for I have not much walking." He tells his father-in-law, June 14th: "I hardly ever see the face of an officer except when they dine with me, and am seldom on deck above an hour in the day, when I go in the twilight to breathe the fresh air."

Let any man take a voyage round the world in a sailing ship—a voyage, let me say, that shall keep him imprisoned betwixt the bulwark rails for nine months—call it nine months—with now and again a sight of land, but never so much as an hour's run ashore; and he shall without difficulty understand the sort of loathing that charged the soul of Collingwood when he wrote that he hardly ever saw the face of an officer, and that he was seldom on deck above an hour in the day. With plenty to do, with a horizon bristling with opportunities, how very much otherwise must it have been with him—with this amiable and gallant gentleman, who, stern as he was in all professional directions, was sociable, hospitable, cheerful, a person of wonderful good temper, of great humour, and of culture in the highest degree! But day after day the same faces—faces flattened and rendered insipid by the absence of everything calculated to colour them with emotion! The same minds to traverse—minds exhausted and without power to supply themselves afresh! The same blue or gray breast of ocean to look at, with its sickening iteration of sea-line, that, by incessant presence, binds up the senses of a man, until his qualities become as a faggot in him, dry and sapless! "How little," Collingwood exclaims in a letter to Lord Radstock, "do the people in general know of war, and of the anxious midnight hours which we experience while they rest as happily in their nests as a full stomach will allow."

There was now, however, to happen a change in the monotony of blockading. In July Collingwood was ordered

Collingwood coming on deck.

to proceed with a squadron to the Dardanelles, where the
Russian fleet was, not to carry on an active war against the
Turks, but rather to conciliate them, and give the Russian
and British Ambassadors an opportunity of making a peace
which should never have been broken. He arrived at
Tenedos on the 9th of August, where he found the
Russians employed in desolating the country. The two
squadrons proceeded, but the Russians were not in sight
when, on the 13th, Collingwood with his ships stood close
in with the castles of the Dardanelles. The Turks thought
the ships meant to attempt the passage; Collingwood,
however, declared it was impossible for them to get in. A
number of flags of truce were exhibited, and a Capagi Bashi
—described by Collingwood as a sort of Lord Chamberlain
of the Seraglio—arrived on board with letters to the British
Ambassador, Sir Arthur Paget, Mr. Arbuthnot having gone
home in Sir John Duckworth's ship.

These letters were of a pacific import. Coffee and sher-
bet were produced, and Collingwood smoked a pipe with
the emissary. Next day an answer to the letters was sent,
and the commander of the ship (Captain Henry) that
carried the communication was invited to dine with the
Capitan Pacha, the Turkish Lord High Admiral. There
were five at table, three of them with beards to their
girdles. Captain Henry minutely observed the social pro-
cedure of this Asiatic entertainment, and Collingwood
appears to have enjoyed his account of it so thoroughly
that he sent it at large in a letter to his wife: "There
were neither plates nor knives and forks, but each had a
tortoise-shell spoon. In the middle of the table was a rich
embroidered cushion, on which was a large gold salver, and
every dish, to the number of about forty, was brought in
singly and placed upon the salver, when the company
helped themselves with their fingers, or if it was fricassee,

with their spoon. One of the dishes was a roasted lamb, stuffed with a pudding of rice : the Capitan Pacha took it by the limbs and tore it to pieces to help his guests ; so that you see the art of carving has not arrived at any great perfection in Turkey. The coffee-cups were of beautiful china, which, instead of saucers, were inserted in gold stands like egg-cups, set round with diamonds, rubies, and emeralds. They drank only water, and were waited on by the Vice and Rear-Admirals, and some of the captains of the fleet." [1] It was observed that these Turks spoke lightly of the Russians, in their very infrequent references to them, and that they seemed to consider themselves as quite a match for them if the English were out of the way. Collingwood foresaw the unsuccessful result of his mission. The Turkish hatred of the Russians was loudly avowed, and the Russians were at no pains to dissemble their enmity. As an example of the style employed by the Turks in their letters, he quotes a passage from a communication of the Capitan Pacha to Admiral Siniavin: "After proper inquiries for your health, we must observe to you, in a friendly way, what yourself must know ; that to lie is forbidden by all religions. Your friend should not receive a falsehood from you, nor can he be a friend who would offer one."

The squadron remained at anchor, and negotiations were continued without an inch of progress being made. Collingwood's patience at last gave way. British ships were everywhere wanted ; yet here was a squadron lying in a state of humiliating idleness. The Turks were effusive in professions of friendship and that was all. At last came news of fresh possessions of the French in the Adriatic, of the disposal of Sicily, of other momentous matters, all which required the fleet, and smarting under

[1] *Correspondence and Memoir*, p. 300.

the indignity of the nothingness of the negotiations with the Turks, and regardless of the views of the British Ambassador, Collingwood, in the hope of bringing affairs to a head, addressed the following point-blank questions to the Capitan Pacha: Will the Sublime Porte accept the friendship offered by England with a renewal of all the relations of peace and amity, the particular terms of which may be settled by the Plenipotentiaries? Or do they reject the proposal and, influenced by malign councils, determine on a state of war? To these questions he informed the Capitan Pacha he expected a prompt, ingenuous, and clear reply. If no answer was returned, he should conclude that the Turkish ministers intended to take such a part as they could not without regret reveal. The Capitan Pacha answered with the assurance that he loved only the real truth, of which he took God to witness; and in a letter, whose evasiveness renders it amusing literature nowadays, though to Collingwood it must have proved in an uncommon degree irritating and perplexing, he begs the British Admiral to believe that there will be no delay on the part of the Turks in communicating the expected answer.

Referring to this correspondence in a letter addressed to J. E. Blackett, dated off the Dardanelles, September 5th, Collingwood says: "The Ambassador (Paget) did not like this; I suppose he thought it was interfering with his treaty, which it was not. I know too well the absolute necessity of each branch of his Majesty's service confining itself to its own proper and peculiar province ever to intermeddle with the duties of another; but it was an effort on my part, as the commander here, to have him accepted as Plenipotentiary, or to make them declare that they would not receive him. I could no longer bear patiently to see the important service of our country

totally at a stand, and not attempt to set it in motion.
I scarce know how this will be received in England,
neither do I care. I considered it well, and shall always
be satisfied with it in my own mind; and if any displeasure be expressed on the occasion, I shall desire to
come home. God knows how truly I have served, how
unremittingly I have studied, my country's interest, and
how I have exerted myself to promote it. What judgment
I have I will use, or have nothing to do with it; and
whenever that day comes when I can retire from the
labours of public service, it will be a happy one indeed.
In bodily strength I am worn out; and whoever enters
so entirely into the state of our country as I do, and have
done, cannot be much otherwise."

There is in this letter—for Collingwood—a warmth and
temper that strongly illustrates the weight and irritation
of the worry of this time. "Tell Sarah," he adds pathetic-
ally, "that I hope she will have a comfortable house for me
when I come home. The farther it is from the sea-shore
the less we shall be annoyed." [1]

By the peace of Tilsit, Russia, like Austria, became the
friend of France, and on the 24th of August in this year,
Vice-Admiral Siniavin, having concluded an armistice with
the Porte, detached a few ships to take possession of the
island of Corfu, that had been ceded to Russia by France,
and then made haste to get away from the Mediterranean
into the Baltic before a war between Russia and England
should have rendered his effort difficult. Collingwood
weighed from Tenedos on the 16th of September, leaving
behind him Rear-Admiral Martin and the *Kent*, until Sir
Arthur Paget should persuade himself that there was
nothing more to be done. He says in a letter to his father-
in-law, dated at Syracuse, October 24th, that "I followed the

---

[1] *Correspondence and Memoir*, p. 310.

Russians down; and being doubtful of the part they were to take, thought it necessary to keep near them; however, they have all sailed, and they said they were destined for the Baltic. Admiral Siniavin and I were great friends; he seemed to like me, and I had a regard for him because he professed to hate the French." [1]   The Russian squadron, after quitting the Mediterranean, deeming it perilous to proceed further north, anchored in the Tagus, where they remained blocked up.

In the life of Sir Jalheel Brenton, who served under Collingwood, there are several references to the Admiral, and one or two anecdotes which are useful as illustrations of Collingwood's character.   There is an incident which fits this date. On the 14th of May in this year, the *Spartan* frigate, commanded by Captain Brenton, fell in with a polacre ship [by polacre is signified a ship whose lower-masts and top-masts are in one; the word simply designates a form of rig], and sent her boats to attack the vessel.   In an order dated the 16th of June, 1806, Collingwood had been express in his instructions respecting the sending of armed boats to a distance from ships, and in a letter to Vice-Admiral Thornborough, written a year later—shortly indeed after this polacre incident—he says: " The practice of detaching boats on a distant service out of the protection of the ship is a cruel thing to gallant young officers, who do not like to return even when their judgment dictates to them that they ought.   They are enterprises highly injurious to the public service, because they disable the ship from performing her real duty; and they are discouraging to the men because they show, even

[1] James says that "Siniavin had been educated in the British Navy, and, if we are rightly informed, subsequently gave a proof of his attachment by retiring from service while hostilities existed between Russia and England."—*Naval History*, vol. iv. p. 233.

to those of the least observation, that they are schemes not directed by judgment."

Captain Brenton sent his boats, but with instructions to the lieutenants in charge not to attack the polacre should she prove a vessel of force. The boats did, nevertheless, attack the polacre. A lieutenant, two midshipmen, and 24 seamen were killed—and another lieutenant and 37 seamen wounded, the officer mortally. Collingwood directed a court of inquiry to be held upon Captain Brenton for this affair, and the court's decision was that Brenton had not deviated from the Commander-in-Chief's order. On Brenton going aboard Collingwood's ship on his arrival off Toulon, the Admiral received him very coolly, and said, "Sir, I am not at all satisfied with the report of the captains who composed the court of inquiry into your conduct."

"And I, my lord," responded Brenton, "am not satisfied with the nature of the tribunal before which it took place, as I should have preferred a court-martial; and I have to request you will be pleased to order one to assemble now for the purpose of trying me."

"No, sir," exclaimed Collingwood, "that is discretional with me, and enough has already been said upon the subject of both; but," he continued, "I have another cause of complaint to bring against you. How came you, whilst senior officer at Malta, to permit a French colonel, a prisoner of war, to return to France on his parole? They did not treat you so when you were a prisoner."

Brenton, who appears to have smiled at this charge, and to have found something entertaining in Collingwood's comment upon it, explained. He said that the colonel was captured out of a small Italian coaster by the *Weazel* sloop-of-war; the colonel's wife and two very young children were with him; the lady was expecting an

addition to her family, and, in fact, when the *Weazel* fired
to bring the little coaster to, a baby was born. The poor
woman died.   Brenton was so much affected by the
colonel's misfortunes that, on the recommendation of
Sir Alexander Ball, he allowed him to go to Naples on
parole on condition that when he had placed his children
in safety he should return unless exchanged.   "Such,"
exclaimed Brenton, in conclusion, "were my reasons, and
in acting as I did, I thought I was only doing what I am
convinced your lordship would have done had you been
there."

This oblique but exceedingly just compliment was
uttered in vain. Collingwood could not be coaxed into
saying yes when he meant no; but we hear no more of
this matter, for the reason perhaps stated by Brenton's
biographer—"that his lordship, with all his dryness of
manner and roughness of exterior, (!) had a kind and
feeling heart, and was a warm and sincere friend. His
prejudices, it is true, were strong and not easily subdued.
. . . His courage was that of a firm, well-disciplined mind
which had been accustomed to view danger with indifference when it came in the way of duty, but which saw no
necessity to go out and brave it when there was no
adequate cause. His professional life had been chiefly
passed in ships of the line as forming parts of great fleets,
and engaged in great movements; and he had therefore
less sympathy with that spirit of adventurous daring which
suited the commander of a cruising frigate; and he was
disposed to look with jealousy if not disapprobation at the
risks which were continually run for the sake of captures
of very little intrinsic value." [1]

In October and November, Collingwood was off Toulon,

[1] *Memoir of the Life and Services of Vice-Admiral Sir Jalheel
Brenton,* edited by the Rev. Henry Raikes, pp. 311—315.

where his ships suffered so heavily from the weather that, on the 6th of December, he put into Syracuse to refit. The following charming letter, addressed to his children, December 26th, refers to this visit to Syracuse :—

"'Ocean' on the Sea, December 26th, 1807.

"MY DEAREST CHILDREN,

"A few days ago I received your joint letter, and it gave me much pleasure to hear that you were well, and I hope improving in your education. It is exactly at your age that much pains should be taken; for whatever knowledge you acquire now will last you all your lives. The impression which is made on young minds is so strong that it never wears out; whereas everybody knows how difficult it is to make an old snuff-taking lady comprehend anything beyond Pam or Spadille. Such persons hang very heavy on society; but you, my darlings, will I hope qualify yourselves to adorn it, to be respected for your good sense, and admired for your gentle manners. Remember that gentle manners are the first grace which a lady can possess. Whether she differ in her opinion from others, or be of the same sentiment, her expressions should be equally mild. A positive contradiction is vulgar and ill-bred; but I shall never suspect you of being uncivil to any person. I received Mrs. ——'s letter, and am much obliged to her for it; she takes a lively interest that you should be wise and good. Do not let her be disappointed. For me, my girls, my happiness depends upon it; for should I return to England, and find you less amiable than my mind pictures you, or than I have reason to expect, my heart would sink with sorrow. Your application must be to useful knowledge. Sarah, I hope, applies to geometry, and Mary makes good progress in arithmetic. Independently of their use in every situation of life, they are sciences so curious in their nature, and so many things that cannot be comprehended without them are made easy, that were it only to gratify a curiosity which all women have, and to be let into secrets that cannot be learned without that knowledge, it would be a sufficient inducement to acquire them. Then do, my sweet girls, study to be wise!

"I am now at sea looking for some Frenchmen whom I have heard of; but I was lately at Syracuse, in Sicily. It was once a place of great note, where all the magnificence and art known in the world flourished; but it was governed by tyrants, and a city which was twenty-two miles in circumference is now inconsiderable. Its inhabitants have great natural civility; I never was treated with so much in my life. The nobility, who live far from the Court, are not contaminated with its vices; they are more truly polite, with less ostentation and show. On my arrival there, the nobility and Senate waited on me in my ship. Another day came all the military; the next the Vicar-General, for the Bishop was absent, and all the clergy. I had a levée of thirty priests—all fat, portly-looking gentlemen. In short, nothing was wanting to show their great respect and regard for the English. The nobles gave me and the officers of the fleet a ball and supper, the most elegant thing I ever saw, and the best conducted. The ladies were as attentive to us as their lords, and there were two or three little *marquisinas* who were most delightful creatures. I have heard men talk of the *dieux de la danse*, but no goddess ever moved with the grace that distinguished the sisters of the Baron Bono. God bless you, my dear girls!"[1]

In the harbour of Toulon there were at this time one ship of 120 guns, another of 80, three of 74, and some

[1] *Correspondence and Memoir*, p. 327.

line-of-battle ships on the stocks nearly ready for launch-
ing. These ships were under the command of Vice-Admiral
Ganteaume, who, on the 6th of February, was reinforced by
a squadron of five sail of the line under the command of
Rear-Admiral Allemand. On the following day Ganteaume
sailed from Toulon with 10 line-of-battle ships, some
frigates and corvettes, and a number of armed transports,
with troops, ordnance, stores, and provisions for Corfu, at
which island the French Admiral arrived on the 23rd.
On this same day the *Porcupine*, a small British vessel
mounting 22 guns, was conveying Captain Duncan to the
Standard, a 64-gun ship stationed off Corfu. The enemy
were descried; Captain Duncan lingered long enough to
clearly ascertain the nationality of the strangers; then
made sail for Collingwood, who was at that time at
Syracuse.

On the 16th of March Ganteaume set sail with his
whole fleet from Corfu and ran along the African, Sicilian,
and Sardinian coasts, watched for some time by Captain,
afterwards Vice-Admiral, Sir Jalheel Brenton, in the
Spartan, a 38-gun frigate, whose name had been already
rendered famous by the bold and fiery spirit of her commander, one of the most gallant of the captains who were
serving in the Mediterranean under Collingwood. There
is something memorably and heroically romantic in the
narrative of Brenton's experiences. He had been directed
to cruise in search of the enemy by Rear-Admiral Martin,
and, on the 1st of April, a fleet of ships was made
out from the deck of the *Spartan* looming large in the
haze to the southward, and heeling over under a fresh
breeze from the north-west. Brenton, who had not heard
of the junction of the French squadrons, was so sure that
the ships which had hove into view were Collingwood's,
that he contented himself with merely making his number

instead of first hoisting the private signal. As the frigate ran down under topsails Brenton, addressing his first lieutenant, who was examining the ships through a glass, exclaimed : " Who is that old-fashioned fellow who carries his mizzen topmast staysail under the maintop ? " The lieutenant answered : " There are three of them that have it." Brenton instantly cried: "It is the enemy's fleet—haul your wind at once." The private signal was also made at the same moment; whereupon all the ships to leeward braced sharp-up in pursuit.

Brenton thrashed his frigate through it under every cloth she could stagger under, and speedily found that his little craft was able to hold her own. He was naturally all anxiety to communicate the position of the French squadron to Rear-Admiral Martin at Palermo, and to Sir Alexander Ball at Malta; but it was also his imperative duty to watch, himself, the Frenchmen, and to dog them wherever they might go. There was nothing for it but to deck the launch with canvas, stretched upon pieces of timber which it was the custom to stow in ships of war for conversion into oars as the occasion for them arose. The little ark was then provided with a carronade, signal flags, ammunition, provisions and water, and at night dispatched to Trapani in charge of the third liĕutenant, Coffin. Scarcely had the launch measured a mile from the *Spartan* when the Frenchmen hove in stays and passed her close; but Coffin, possibly remembering the old West Indian privateering ruse, let fall his sail, leaving nothing showing but a mere filament of mast, and the enemy swept by without observing him.[1]

The launch reached Trapani on the evening following the night of its departure from the frigate. She was at

---

[1] *Life and Services of Vice-Admiral Sir Jahleel Brenton*, by the Rev. Henry Raikes, p. 328.

once dispatched to Malta, and Coffin started for Palermo, where he gave the intelligence to Rear-Admiral Martin. From Malta, on Sir Alexander Ball receiving the news, vessels were sent in all directions to convey the information of the whereabouts of the Frenchmen to Collingwood. Brenton continued to dog Ganteaume. Never did British seamanship exhibit greater intrepidity and more consummate skill than Brenton's manœuvrings. At night he would place himself abeam with the French Admiral, and at daylight haul away a bit to enlarge his horizon and improve his chance of falling in with Collingwood. Once he was almost taken; the frigate was becalmed, and the French liners were coming down upon her, carrying with them a breeze; but the wind travelled faster than the enemy, it swept into the canvas of the *Spartan*, and again she took up her position on the Admiral's weather beam. For three days the frigate stuck to the Frenchmen, and every effort to capture her or to shake her off on their part was defied by the saucy and magnificently-handled British ship. Towards the close of the third day Brenton observed that the French line-of-battle ships were spoken in succession by a frigate that ran along the line of them, and soon after the enemy bore up, steering with the wind abeam. Captain Brenton, concluding that the French Admiral had shaped a course for the Gut of Gibraltar, headed the same way. The night gathered very black, with a strong breeze out of the north and west, and, as may be supposed, aboard the British frigate a sharp and anxious look-out was kept for the enemy. On a sudden the pale shadow of the Frenchmen's canvas glimmering out of the darkness was discovered close aboard on the lee-quarter. It was a stratagem of Ganteaume—clever enough to deserve success: but all the same it failed. In an instant the helm of the *Spartan* was put up, and the frigate sweeping past the enemy within gunshot, went clear of them with the squadron in full chase before the Frenchmen seemed quite to realize what had happened. Next day the ships of the enemy were hull down, and when the night came Captain Brenton lost sight of them.[1]

Collingwood, as we gather from his letter to Lord Radstock, dated April 4th, did not hear of the arrival of the Rochefort squadron, under Allemand, in the Mediterranean until the 22nd of February, nor was he made certainly acquainted with the fact of their junction with the squadron at Toulon until April 3rd. On hearing that the enemy had sailed to Corfu, he most reasonably construed the movement into a device to withdraw the British force from Sicily. He had hunted for the Frenchmen at Naples, and had sent frigates everywhere to discover them; but he could obtain no intelligence, and such gossip as might reach him was not to be depended upon. He was possessed with the conviction that Sicily was their destination, and that every step they took must be a ruse to withdraw his ships from the defence of that island. Writing to Viscount Castlereagh on the 13th of March, he says that he came to Naples in the hope of obtaining intelligence of the Toulon ships. "I am come here for the purpose," he says, "and afraid at the same time of being too distant from Sicily. It is exceedingly distressing to be so entirely without any knowledge of them, either where they are or what their force is." The Duke of Clarence, in replying to a letter that Collingwood had sent him on March 30th, reiterates with emphasis the opinion he had found in the Admiral's communication. "From the secrecy of those Frenchmen," the Duke says, "and their power on the Continent, which are equally known to your lordship and myself, the affairs of war are more intricate than ever; but in your lordship's

[1] Brenton's *Naval History*, vol. ii. p. 239.

hands the interests of our country are safe. The great
object of the enemy must be Sicily, for your lordship
observes with as much truth as wisdom that we cannot
maintain ourselves in the Mediterranean without that
island. I sincerely trust that the next time the French
venture out your lordship will fall in with them. The
event will speak for itself—another Trafalgar. All I ask
is that the life of the gallant Admiral may be spared to
his grateful country."[1]

There runs through James' narrative of Collingwood's
pursuit of the French fleet the suggestion that the naval
historian cannot persuade himself the Admiral was very
much in earnest. He allows Nelson's enthusiasm; yet
omits to cavil at the difficulties which hindered the Hero
of the Nile from swift detection of the lurking-place of
the enemy's ships. James would have us believe that
Collingwood addressed himself very leisurely to this task
of chasing; that he thought more of balancing a period
than of keeping a bright look-out. It is surely wholly
needless to say that no admiral ever panted to get at an
enemy as Collingwood did; that no commander-in-chief
ever more fully exhausted every appliance at his disposal
to achieve his end; that no hero ever looked from the
quarter-deck of a British ship across the ocean with a
nobler and more impassioned desire to add to his country's
glory than did Collingwood during the exhausting weeks
he was now spending in pursuit of the Frenchmen. What
sort of spirit, one would like to ask, breathes in the letter
he addressed to his wife in March, and at a date when, as
we know by the date of the General Order he issued, he
was daily, indeed in hourly, expectation of meeting with
the enemy? "I am just now cruising with my fleet off
Maritimo, and intend continuing here until I get inform-

[1] *Correspondence and Memoir*, p. 358.

ation to lead me to the French, which I expect very soon, and then hope that God will bless me. Our country requires that great exertions should be made to maintain its independence and its glory. You know when I am in earnest on any subject how truly I devote myself to it; and the first object of my life, and what my heart is most bent on (I hope you will excuse me), is the glory of my country. To stand a barrier between the ambition of France and the independence of England is the first wish of my life; and in my death I would rather that my body, if it were possible, should be added to the rampart than trailed in useless pomp through an idle throng."

This is not a letter written with an eye to the public prints; it is a whisper to his wife, a secret delivery of his heart's passionate desire to one who knew his nature as no one else did, whose opinion of him he was not a man to trouble himself to endeavour to exalt by such high-sounding resolutions of " I'll do, and I'll do, and I'll do!" as may be found in the letters of other admirals and captains addressed to their wives or their sweethearts or their mistresses. Much has been made of his neglect to communicate with the *Standard* line-of-battle ship, which, as we have seen, had promptly sailed from off Corfu to join Collingwood, and communicate the important intelligence that the French fleet was in that neighbourhood. The incident is as follows: On the 24th of February—that is to say, on the day following the date of the arrival of Ganteaume at Corfu—Collingwood was lying at Syracuse, with the *Canopus* and *Malta*, 80's, and the *Repulse* and *Montague*, 74's. In the course of the day he weighed for Palermo, leaving the *Repulse* behind him. On that same evening, a line-of-battle ship was observed in the east, heading for Syracuse. She was the *Standard*, but Collingwood's squadron was unseen by her, owing to the ships being under the land. It was a dark night when the *Standard* entered Syracuse, and owing to the breeze continuing to blow inshore, she was unable to sail again for two or three days. On the arrival of the *Standard* at Syracuse, Captain the Honourable A. K. Legge, of the *Repulse*, sent an express to Cape Passaro, in the hope of intercepting Collingwood, who had, however, by this time passed to the westward.

"Most unfortunately," says James, " his lordship"— meaning Collingwood—" could not be persuaded that there was the least necessity for communicating with Captain Harvey "[1]—that is, with the *Standard.* How did James know that his lordship could not be persuaded ? There is a cocksureness in writing of this sort which would make one almost suppose that the author had been aboard at the time, that he was not only exactly informed of all that had passed, but was himself an eye-witness of most of the striking occurrences he relates. There is, indeed, what Coleridge would call a pleonasm of nakedness about James' "facts." He will not have them bare only, he must have them bald also. Does he wish us to believe that this same Admiral Lord Collingwood, whose passion to hear of the French and to get at the French was consuming his heart; that Collingwood at the time the *Standard* was sighted was in his cabin producing one of the many delightful letters which his son-in-law afterwards collected, having given strict injunctions, which the sentinel at his door was to enforce with his musket, that he was on no account whatever to be disturbed, no, not even if Ganteaume himself came alongside of him ? What does Mr. James want posterity to imagine of Collingwood's behaviour on this occasion ? That he deliberately refused to communicate with the *Standard ?* He says so. But this is con-

[1] *James,* vol. iv. p. 292,

jecture, and conjecture that is absolutely repugnant to what we know of Collingwood's character, and of the desires by which he was then governed. Every theoretical solution of the problem that does not absolve Collingwood from the charge of neglect must fail. The omission to communicate must be accounted for by some cause outside the sphere of the control of even a British Admiral aboard his own ship. We need but figure Collingwood alive to hold that by a single sentence of explanation he would extinguish for ever, under the head of this incident, the two or three land-going writers who have settled upon this page of his stainless story, straining their little best to fly-blow it.[1] "I know," he wrote to Lord Radstock in June, "that success, or the want of it, is the scale on which all men's merits are measured, and that the French flying from one end of the Mediterranean to the other will be imputed to great stupidity and want of judgment by those who are not capable of forming a true estimate of circumstances; and as they compose a large majority, the unfortunate, however great their exertion may have been, will suffer in the general opinion."

[1] Collingwood makes a single reference to the subject in a letter to Lord Radstock, dated August 15th, when he was off Cadiz. "The *Standard*," he says, "arrived at Syracuse on the very evening that we sailed in the morning; or, instead of going off to Maritimo, I should probably have gone to Corfu with my few ships."—*Correspondence and Memoir*, p. 436. This certainly reads as though the fact of the *Standard* having hove into sight was unknown to the squadron, or had not been communicated to the Admiral.

CHAPTER XI.

ON the 2nd of March, when some thirty or forty miles to the north-westward of Maritimo, Collingwood was joined by Vice-Admiral Thornborough and Rear-Admiral Sir Richard Strachan. This reinforcement swelled the total of the ships under him to fifteen sail of the line and some frigates. The fleet proceeded towards Palermo; but four days later, when off Cape St. Vito, the *Apollo* was fallen in with. She gave the news of Ganteaume having sailed from Toulon a month previously. A little later the *Standard's* intelligence reached Collingwood, and he made sail to the southward round the west end of Sicily. Having no doubt of the enemy's intentions, he consistently and wisely clung to the coast of Sicily. He must be governed by one theory or nothing: for more than one must distract him; whilst, without a theory, everything must be left to chance, and the chance that the Mediterranean was to provide was slender indeed. "At sea," he wrote to his wife, May the 15th, "there is no getting intelligence as there used to be on former occasions, for now there is not a trading ship upon the seas—nothing but ourselves. It is lamentable to see what a desert the waters are become. It has made me almost crazy, and if I had not a very good constitution, would have worn me quite out, for I know that in England success is the only criterion by which people judge, and to want that is always reckoned a great crime. But I have felt the service in my heart, and have left nothing undone that my anxious mind suggested." [1]

Having formed his opinion, he made an iron-hard resolution of it. Referring to Sicily, in a letter to Lord Radstock, April 4th, he writes: "From all quarters I hear that their object is the reduction of this island, and have therefore little doubt that I shall before long find them, and find them confident of their own strength and therefore in no haste to go off. Sir Richard Strachan, having pursued them to this station, makes the fleet strong enough for anything; but Sicily itself is as weak as it can be." On the 22nd the fleet approached the Adriatic, and next day we find Collingwood with twelve sail of the line—having sent Rear-Admiral Martin with three ships to Palermo—in hourly expectation of falling in with Ganteaume. On this day, March 23rd, he issued his General Order, from which I shall quote only those passages which directly and essentially illustrate the tactics he designed to employ.

"Should the enemy be found formed in order of battle with his whole force, I shall, notwithstanding, probably not make the signal to form the line of battle; but, keeping the closest order, with the van squadron attack the

[1] *Correspondence and Memoir*, p. 355.

van of the enemy, while the commander of th
division takes the proper measures, and makes t
ships of his division the necessary signals for comme
the action with the enemy's rear, as nearly as possil
the same time that the van begins; of his signals, 1
fore, the captains of that division will be partic
watchful.

"If the squadron has to run to leeward to close
the enemy, the signal will be made to alter the
together, the van division keeping a point or two
away than the lee, the latter carrying less sail; and
the fleet draws near the enemy, both columns a
preserve a line as nearly parallel to the hostile fl
they can.

"In standing up to the enemy from the leeward, u
contrary tack, the lee line is to press sail, so tha
leading ship of that line may be two or three
before the beam of the leading ship of the weathei
which will bring them to action nearly at the
period.

"The leading ship of the weather column will ende
to pass through the enemy's line, should the weath
such as to make that practicable, at one fourth fro
van, whatever number of ships their line may be
posed of.

"The lee division will pass through at a ship o
astern of their centre; and whenever a ship has weat
the enemy, it will be found necessary to shorten s
much as possible, for her second astern to close wit
and to keep away, steering in a line parallel to the en
and engaging them on their weather side."

A dissertation on the relative merits of Nelson'
Collingwood's General Orders before battle would, i
iron age of steam and torpedoes and 100-ton guns,

about as profitable and interesting as a discussion on the merits of the 42-pound carronade compared with those of the long 36-pounder gun. The chapter is ended. The volume containing it is closed!

> " Men are we, and must grieve when even the shade
> Of that which once was great has passed away."
>
> WORDSWORTH.

But we must submit to transformations even more lamentable and more afflicting to the romantic spirit than the conversion of the topsail into the propeller. The seaman, however, who reads the extracts I have just made from this General Order will probably judge of Collingwood's views and intentions thus :—he will hold that reflection had persuaded the Admiral that the tactics of Howe were superior to the tactics of Nelson—as illustrated by the Battle of the First of June and by the Battle of Trafalgar—*now* that the spirit and the fire of the incomparable Nelson's example, bequeathed by him in the memory he left, were the animating principle of the British ocean warrior. Collingwood could have little doubt of the issue of the combat, be his tactics what they might, should he fall in with the French; but he probably hoped to render that issue even more decisive than Trafalgar— having regard to the proportion of vessels engaged—by attacking the whole line and so providing against such hovering withdrawals as those of Gravina and Dumanoir. Had he not doubted the value of the Nelson tactics, he would certainly have adopted them. He desired victory before all things, and the best method to achieve it would certainly be the one and only method with him, no matter with whom it originated.

But he would remember the part he had himself played at Trafalgar: how Nelson's order of battle might have resulted in the *Royal Sovereign* being cannonaded into staves whilst the British fleet, swarming slowly down, could only idly look on. When once the battle had opened, every captain was a Nelson, and Nelson did no more than any of his captains. Had the great Admiral remained on board a frigate, and at a distance directed his fleet by signals, as a General directs his army from some vantage point, whence he may command a view of the whole scene, then undoubtedly the Nelson tactics might be a subject tangible enough to enable a writer to deal with it. But the contest was far from being decided when the Hero was mortally wounded; no directions, saving the "If I live, I'll anchor, Hardy," proceeded from him. His ships having floated into the enemy in the manner pre-arranged by him and Collingwood, engaged without order, without confusion, with lawless choice of what was next them. In short, the noble and heroic Nelson "left it to his captains," and he fought as one of them.[1]

Collingwood, who knew what the influence of Nelson as an impulse had achieved for the British Navy, Collingwood, who also knew that there was now to be depended on the spirit that was wanting in the Battle of the First of June, had resolved by the disposition of his force to render the blow he meant to deal effective to annihilation. But the chance he thirsted for did not befall him. Five days after the date of his General Order, when he was within

[1] Lord Dundonald has for all time summed up the Battle of Trafalgar : "Trafalgar itself is an illustration of Nelson's peculiar dash. It has been remarked that Trafalgar was a rash action, and that had Nelson lost it and lived, he would have been brought to a court-martial for the way in which that action was conducted. But such cavillers forget that from previous experience he could calculate both the nature and amount of resistance to be expected ; such calculation forming as essential a part of his plan of attack as even his own means for making it. The result justified his expectations of victory, which were not only well-founded but sound."—*The Autobiography of a Seaman*, p. 55.

a few miles of Cape Rezzuto, he learnt that the French fleet had left the Adriatic for the Mediterranean.   He forthwith steered west, and cruised until the 28th between Sardinia and Sicily, when news was brought by a frigate that Ganteaume was at anchor at Toulon.   The whole story of this fruitless pursuit is summed up by Collingwood himself in a couple of sentences : " Their escape was by chance ; for at one time we were very near them without knowing it."   It is hard to understand why James should witness " a very extraordinary circumstance " in the fleets having missed each other.   The horizon is wide, and even a line-of-battle ship makes but a minute speck upon the surface of a few miles of ocean.   From the top-gallant mast-head of a tall ship of war one should indeed be able to command a wide expanse of water— calculating dimensions by the standard of man and his structures ; yet so broad is the surface of the sea, that two fleets of ships may, comparatively speaking, be close together and yet out of sight ; though had the look-out, stationed, let us say, on the foretop-gallant yard, climbed to the starry altitude of the truck, the royals of the ships behind the horizon might have been seen " dipping," as sailors term it ; for a few feet of elevation will extend the gaze by some leagues.   Captain Edward Brenton, however, who was a sailor, puts the case as every seaman would : " That Admiral Ganteaume did relieve Corfu is most true ; but that he cruised a few days on the coast of Africa, as has been asserted, is very improbable.   We know that he carried all possible sail against a north-west wind, and was unable to weather Sardinia.   A landsman might perhaps call this cruising ; we do not so consider it in the navy. That two hostile fleets should be at sea and not fall in with each other, even if both were anxious to meet, might appear strange to any person unacquainted with the subject. We can therefore easily account for Mr. James' wonder. But there was no want of vigilance or attention on the part of our naval officers in the Mediterranean as far as regarded the escape of Ganteaume, who was as anxious to avoid an interview as Lord Collingwood was to get sight of him." [1]

In June Collingwood quitted the Mediterranean for his old cruising station off Cadiz, but no longer to block the port. The Spaniards had taken up arms for the recovery of their independence, and in the earliest throes of their struggle to free themselves from the yoke of France, were pleading to England for support. "I left a station," Collingwood wrote to his wife on June 15th, from off Cadiz, "which had almost worn me out with care, to be upon the spot where a great revolution was taking place in Spain, and to give my aid to it. Everybody here was very glad to see me, both English and Spanish. The French at Toulon had heard, I believe, what was going on before we did; for suddenly they seemed to give up their preparations for sea and moved several of their ships into an inner harbour. I left Admiral Thornborough to look after them, and came to see what good I could do here."

It is in his letters to his wife that one sees most of what is going forward; they are transcripts of his secret opinions, unembellished, save by the natural graces of his style and by the native elegance of his turn of thought. He writes with a masked countenance to most of his correspondents, who are all sorts of important people, Kings and Queens, Emperors and Beys, Ambassadors, Ministers of State, Lords of the Admiralty, and so on; but with his wife he sits and prattles, pen in hand, and in the intellectual atmosphere these letters create, we witness him in all the fullness of his racy and noble individuality—humorist, philosopher,

[1] *Naval History*, vol. ii. p. 240.

statesman, diplomatist, sailor, all delightfully blending in a flow of loving and often impassioned communication. You notice, also, a pardonable note of pride, almost shy in its way, in his letters to his lady; it is his enjoyment of *her* enjoyment of the dignity of his position, with its almost royal responsibilities and obligations. One can appreciate the staggering effect of the change upon his mind—this change at Cadiz, which he can only think of as a port that he is heart-sick of blockading, whose forests of masts it has been his distressing duty to watch for months and months. "We are doing everything for them that we can," he writes. "Yesterday we supplied them with gunpowder for their army, and their cause and ours are now the same."

No doubt it was in one of his letters to his wife that he related the little anecdote his son-in-law makes a note of; how that when gunpowder was first furnished by the English fleet to the Spaniards, it was instantly fired away by them in honour of a saint, whose festival they were then celebrating; and how, when a fresh supply was asked for, Collingwood told them that he could spare no more unless they would promise to reserve it for sinners and not for saints. "They consult us on everything," he writes, "and I do what is in my power for their aid and succour. When our officers land at Cadiz, which they do every day, they are surrounded by multitudes crying, ' *Vivan los Ingleses! Viva King George !* ' "

When he himself goes ashore he is received with military honours, and forty thousand men and women turn out to welcome him. He is met by crowds of volunteers—gentlemen of the city; the cavalry clear the streets for him to pass through; the whole city resounds with cries of " *Viva King George ! Viva Collingwood !*" Magnificent entertainments are given to him, and the company are people of the first rank. He goes to the opera, and when he enters the Governor's box the crowded audience rise *en masse* and clap their hands for a quarter of an hour. A change indeed from the weary old business of cruising to and fro, during which, as Nelson was wont to say, every wind that blows is a foul one, whilst the delightful word "Steady!" is never to be heard![1]

Collingwood's health, however, was now giving him much anxiety. When at Syracuse he sat for his portrait, and on the picture being finished he sent it to his wife. But he was hardly conscious of the change that had been wrought in his appearance since he bade her farewell at Morpeth. The letter in which Lady Collingwood acknowledged the picture expressed her concern, if indeed no deeper emotion were conveyed; for, in writing to her on July 18th, he says: "I am sorry to find my picture was not an agreeable surprise. I did not say anything to you about it, because I will always guard you as much as I can against disappointment; but you see with all my care I sometimes fail. The painter was reckoned the most eminent in Sicily; but you expected to find me a smooth-skinned clear-complexioned gentleman, such as I was when I left home, dressed in the newest taste, and like the fine people who live gay lives ashore. Alas! it is far otherwise with me. The painter was thought to have flattered me much; that lump under my chin was but the loose skin from which the flesh has shrunk away; the redness of my face was not, I assure you, the effect of wine, but of burning suns and boisterous winds; and my eyes, which were once dark and bright, are now faded and dim. The painter represented

[1] "Steady!"—that is, "Keep her as she goes"—which implies that the ship is to her course, or as near it as the officer of the watch chooses to jam her. But in blockading there is no course—nothing but directions to be avoided, such, for instance, as those which lead ashore.

me as I am; not as I once was. It is time and toil that
have worked the change, not his want of skill. That the
countenance is stern will not be wondered at, when it is
considered how many sad and anxious hours and how
many heartaches I have." [1]

A handsome man such portraits as I have seen of Collingwood do not represent him as having been; but his large,
full, dark eyes glow with intellect and sensibility; his face
is strong and firm with character—it is such a face as being
encountered would detain the attention and be recalled
with interest and speculation.   He is described as having
been rather above the middle stature, slender and well-
proportioned. But by this time the sea had done its work
with him; it had stooped his form, withered his features,
dimmed his vision. In August the prospect of another
long blockading cruise off Toulon had forced him into a
serious contemplation of his condition, and on the 26th of
that month, shortly before proceeding to the Mediterranean,
he communicated to the Admiralty the delicate state of
his health, and, claiming that the service he was upon
exacted more strength and spirits than he had power to
give to it, he begged to be relieved for such time as might
be necessary to restore his health and strength in England.
He wrote to the same effect to Lord Mulgrave, attributing
the state of his health to the long years he had been at
sea and to the heavy and continuous pressure of anxiety.

Lord Mulgrave, in reply, said : " I have read with great
uneasiness and regret the concluding part of your letter, in
which you express some doubts of the continuance of your
health to the end of the war, and I earnestly hope that the
service of the country will not suffer the serious inconvenience of your finding it necessary to suspend the exertion
of your zeal and talents. It is a justice which I owe to you

[1] *Correspondence and Memoir*, p. 415.

R

and the country to tell you candidly that,I know not how
I should be able to supply all that would be lost to the
service of the country, and to the general interests of
Europe, by your absence from the Mediterranean.   I trust
you will not find the necessity, and, without it, the whole
tenor of your conduct is a security that you will not feel
the inclination, to quit your command while the interests
of your country can be so essentially promoted by your
continuing to hold it."   The impression, Collingwood says,
produced upon him by Lord Mulgrave's letter, was one of
grief and sorrow: "First, that with such a list as we have,
there should be thought to be any difficulty in finding a
successor of superior ability to me; and next, that there
should be any obstacle in the way of the only comfort
and happiness I have to look forward to."

His bad health was known in England amongst his
friends, as I find by the following letter, dated July 21st,
in this year, addressed to Sir Edward Blackett, by his
brother, the Rev. Henry Blackett: "I am sorry Lady
Collingwood is gone to Brighton.   I would by no means
have her sequester herself and daughter from company ;
but in the situation her husband is at present (in) she had,
I think, better not have chosen the most public of them all,
where she is sure to be particularly noticed by the Prince
and all his circle, and invited to all his balls and concerts,
which she and her daughters cannot help going to.   It
shows too great a fondness for popularity, and is enough to
turn the heads of the girls, and I am sure it would have
pleased Lord Collingwood more to hear that they were at
a less public place than that they were at the Prince's
ball, and danced with such and such a lord.   I hear Lord
Collingwood is very weak and has complaints in his
stomach.   He must soon come home, and will be ordered
to Bath, and will not be able to come to Chirton this

autumn or winter. After being so long in a hot climate, the cold northern blasts here would not agree with his constitution."[1]

Before we follow Collingwood to Toulon, a short retrospective glance at a few of the features of the business which occupied him during this term of command off Cadiz will enable us to appreciate his desire to relinquish his duties. "The variety of subjects," he tells his wife, "all of great importance, with which I am engaged, would puzzle a longer head than mine. The conduct of the fleet alone would be easy; but the political correspondence which I have to carry on with the Spaniards, the Turks, the Albanians, the Egyptians, and all the States of Barbary gives me such constant occupation that I really often feel my spirits quite exhausted, and of course my health is much impaired; but if I must go on I will do the best I can." When he had arrived off Cadiz there were then in that port, under the command of Vice-Admiral Rosily, five ships of the line, one of them of 80 guns, and the others of 74 guns, together with a frigate and a brig. On the 4th of June the Supreme Junta at Seville declared

---

[1] From letters in possession of J. C. Blackett, Esq. Clavell, an officer who was much esteemed by Collingwood, though he was never able to procure him an Admiralty appointment—Clavell, who at this time was a Post-Captain by a death vacancy, on his arrival in England in July, appears, from an amiable anxiety not to cause alarm, to have misrepresented the state of Collingwood's health. Writing to his brother, Sir Edward, from Newcastle on July 10th, 1808, Mr. J. E. Blackett says : "My daughter Collingwood went south on Monday last, and I trust would arrive at the Royal Hotel, Pall Mall, on Friday, where I expect she would meet her sister Stead, and I hope may find her daughters in good health and much improved. Captain Clavell, who is lately arrived in town, writes her that he left Lord Collingwood perfectly well. He was Lord C.'s first lieut. at the action off Trafalgar, was promoted by him to Post-Captain, and has come home on account of his health. I direct my letters to Lord Collingwood, Plymouth Dock, Port-Admiral's office."—*MSS. Letters.*

war against France in the name of their imprisoned king, Ferdinand; on which, and immediately, Rosily shifted the position of his ships clear of the guns of the town batteries, and brought up in a defensive position in the Caraccas Channel. At this time Rear-Admiral Purvis, with eleven sail of the line, was cruising off the harbour, and he expressed his willingness to the Spanish authorities on shore to help them to bring the French Admiral to terms. The Spaniards, however, determined to manage without aid from the British. The first act of General Thomas de Morla, the Captain-General of Andalusia, was to send a summons of surrender to Rosily. He seemed to shrink from the idea of firing upon people who were just now the allies of his country against the nation whose ships for months, and indeed for years, had been hostilely haunting the Cadiz waters—most disastrously to Spanish interests, as De Morla would remember, when his mind went to the 14th of February, 1797, and to October 21st, 1805. He and Rosily had smoked many a cigar together, tossed down many a bumper of the wines of Spain and Portugal to the destruction of those British ships whose canvas was for ever whitening the blue sea off Cadiz; and now to turn the cannons of Spain, loaded perhaps with British gun-powder, upon Rosily and his fellows!

The General sent a copy of the summons to Admiral Purvis, who forwarded it to Collingwood. It was necessary to encourage the Don to maintain the warlike posture he had put himself into three days before Collingwood wrote; and dating his letter from the *Occan*, off Cadiz, June 12th, our hero says: "It may be true that Admiral Rosily feels no hostility towards the Spanish nation; but when his Government are taking the most active measures to sub-jugate your country, and have led your Princes captive to their capital, there needs no more to prove the violation of every friendly connection and alliance. The proposal which the Admiral makes to your Excellency's second summons appears to me to be merely an expedient to gain time, as he has no reason to believe that his squadron can pass the English without being assailed."[1] The expedient to which Collingwood refers was Rosily's proposal to quit the Bay, provided the British would permit him. On the 9th hostilities had been commenced against the French ships. The fire was returned; and powder was burnt without intermission until night. The French Admiral then offered to disembark his guns and ammunition on condition that he retained his men and showed no colours. These terms were refused, and Rosily, finding further resistance hopeless in face of the increased force with which the Spaniards were prepared to renew the attack, struck his colours.

Collingwood s eyes were everywhere; they glanced from China to Peru. As we have seen, the Russian Vice-Admiral Siniavin had taken refuge in the Tagus, where he was watched by Admiral Sir Charles Cotton, who cruised off the mouth of that river with a British squadron. In a letter to Sir Charles, dated July 20th, Collingwood advises. a subtlety of behaviour which one would not suppose his nature capable of suggesting, to judge of it as one finds it on the face of his correspondence. "If," says he, "you can open a correspondence with Siniavin, I think it would have the effect of detaching him from the French; and if it did not you might make him suspected by them and cause a breach. If your ships inshore were to answer his signals with the Russian flag displayed, all he could say would not convince Junot that he has not communication with you." But almost before this hint could find time to operate in the literal mind of its stout-hearted

[1] *Correspondence and Memoir*, p. 372.

recipient, Sir Arthur Wellesley had landed; on the 21st Vimiera was fought; on the 22nd Sir Hew Dalrymple took command of the British troops; and on the 30th the convention of Cintra was concluded, which *inter alia* consigned Siniavin's squadron in the shape of a deposit to his Britannic Majesty to be held until six months should have expired from the date of the conclusion of peace between Russia and England; the officers and men of the squadron to be conveyed to Russia at England's expense!

Collingwood had very little hope for Spain, despite her convulsive struggle after independence. He admired what he terms "the glorious efforts" of the Spaniards to expel the enemy; but he dreaded lest the Juntas, with their cabals and contentions for superiority, should result in an anarchy that must prove more terrible to the nation than the presence of the French. There was an inertness that vexed and angered him, as at Naples the same quality had vexed and angered Nelson. "To the eastward," he says, "they are in great want of cannon. Here is their foundry, and they have the most abundant store; yet they will not send them any. I have told them a ship of war shall carry the guns, and the Governor replies that they are an ingenious people, and have abundance of resources. In a word there never was a nation more disjointed, and I consider its safety is very doubtful. If they do not constitute one sole government which will combine the powers of the country, it will be lost. These subjects and my cares for them are wearing me to death."

Whilst off Cadiz he was somewhat perplexed by the action of the Queen of Sicily, who had sent her son, Prince Leopold, to Gibraltar, to offer himself as Regent of Spain. Collingwood regarded this step as the height of folly. The Prince had left Palermo without any knowledge of the state of Spain; moreover, a number of those who accompanied him were French, and there was no government to furnish protection to Frenchmen against the insults of the populace. Whilst the Prince was at Gibraltar the Duke of Orleans arrived off Cadiz in the *Thunderer*, and expressed his intention of remaining there that he might support what he called "the claims" of Prince Leopold. Collingwood waited upon the Duke, and told him very plainly that his orders from his Majesty's ministers were to give all possible assistance to the Spanish people to defend their country, and maintain their independence as a nation. The conduct of their affairs, he said, was to be left entirely to their own judgment. The Junta had no correspondence with any other nation than England, and it was therefore impossible for any proposals to be made from the ships or from the garrison, until instructions had been received from the British Government. He also pointed out that there was no power in Spain at that time to which Prince Leopold could address himself. If he approached a provincial Junta the others might disapprove. Discussions would follow, and troubles and difficulties. If he went to the people at large he opposed the constituted authorities. Collingwood's masterful judgment quickly made the Duke see that there was nothing to be done, at all events just then. Referring to this complicated and yet momentous business in a letter to his wife, Collingwood wrote: "The Duke professed to be much taken with me, though I had to argue against his object and to put him from his purpose. He said when we parted that he should never forget the day that made him acquainted with me. The service has become very arduous. I cannot tell you all about it in a letter; but some long winter's evening I will give you the whole history."

At the beginning of September Collingwood was again

off Toulon. On September 20th he wrote to his wife: "I am returned to watch the French in this port; but it is impossible to devise or form the smallest judgment of what they will do, or what project they may have in view; so that all I can do is to watch them on this stormy coast. Since I have been here we have only had two days of weather in which boats could pass from ship to ship; and so you may judge with how little effect this service can be done. It is not practicable; but this the people on shore cannot comprehend; and I fear in the perseverance both ships and men will be worn out. I will do what is possible. It will be a great relief to get hold of them before the winter be advanced."

His illness was still gaining upon him. In October he describes himself as exceedingly weak and languid, incapable of exerting himself to the degree of his wishes, and to the height of his responsibilities and obligations; but he tells Lord Mulgrave that having submitted his motive and reason for desiring to withdraw from his command, he has no more to add than that his best service is due to his country as long as he lives, and that all else he leaves to the Earl's consideration and convenience. He seems not to have suspected the cause of his complaint. It was strange that there was no surgeon in the fleet to give him the truth, and advise him before advice should be too late. He attributed his general weakness, and the particular infirmity of his limbs, to time having worn him out; yet, saving the one source of illness—a weakness still (at this time) within reach of medical skill—he was perfectly sound, possessed of an iron constitution, comparatively young, though two years older than his son-in-law believed him to be, his faculties unimpaired, as his correspondence down to the last of his printed letters proves. Even now there might have been time to preserve his life had he chosen to quit his post. No man then afloat, no man who had ever served his country at sea, more richly merited the enjoyment of all that home could yield him. But his sense of duty was inflexible. He had been asked to stay where he was, in language whose note of almost special command is scarcely to be missed. But this was not all: fagged, worn out as he was by incessant harassing, distracting service, the animation of the old noble heroic spirit beat like pulses of fire in the motives of his compliance. There was still a chance of his meeting the French! and this was such a hope as must appease his tenderest home-yearning, and dominate, indeed eclipse all perception of the condition of health to which devoted duty had reduced him.

An admirable letter, addressed to Lady Collingwood, belongs to this period. On board the *Ocean* off Toulon, on November 8th, he says: "You cannot conceive how I am worried by the French; their fleet is lying in the port here with all the appearance of sailing in a few hours; and God knows whether they will sail at all, for I get no intelligence of them. Their frigates have been out in a gale of wind, were chased by some of our ships, and got in again. We have had most frightful gales, which have injured some of my ships very much, but now that the Alps have got a good coat of snow on them, I hope we shall have more moderate weather. I have a double sort of game to play here; watching the French with one eye, while with the other I am directing the assistance to be given to the Spaniards. . . . Perhaps you may think I am grown very conceited in my old age, and fancy myself a mighty politician; but indeed it is not so. However lofty a tone the subject may require and my language assume, I assure you it is in great humility of heart that I utter it, and often in fear and trembling lest I should exceed my bounds. This must always be the case with one who, like me, has been occupied in studies so remote from such business. I do everything for myself, and never distract my mind with other people's opinions. The credit of any good which happens I may claim, and I will never shift upon another the discredit when the result is bad. But now, my dear wife, I think of you as being where alone true comfort can be found, enjoying in your own warm house a happiness which in the great world is not known. Heaven bless you; may your joys be many and your cares few. My heart often yearns for home; but when that blessed day will come in which I shall see it God knows." [1]

When this was written he had not received a very flattering letter from the Earl of Mulgrave, dated September 25th. The Earl repeated what he had said in his earlier letter, that he was so much impressed by the difficulty of supplying the place of Collingwood that he was unable to forbear suspending the solicited recall till he should hear again from him, and learn once more that a longer continuance at sea would be injurious to his health. The Earl added that if this proved the case he should consider it highly advantageous to the service if Collingwood would take the command at Plymouth, the centre and spring of the most active points of naval operations.

It has been urged, as though it were positively a blot on the character of Collingwood, that he clung to his Mediterranean post despite Lord Mulgrave's offer of the port of Plymouth; that his murmurs and complaints were insincere; and that he stuck to a command to whose duties he knew himself to be unequal, because he abhorred the notion of a successor. Those who thus reason do not appear to have read his answer to Lord Mulgrave, which,

---

[1] *Correspondence and Memoir*, p. 470.

to my mind, is so explicit, is so ample and conclusive a rejoinder to the perfidious hypotheses of those who are unable to understand the character of Collingwood, that, having quoted it, I shall dismiss the subject:

"*January* 10*th*, 1809.

" My long continuance at sea has made me very feeble; and the fear of my'unfitness, which I know people are often the last to discover in themselves, induced me to make the application. My situation requires the most vigorous mind, which is seldom possessed at the same time with great debility of body. Since my letter of the 30th October to your lordship on this subject, the vexations which I have had on account of the affairs in Catalonia, and the violent stormy weather which has done much injury to some of the ships, particularly to the *Ocean*, have increased my infirmity, but on this subject I have nothing to add to what was said in that letter. I have no object in the world that I put in competition with my public duty; and so long as your lordship thinks it proper to continue me in this command, my utmost efforts shall be made to strengthen the impression which you now have. But I still hope that whenever it may be done with convenience your lordship will bear in mind my request. On the subject of Plymouth I have only to say that wherever I can best render my service I shall be at your lordship's command. I would not have requested to be called from hence on any account but that which I have stated; and when my health is restored I shall be perfectly at your lordship's disposal, but with the little that I have ever had to do with ports I should enter on that field with great diffidence." [1]

[1] *Correspondence and Memoir*, p. 481.

CHAPTER XII.

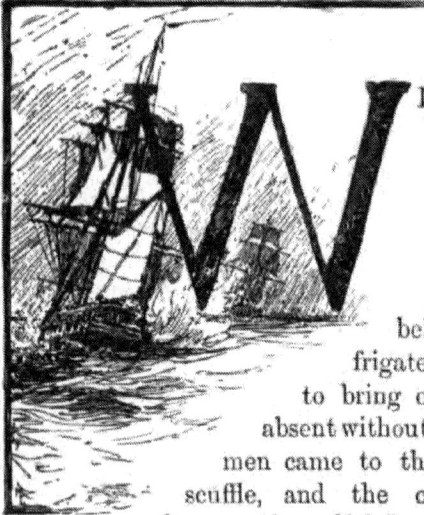

HILST Collingwood
was at Malta, in
February 1809, he
was amused by a
singular instance of
forecastle superstition.
A corporal of marines
belonging to the *Spartan*
frigate had been sent on shore
to bring off a marine who was
absent without leave. Some drunken
men came to the rescue, there was a
scuffle, and the corporal, drawing his
bayonet in self-defence, killed the marine.
The magistrates investigated the affair, and the corporal
was acquitted of all blame and sent on board the
Spartan, which sailed a day or two after. During
the cruise of the frigate nothing but heavy weather
was experienced, and not a prize was taken. The Jacks,
casting their eyes upon the corporal, considered him as
having been guilty of murder, and therefore responsible in

the first degree for the ill-luck that was attending the ship; they pronounced him, in short, a Jonah. There could be no more good fortune, they said, whilst Corporal Mantle remained on board. Captain Brenton, the commander of the frigate, inclined his ears to these forecastle murmurs, without appearing to heed them. But on his arrival at Malta he mentioned the matter to Collingwood, and suggested that the man should be tried by a court-martial. His acquittal he thought was certain, and the issue would be the means of whitewashing him in the eyes of his shipmates, who were not disposed to accept the decision of land-going magistrates. No man better knew the sailor's character than Collingwood, who at once assented; the court was ordered, and the corporal fully acquitted. This broke the spell; fine weather followed, a prize was taken, and Corporal Mantle was himself again.[1]

By a letter addressed to him in January by the Earl of Mulgrave, Collingwood found himself appointed Major-General of Marines, vacant by the death of Admiral Lord Gardner, of whom, as a sea-officer, he had been wont to speak as though no greater man was then alive. This appointment was exceedingly flattering, because of the many candidates for the position. Collingwood never asked for any favour in his life saving the perpetuation of his title through his daughters, and this appointment was grateful to him as coming to one who " never solicited anything pecuniary or for myself." To a man whose state of health was exceedingly infirm, the furious weather encountered by the fleet off Toulon was a punishment cruelly severe. The succession of storms blew the ships away. The *Ocean*, aboard which Collingwood still continued, came very near to going to pieces; her copper bolts might as well have been of lead, so useless were they

[1] *Memoir of Sir Jalheel Brenton*, p. 345.

as fastenings. He sailed her to Malta, to secure her with iron bolts. The *Ocean*, like other ships at that time, upon whose durability and seaworthy qualities the security of the country depended, was the outcome of an experiment which the surveyors of the navy were making in the mode of securing vessels. Collingwood declared that had the French devised a plan for the destruction of the British Navy, they could not have lighted upon anything more effectual than this experiment of the surveyors with copper instead of iron bolts.

His duties chained him to his desk; his bad health rendered him unequal to all social demands. He tells his father-in-law that his time is so occupied, even the common visits of civility are inconvenient to him. Malta he describes as made up of gossip and gormandizing. "The ladies who have so lately emerged from the humblest duties of domestic industry," he writes, "now vie with each other in all the shining finery of tassel and tinsel, and pass their nights in routs and revels; their days go for nothing. I just saw enough of it to know that it would not do for me. Neither my health nor my occupations were suited to it, and I declined all invitations."

He was vexed about this time by the publication of his life in a naval magazine. To what publication he refers, unless it be the *Naval Chronicle* for 1806, I am unable to discover. He complains of this biography in February 1809. Two points he might find distasteful in the publication in the *Naval Chronicle*—the first is his portrait, which is an ill-executed caricature; and the second is the reference to his birth and antecedents, in which his parents are termed in effect poor but respectable, and where it is affirmed that he was not descended from a long train of ancestors. If this biography be the account he speaks of, posterity should be cautious in drawing upon it for

information about him, " for," says he, " it related a heap
of stuff that had not the least foundation in truth, and
was in many parts exceedingly offensive to me." He
also refers satirically in this letter to a Scotchman who
wrote to inform him that he was about to publish a
Memoir of the House of Drummond, and that as he
(Collingwood) was immediately descended from it, and
closely allied by intermarriage, would he give him the
honour of his support? "I shall answer him," says
Collingwood, "that I apprehend his letter must have
been intended for some other person, as I have not the
honour of being connected in the most distant degree
with any family or person north of Tweed."

He had long wished to visit the King and Queen of
Naples, and having arrived at Palermo from Malta, he was
invited, on the *Ocean* anchoring, to a grand ball and
supper given by the Queen to the nobility on Ash Wednes-
day, the last day of the Carnival. He was very graciously
received. The King, he thought, had the air and manners
of a worthy, honest, country gentleman. The Queen
struck him as a lady who was consuming her life with the
effort to read the thoughts of everybody who approached
her. "She would be thought a deep politician; yet all
her schemes miscarry. She broods over what is imprac-
ticable with her little means, and frets herself continually
that others are not as dim-sighted as herself. Her lot
also has been cast awry, or in the distribution of stations
for this world so loose a morality and such depravity
of manners would never have been found perched upon
a throne, from whence should issue the bright example
of all that is good and great." This is the language in
which he conveys his impression of the Queen of Naples
to Lady Collingwood. He dined with the King at his
country house, and his Majesty carried him over the little

building, and showed him rooms not much larger "than ours at Morpeth." "I have also seen a great deal of the Princesses and Duchesses of Sicily, and all I shall say of them at present is that the more I see of them the more I bless my stars that I was born in England, and have got a darling wife who is not a princess."

He thought the Queen looked pleased when he took leave of her, and attributed her manner to falsehoods which had been told to her—that he had opposed Prince Leopold's going to Spain, that he had been the cause of Saint Clair's sudden withdrawal from Gibraltar, and so forth. Though he was handsomely entertained, he noticed that some consternation was excited by his arrival, due, as he concluded, to Lieut.-General Sir John Stuart having come to Palermo to meet him; whence the Queen inferred that the object of Collingwood's visit was to clear Sicily of all her French favourites. "They never desire," says he, "I am sure, to see my face again." The shade of Nelson seems, as one reads, to stalk in upon this stage of dim gilt and faded finery, the noxiousness of whose atmosphere of lies, deceit, false sentiment, and buffoon Italian sensibility is not to be neutralized by the savour of the feast and the perfume of the exotic. The Queen does not ask Collingwood how Lady Hamilton is. The clear, calm, austere gaze of this New-castle man pierces through and through her. She is very glad when he bows himself out of her presence. His cold demeanour, his air of dignified reserve, is insipid to a degree to this emotional woman. But her sharp eye, penetrating beneath the surface, also witnesses or suspects qualities which, as she cannot understand them—for they are solid old-fashioned English virtues, whose central pulses, deep-seated, leave them exteriorly cold and im-passive—alarm her, and glad as she always is to hear the thunder of his cannon in her defence, she never wishes to see his face again.[1]

On April 5th or 6th, the *Ocean*, having some days previously put into Port Mahon through stress of weather, which had shaken her very nearly to pieces, Collingwood shifted his flag into the *Ville de Paris*, a vessel which, he said, he liked very much after a brief experience of her, though, as he wrote to his wife, all ships which sailed well and were put together in a manner fit to defy the sea were alike to him. " I see little of them, seldom moving from my desk." What he said he required was not so much a stout ship as a new pair of legs and a new pair of eyes. Whilst he was at Port Mahon with the blockading fleet, a French squadron of five sail of the line, two frigates, one corvette, and sixteen brigs and settees, under the command of Rear-Admiral Baudin in the *Robuste*, an 80-gun ship, sailed from Toulon with troops and provisions for the relief of Barcelona. Baudin landed his succours and returned to Toulon in the middle of May. At the time the British ships had made good the injuries they had sustained in the gale, and the fleet were under sail from Port Mahon, a message reached Collingwood stating that a squadron of the enemy's ships had appeared before Barcelona four days before. He at once headed on a course with the hope of intercepting them on their return. Next day the fleet captured two French ships with a number of invalid soldiers on board, fresh from Barcelona, and from them

[1] He has more to say about the Sicilian Royal family in a letter to Rear-Admiral Sotheby, June 30th, 1809 : " It is a great mistake for an officer to come here with his wife and family. Who would think of bringing a poor woman from the society of her friends to live where ?—at Malta ? All his pay would not pay her house-rent. At Palermo among the Princesses ? That, in my opinion, whatever she might think of it, is worse ; unless she can paint her face well, and intrigue by moonlight, she will be nobody there."— *Correspondence and Memoir*, p. 534.

Collingwood learnt that Baudin had returned to Toulon. It seems that the British had crossed the Frenchmen's route about ten hours after they had passed! On arriving off Toulon on the day following, Collingwood found Baudin and his ships safe at anchor there.

He could not disguise his mortification. "I have an artful, deceptious, and timid foe to deal with. They are as secret as the night, and ingenious in devices; yet my perseverance may at last avail me. My constant study is how to counteract them, and I hope that my good fortune will one day be predominant. I would rather die anyhow than with grief and disappointment." He justly points out, however, to Lord Mulgrave, that the catching of a small squadron of the enemy in such short expeditions—as, for example, from Toulon to Barcelona—must ever be a matter of chance. Opportunities, and such opportunities as no vigilance could extinguish or provide against, were watched for and eagerly seized. The *Unité* and *Cambrian*, two smart frigates, had been left by Collingwood off Toulon; yet the first news he received of the escape of the French squadron was from Tarragona. Baudin was also fortunate in winds, and in those days wind at sea meant a very great deal more than ever steam is likely to signify, at all events in our time.

But full as his hands are of business, miserably ill as he now is, vexed to the heart, too, by the repeated disappointment of a great and cherished hope—the hope that was keeping him away from his home, and yoking him to a command which his letters clearly show he knew meant certain death to him—the hope, in a word, of getting at the French, and striking a final magnificent blow for the country he loved and was serving with a devotion unparalleled in the annals of the most brilliant and heroic of her ocean children—he could still find love and leisure for

such a message as this (June 17th): "I am writing you a
letter, my love, because there is nothing I so much delight
in as a little communication with her on whom my heart
for ever dwells. How this letter is to go to you I know
not. I never hear from your world, and cannot tell
whether anything from ours ever reaches you; but I take
the chance of sending you my blessing. I am pretty well
in health," adds the noble soul, anxious to soften to the
uttermost degree all anxiety in his wife, "but have fatigue
enough; nothing that is pleasurable ever happens to me.
I have been lamenting our ill-luck in not meeting the
French ships, the only time perhaps that they will show
themselves out of port for the summer; but it was not to
be avoided; they never come out but with good assurance
of being safe." [1]

According to James the fleet at anchor in Toulon road
during the early part of October in this year (1809)
consisted of 15 sail of the line, exclusive of six Russian
sail of the line, six or seven French frigates, and a number
of armed transports and store-ships. "And either the
whole fleet," he says, "or a division of it, were waiting for
a second opportunity to throw supplies into Barcelona.[2]
In the previous September Collingwood had formed a
plan of action, which he had communicated to the
Admiralty, and he now proceeded to the execution of it.
He was aware from the intelligence which he had received
that the French were all anxiety to supply Barcelona with
provisions, but that the attempt would not be made whilst
his fleet continued off Toulon. Nothing was likely to coax
them out but a gale of wind that should blow the British
ships away. Such a gale arose, and Collingwood withdrew
to Minorca, and sent several of his ships into harbour,

[1] *Correspondence and Memoir*, p. 528.
[2] *James*, vol. iv. p. 444.

where they remained long enough to suggest that they
were settled and in no hurry to weigh, and for news of
their being snug in harbour to reach Toulon.   Collingwood
then called them out and sailed for Cape Sebastian, where
the frigates, which he had left stationed at Toulon, were
to bring him intelligence of the enemy's movements.

On the 21st of October, Baudin sailed from Toulon with
the *Robuste, Borée,* and *Lion,* two frigates, the *Pauline* and
the *Pomone,* and a fleet of armed store-ships and transports;
the whole bound to Barcelona.   On the same afternoon
the enemy was descried by one of the British frigates,
which next morning fell in with Collingwood, who was
cruising, as we have seen, off Cape San Sebastian, with 15
sail of the line, three frigates, and a sloop.   Collingwood
prepared his fleet for battle, taking care to so station his
frigates as to enable them to swiftly communicate intelligence of the enemy's approach.   On the morning of the
23rd, one of these frigates signalled a fleet in sight to the
eastward.   Instead of a fleet, the approaching craft proved
the three liners, the frigates and store-ships and transports
under Baudin, who, on catching sight of the British, shifted
his helm and braced up his yards, and the whole pack of
them made off, pursued by Rear-Admiral Martin with
eight of the fastest of the ships.   In the afternoon, the
chase still continuing, the French battle-ships and frigates
quitted the convoy, which went steering in wild and
scattering confusion to the north and west, while Baudin's
ships of war headed south and east.   An English frigate
that was well to windward bore down upon the convoy and
destroyed four or five of the small vessels; but the rest got
away, and with the five men-of-war were lost sight of.

Admiral Martin, always on the look-out, made for the
French coast, guessing the enemy would head in that.
direction, and late in the afternoon of the following day,

having then six sail of the line (for two of the chasing ships had parted company during the previous night), he was signalled by the *Tigre*, the headmost ship, that there were four sail in the north-north-east. They proved the French liners, and one of the frigates, the *Pauline*. Martin's ships cracked on, but nothing could be done that night. Next day the Frenchmen were again in sight, running along shore. Sail was immediately made in chase, and for a few hours the pursuit continued, until, at about midday, the *Robuste* and *Lion* were run ashore by their people, within pistol-shot of each other, some few miles from the harbour of Cette. The third liner, the *Borée*, and the frigate *Pauline*, with the British ships *Tigre* and *Leviathan* clinging to their skirts, and firing into them as they swept along, succeeded breathlessly in reaching Cette harbour. Meanwhile the *Robuste* and *Lion*, having been dismantled and their crews landed, were fired by their own people, and shortly before eleven o'clock at night blew up with a prodigious explosion and a mighty volcanic upheaval of flame, to the great satisfaction of the English Jacks, who were watching the fine show at a distance of five or six miles from the shore, where the British squadron were lying nearly becalmed.

Admiral Martin, on the 30th, rejoined Collingwood, who, learning that the five ships of war which Martin had pursued were all that had sailed out of Toulon, resumed the blockade of the port. The *Borée* and the frigate which had entered Cette were preserved by the enemy, who, however, were not so fortunate with the convoy; for when it was known that these ships had put into the Bay of Rosas, Collingwood detached Captain Hallowell[1] with a

---

[1] Captain Hallowell, now the intimate friend of Collingwood, had been also one of the captains most valued by Nelson. He is a brilliant figure in the annals of those times, and is also memorable

number of vessels to capture or destroy them, with the result that by dawn on the first of November every one of them was either burnt or brought off, though at the cost to the British of many killed and wounded.

Collingwood wrote of this affair to his wife with delight. "You will have great pleasure in hearing of my success," he says (writing prior to the attack upon the convoy), "and particularly of its having been effected without a hair of anybody's head being hurt, and almost without a shot being fired. . . . On Sunday night, the 22nd, one of them (*i. e.* the frigates) came with a signal that the enemy was approaching. Every soul was in raptures; I expected the whole fleet, and that we should have had a dashing business." He then tells the story, and goes on to say that he has sent a squadron to capture the remainder of the convoy. His eagerness to communicate good news to his Sarah is illustrated by the date of this letter. He wishes to justify to her his resolution to remain at his post by making her see that the field of honour and of glory is still a wide one, that opportunities are offering, and that some final brilliant achievement may be his before he turns his face to the wall. "To you, my dear Sarah," he says, "I am sure it will be a gratification that I am usefully employed, and that although we cannot always command success, I spare no pains to deserve it." The Duke of Clarence sent him a congratulatory and cheering letter on this action; but it was dated December 9th, and when Collingwood received it, the eyes with which he perused it were growing dim with death. "It is odd," wrote the Duke, "that the enemy should have selected the 21st October for sailing; and extraordinary

---

for the singular gift of a coffin to Nelson—a ghastly relic formed of a fragment of *L'Orient*. This strange shell contains the dust of the hero.

also that the French should build such fine ships and handle them so ill. I am glad that your lordship is satisfied with the conduct of our officers and men on this occasion; and am clearly of opinion that the lieutenants deserve and ought to be promoted. I am for liberal rewards; the gallant Raitt[1] of course comes within my ideas of promotion and gratuities. I have ever been, and ever shall be, of opinion that zeal and bravery ought to be the great and sole causes of promotion. Your former favourite, the Empress Catherine, knew well this secret of State; and your lordship's observation is quite correct, that her Imperial Majesty carried the same notions even into her private amusements: 'None but the brave,' my dear lord!"

Collingwood's end was now close at hand. Writing on the 1st of January, 1810, from Minorca, he tells his father-in-law that he has been and still is very unwell, and that the doctors attribute his illness to his constant confinement, which distresses him to learn, as, he says, there is little chance of his being able to change the conditions of his life. Again, on the 10th of February, he writes to his old friend, Captain Clavell, that lately he has had a very severe complaint in his stomach, which has almost prevented him from eating. "It is high time," he says, "I should return to England, and I hope that I shall be allowed to do so before long. It will otherwise be soon too late." It was already too late, and his last letter to

---

[1] Captain Raitt was one of the heroic skirmishing band under Collingwood, in which were included Brenton, Hoste, Pearse, Cochrane, Maxwell, Staines, and others. Of them Collingwood wrote in June 1809: "The activity and zeal in those gallant young men keep up my spirits, and make me equal to bear the disagreeables that happen from the contentions of some other ships. . . . Those who do all the service give no trouble; those who give the trouble are good for nothing."

the Earl of Mulgrave, dated February 22nd, renders it evident that he knew it to be so, though with a sort of languishing hope in his dying mind, he writes as though possessed by some dream of amendment should he be able to land. Three days later, that is to say, on the 25th of February, his sufferings were so keen, his exhaustion so great that, the *Ville de Paris* having moored in the harbour of Port Mahon, Collingwood immediately went on shore, urged to this step by the persuasion, indeed by the commands, of his medical attendants. His friend Captain Hallowell accompanied him. Nothing, however, could now be done. He was incapable of bearing the slightest fatigue, and on the 3rd of March he surrendered his command to Rear-Admiral Martin, and was conveyed on board the *Ville de Paris.*

For two days the crew were employed in trying to warp the ship clear of the harbour; on the 6th the wind shifted, and at sunset sail was made, and the vessel proceeded on her passage to England. The narrative of Collingwood's closing hours has been related by his son-in-law. When lying below in his cot he was told that he was again at sea; a light kindled in his eye, a momentary vigour of life possessed him, and addressing those who stood near, he exclaimed, "Then I may yet live to meet the French once more." There is a greatness in his manner of meeting death that is very impressive. All is calmness and resignation. He told Captain Thomas on the morning of the 7th, in reply to that officer's expression of fear that he was incommoded by the heavy swell on which the ship was then rolling: "No, Thomas; I am now in a state in which nothing in this world can disturb me more. I am dying; and I am sure it must be consolatory to you and all who love me, to see how comfortably I am going to my end." He sometimes mentioned his family; but this

was a subject which one may imagine he would choose to
think of rather than talk about. He very well knew that
he would never again see his wife and daughters in this
world. Every thought of them would be sanctified by a
degree of emotion that would render all reference, saving
such messages as he might have to send, a kind of
profanity. Only those who closely study his letters can
to any extent understand the depth of this great man's
love for those from whom his duty to his country had
kept him absent for years, and whom that duty was to
deny him the joy of again clasping to his heart. As we
stand by the side of the dying Nelson we hear the
thunder of the ship's artillery, the huzzaing of the con-
quering sailors; he is the hero of a prodigious victory;
his death is an apotheosis—it is a translation. But
Collingwood! He has worn out his heart in the service
of his country; earthly distinctions indeed have been his,
but they have been as dust in his mouth; for such honours
as he obtained are useful only for enjoyment in one's own
country, and years, many long years, had passed since
Collingwood had set foot in his native land. It was a
hard death for this great soul to die. It was hard to
expire after a prolonged term of banishment remorse-
lessly enjoined and rigorously executed by his inflexible
sense of duty. The surgeon who attended him in his
dying moments would afterwards say that those who
witnessed the composure and resignation with which he
met his fate must long remember the scene with wonder
and admiration. "In no part of his lordship's brilliant
life did his character appear with greater lustre than when
he was approaching his end. It was dignified in the
extreme. If it be on the bed of sickness, and at the
approach of death—when ambition, the love of glory,
and the interests of the world are over—that the true

character is to be discovered, surely never did any man's appear to greater advantage than did that of my Lord Collingwood. For my own part I did not believe it possible that any one, on such an occasion, could have behaved so nobly. Cruelly harassed by a most afflicting disease, obtaining no relief from the means employed, and perceiving his death to be inevitable, he suffered no sigh of regret to escape, no murmuring at his past life, no apprehension of the future. He met death as became him, with a composure and fortitude which have seldom been equalled and never surpassed." [1]

He died on the evening of the 7th of March, 1810. The immediate cause of his death was contraction of the pylorus, due to long confinement on board ship, and to his habit of bending over his desk whilst engaged on his multifarious correspondence. It was found that with the exception of the stomach all the organs of life were sound and unimpaired, and his son-in-law, writing in 1827, declares that had Collingwood been earlier relieved from his command, "he would have still been in the enjoyment of the honours and rewards which would doubtless have awaited him on his return to England." The *Ville de Paris*, with his remains on board, arrived at Gibraltar on the 25th; the body was then transferred to the *Nereide* frigate, which reached England about the middle of April.

Collingwood was buried in St. Paul's Cathedral on Friday 11th of May. The body had been landed at Greenwich Hospital on the 26th of the previous month, and the flag of the *Ville de Paris* was hoisted over his coffin, which was placed under the stern of Nelson's funeral car. On the morning of the funeral there were drawn up at Greenwich, in two lines, five hundred pen-

[1] *Correspondence and Memoir*, p. 563.

sioners. The coffin was carried by twelve veterans, and there were eight naval officers as pall-bearers, the pall being Collingwood's flag; and it remained in St. Paul's Cathedral, with the standard lowered and the coronet placed on the pall, till the service had been read; it was then removed to the vault under the dome and placed by the side of Nelson's. Collingwood's servant, or steward, named Smith, a man, to judge from certain passages in the Admiral's letters, superior to his situation, was suffered, at the request of Lady Collingwood, to perform the last office to the remains of his master by placing the coronet on the coffin. Amongst those present was Collingwood's old schoolfellow, Lord Eldon, who, in speaking to Mrs. Foster about the funeral, said: "It was very affecting—his sailors crowded so around all anxious to see the last of their commander. One sailor seized me by the arm, and entreated that I would take him in with me that he might be there to the end. I told him to stick fast to me, and I did take him in; but when it came to throwing some earth on the coffin (you know the part of the service 'dust to dust'), he burst past me and threw himself into the vault." [1]

It is said that the remains of Collingwood were deposited in the stone coffin which Cardinal Wolsey had prepared for himself. "It had remained as lumber in a room adjoining St. George's Chapel, Windsor; and for its last purpose was given as a present by his Majesty." [2]

Lady Collingwood sent a memorial mourning ring to the Duke of Clarence, who thanked her for it in a letter in which he expressed great concern at having been prevented from attending the funeral. "I was informed that the interment was to be quite private, or else I should have made a point of attending the remains of my

[1] Twiss's *Life of Lord Eldon.* [2] *Naval Chronicle,* vol. xxiii. p. 448.

departed friend to the grave. No one could have had a more sincere regard for the public character and abilities of Lord Collingwood than myself; indeed, with me it is enough to have been the friend of Nelson to possess my estimation. The Hero of the Nile was a man of great mind, but self-taught; Lord Collingwood, the old companion in arms of the immortal Nelson, was equally great in judgment and abilities, and had also the advantage of an excellent education. Pardon me, madam, for having said so much on this melancholy occasion; but my feelings as a brother officer, and my admiration of the late Lord Collingwood, have dictated this expression of my sentiments. I will now conclude, and shall place on the same finger the ring which your ladyship has sent me with the gold bust of Lord Nelson. Lord Collingwood's must ever be prized by me as coming from his family; the bust of Lord Nelson I received from an unknown hand on the day the event of his death reached this country. To me the two rings are invaluable; and the sight of them must ever give me sensations of grief and admiration." [1]

Lady Collingwood survived her husband nine years. She died September 16th, 1819.

A monument was erected to Collingwood, by a vote of Parliament, in St. Paul's Cathedral. Proud as Newcastle-on-Tyne was of him, there was a tardiness as of reluctance almost in her method of doing him honour. A cenotaph, containing a medallion and a tediously long inscription, was indeed placed in the nave of St. Nicholas' Church; and a whole-length likeness of the hero, painted by Lonsdale, was hung up at the east end of the great hall of the Exchange on the Sandhill, together with portraits of Lord-Chancellor Eldon and Lord Stowell.[2] But so

---

[1] *Correspondence and Memoir*, p. 568.
[2] *Newcastle Chronicle*, November 28th, 1885.

great a man as Collingwood deserved at least a statue at the hands of the people of the district in whose flourishing central manufacturing capital he was born; and this was long in coming. In 1838 a meeting was held, Admiral Sir Charles Ogle in the chair, to consider the "propriety" of erecting a monument to the memory of Collingwood. But nothing further appears to have been done till October 1840, when another meeting was held, with Mr. M. Bell in the chair, and it was then resolved to commission Lough the sculptor to execute a monument. The business languished till 1845, and then a statue was erected, not in Newcastle-on-Tyne, but at Tynemouth. The site was ill-chosen; the angry feelings occasioned by difference of opinion influenced the subscriptions, and the sum furnished was inadequate to the erection of such a memorial as the fame and genius of Collingwood merited. Three years later, four 32-pounder guns, which had formerly belonged to the *Royal Sovereign*, were landed at Shields, and placed upon the base of the monument.[1]

"My life," wrote Collingwood to Gold, the publisher of the *Naval Chronicle*, in answer to a request for an account of his career, "has been a continued service at sea, but unmarked by any of those extraordinary events or brilliant scenes which hold men up to particular attention and distinguish them from those officers who are zealous and anxious for the public service." The truth of this all who have occasion to deal with his professional services must feel. There have not been wanting writers who contend that Collingwood was created by Nelson; that without Nelson Collingwood would have been a comparatively insignificant unit in the crowd of the sea-officers of his time. Therefore, it is urged, he was extremely fortunate in his association with Nelson. But then scores were the companions

---

[1] Latimer's *Local Records.*

of Nelson who were yet not Collingwoods. The argument is, indeed, a ridiculous one. For others Nelson provided such opportunities as never happened to Collingwood, and yet Collingwood was greater than any of those men, and in many respects the equal of Nelson, and in some respects superior to him. Collingwood's shining light was to his contemporaries, and still is to posterity, somewhat dimmed by Nelson's sun-like blaze. Therefore I cannot see that it was fortunate for Collingwood that he should have been associated with Nelson. Had he held independent command in a field of action where Nelson was *not*, but where the occasions out of which Nelson created himself *were*, Collingwood would certainly have proved himself his friend's peer in every conceivable regard of heroism, judgment, dutifulness, devotion, and minute professional knowledge.

But to what purpose are they compared? It is enough that we should recognize in Collingwood all those great professional qualities which are claimed for him by those who regard comparative criticism as worthless when individual excellence is to be considered. It matters nothing in our estimate of Milton that Shakespeare should be deemed the greater poet. Was Milton a poet? Was he a great poet? This weak attempt to submit the character of one of England's Admirals must surely fly very wide of its mark, short as is the flight that the feeble string impels it into, if it do not suggest or submit a great and shining character, and if it do not convince the reader that Collingwood ranks among the very first of those British sea-chieftains who have fought for, and who have bled for, and many of whom have died for, their country; who have magnificently, heroically, and, with matchless devotion, maintained her honour, promoted her greatness, and hoisted her flag to the dominating altitude at which it flies amongst the mastheads of the world.

All the golden threads of the virtuous qualities entered into the strands which nature had "laid up" for the formation of this Sailor's character. The closer you look into his life the deeper grow your affectionate respect and admiration. He is the most absolute embodiment of the solid, the elegant, and the affecting English virtues that I am acquainted with, be the walk of life at which I direct my gaze what it will. His career is a noble enrichment of the annals of the glorious Service he passed his life in. He was equal to the greatest performances; yet never did any man illustrate with more exquisite modesty that philosophy of patient, obscure, but all-important heroism which is expressed by Milton in the line :

"He also serves, who only stands and waits."

COLLINGWOOD'S STATUE.

A LIST OF NEW BOOKS
AND ANNOUNCEMENTS OF
METHUEN AND COMPANY
PUBLISHERS : LONDON
36 ESSEX STREET
W.C.

CONTENTS

OCTOBER 1894

MESSRS. METHUEN'S
ANNOUNCEMENTS

Poetry

Rudyard Kipling. BALLADS. By RUDYARD KIPLING. *Crown 8vo. Buckram. 6s.* [*May 1895.*

The announcement of a new volume of poetry from Mr. Kipling will excite wide interest. The exceptional success of 'Barrack-Room Ballads,' with which this volume will be uniform, justifies the hope that the new book too will obtain a wide popularity.

Henley. ENGLISH LYRICS. Selected and Edited by W. E. HENLEY. *Crown 8vo. Buckram. 6s.*

Also 30 copies on hand-made paper *Demy 8vo.* £1, 1s.
Also 15 copies on Japanese paper. *Demy 8vo.* £2, 2s.

Few announcements will be more welcome to lovers of English verse than the one that Mr. Henley is bringing together into one book the finest lyrics in our language. Robust and original the book will certainly be, and it will be produced with the same care that made 'Lyra Heroica' delightful to the hand and eye.

"Q" THE GOLDEN POMP: A Procession of English Lyrics from Surrey to Shirley, arranged by A. T. QUILLER COUCH. *Crown 8vo. Buckram. 6s.*

Also 30 copies on hand-made paper. *Demy 8vo.* £1, 1s.
Also 15 copies on Japanese paper. *Demy 8vo.* £2, 2s.

Mr. Quiller Couch's taste and sympathy mark him out as a born anthologist, and out of the wealth of Elizabethan poetry he has made a book of great attraction.

Beeching. LYRA SACRA: An Anthology of Sacred Verse. Edited by H. C. BEECHING, M.A. *Crown 8vo. Buckram. 6s.*

Also 25 copies on hand-made paper. 21s.

This book will appeal to a wide public. Few languages are richer in serious verse than the English, and the Editor has had some difficulty in confining his material within his limits.

Yeats. A BOOK OF IRISH VERSE. Edited by W. B. YEATS. *Crown 8vo. 3s. 6d.*

Illustrated Books

Baring Gould. A BOOK OF FAIRY TALES retold by S. BARING GOULD. With numerous illustrations and initial letters by ARTHUR J. GASKIN. *Crown 8vo. 6s.*

Also 50 copies on hand-made paper. *Demy 8vo. £1, 1s.*

Also 15 copies on Japanese paper. *Demy 8vo. £2, 2s.*

Few living writers have been more loving students of fairy and folk lore than Mr. Baring Gould, who in this book returns to the field in which he won his spurs. This volume consists of the old stories which have been dear to generations of children, and they are fully illustrated by Mr. Gaskin, whose exquisite designs for Andersen's Tales won him last year an enviable reputation.

Baring Gould. A BOOK OF NURSERY SONGS AND RHYMES. Edited by S. BARING GOULD, and illustrated by the Students of the Birmingham Art School. *Crown 8vo. 6s.*

Also 50 copies on Japanese paper. *4to. 30s.*

A collection of old nursery songs and rhymes, including a number which are little known. The book contains some charming illustrations by the Birmingham students under the superintendence of Mr. Gaskin, and Mr. Baring Gould has added numerous notes.

Beeching. A BOOK OF CHRISTMAS VERSE. Edited by H. C. BEECHING, M.A., and Illustrated by WALTER CRANE. *Crown 8vo. 6s.*

Also 50 copies on hand-made paper. *Demy 8vo. £1, 1s.*

Also 15 copies on Japanese paper. *Demy 8vo. £2, 2s.*

A collection of the best verse inspired by the birth of Christ from the Middle Ages to the present day. Mr. Walter Crane has designed some beautiful illustrations. A distinction of the book is the large number of poems it contains by modern authors, a few of which are here printed for the first time.

Jane Barlow. THE BATTLE OF THE FROGS AND MICE, translated by JANE BARLOW, Author of 'Irish Idylls,' and pictured by F. D. BEDFORD. *Small 4to. 6s. net.*

Also 50 copies on Japanese paper. *4to. 30s. net.*

This is a new version of a famous old fable. Miss Barlow, whose brilliant volume of 'Irish Idylls' has gained her a wide reputation, has told the story in spirited flowing verse, and Mr. Bedford's numerous illustrations and ornaments are as spirited as the verse they picture. The book will be one of the most beautiful and original books possible.

Baring Gould. A GARLAND OF COUNTRY SON
English Folk Songs with their traditional melodies. Collected
arranged by S. BARING GOULD and H. FLEETWOOD SHEPP/
Royal 8vo. 6s.

In collecting West of England airs for 'Songs of the West,' the editors came a
a number of songs and airs of considerable merit, which were known throu
England and could not justly be regarded as belonging to Devon and Cor:
Some fifty of these are now given to the world.

Oliphant. THE FRENCH RIVIERA. By Mrs. OLIPH.
and F. R. OLIPHANT. With Illustrations and Maps. *Crown*
6s.

A volume dealing with the French Riviera from Toulon to Mentone. Withou
ing within the guide-book category, the book will supply some useful pra
information, while occupying itself chiefly with descriptive and historical m:
A special feature will be the attention directed to those portions of the Ri\
which, though full of interest and easily accessible from many well-frequ
spots, are generally left unvisited by English travellers, such as the M:
Mountains and the St. Tropez district, the country lying between Cannes, G
and the Var, and the magnificent valleys behind Nice. There will be se
original illustrations.

George. BATTLES OF ENGLISH HISTORY. By H.
GEORGE, M.A., Fellow of New College, Oxford. *With nume*
Plans. Crown 8vo. 6s.

This book, by a well-known authority on military history, will be an impo
contribution to the literature of the subject. All the great battles of En
history are fully described, connecting chapters carefully treat of the cha
wrought by new discoveries and developments, and the healthy spirit of patri<
is nowhere absent from the pages.

Shedlock. THE PIANOFORTE SONATA: Its Origin .
Development. By J. S. SHEDLOCK. *Crown 8vo.* 5s.

This is a practical and not unduly technical account of the Sonata treated hi:
cally. It contains several novel features, and an account of various works
known to the English public.

Jenks. ENGLISH LOCAL GOVERNMENT. By E JEN
M.A., Professor of Law at University College, Liverpool. *Cr.*
8vo. 2s. 6d.

A short account of Local Government, historical and explanatory, which will ap
very opportunely.

Dixon. A PRIMER OF TENNYSON. By W. M. DIXON, M.A., Professor of English Literature at Mason College. *Fcap. 8vo.* 1s. 6d.

This book consists of (1) a succinct but complete biography of Lord Tennyson; (2) an account of the volumes published by him in chronological order, dealing with the more important poems separately ; (3) a concise criticism of Tennyson in his various aspects as lyrist, dramatist, and representative poet of his day; (4) a bibliography. Such a complete book on such a subject, and at such a moderate price, should find a host of readers.

Oscar Browning. THE AGE OF THE CONDOTTIERI : A Short History of Italy from 1409 to 1530. By OSCAR BROWNING, M.A., Fellow of King's College, Cambridge. *Crown 8vo.* 5s.

This book is a continuation of Mr. Browning's 'Guelphs and Ghibellines,' and the two works form a complete account of Italian history from 1250 to 1530.

Layard. RELIGION IN BOYHOOD. Notes on the Religious Training of Boys. With a Preface by J. R. ILLINGWORTH. By E. B. LAYARD, M.A. *18mo.* 1s.

Chalmers Mitchell. OUTLINES OF BIOLOGY. By P. CHALMERS MITCHELL, M.A., F.Z.S. *Fully Illustrated. Crown 8vo.* 6s.

A text-book designed to cover the new Schedule issued by the Royal College of Physicians and Surgeons.

Malden. ENGLISH RECORDS. A Companion to the History of England. By H. E. MALDEN, M.A. *Crown 8vo.* 3s. 6d.

A book which aims at concentrating information upon dates, genealogy, officials, constitutional documents, etc., which is usually found scattered in different volumes.

Hutton. THE VACCINATION QUESTION. A Letter to the Right Hon. H. H. ASQUITH, M.P. By A. W. HUTTON, M.A. *Crown 8vo.*

Leaders of Religion

NEW VOLUMES

Crown 8vo. 3s. 6d.

LANCELOT ANDREWES, Bishop of Winchester. By R. L. OTTLEY, Principal of Pusey House, Oxford, and Fellow of Magdalen. *With Portrait.*

ST. AUGUSTINE of Canterbury. By E. L. CUTTS, D.D. *With a Portrait.*

THOMAS CHALMERS. By Mrs. OLIPHANT. *With a Portrait. Second Edition.*

JOHN KEBLE. By WALTER LOCK, Sub-Warden of Keble College. *With a Portrait. Seventh Edition.*

English Classics

Edited by W. E. HENLEY.

Messrs. Methuen propose to publish, under this title, a series of the masterpieces of the English tongue.

The ordinary 'cheap edition' appears to have served its purpose: the public has found out the artist-printer, and is now ready for something better fashioned. This, then, is the moment for the issue of such a series as, while well within the reach of the average buyer, shall be at once an ornament to the shelf of him that owns, and a delight to the eye of him that reads.

The series, of which Mr. William Ernest Henley is the general editor, will confine itself to no single period or department of literature. Poetry, fiction, drama, biography, autobiography, letters, essays—in all these fields is the material of many goodly volumes.

The books, which are designed and printed by Messrs. Constable, will be issued in two editions—

(1) A small edition, on the finest Japanese vellum, limited in most cases to 75 copies, demy 8vo, 21s. a volume nett;

(2) The popular edition on laid paper, crown 8vo, buckram, 3s. 6d. a volume.

The first six numbers are :—

THE LIFE AND OPINIONS OF TRISTRAM SHANDY. By LAWRENCE STERNE. With an Introduction by CHARLES WHIBLEY, and a Portrait. 2 vols.

THE WORKS OF WILLIAM CONGREVE. With an Introduction by G. S. STREET, and a Portrait. 2 vols.

THE LIVES OF DONNE, WOTTON, HOOKER, HERBERT, AND SANDERSON. By IZAAK WALTON. With an Introduction by VERNON BLACKBURN, and a Portrait.

THE ADVENTURES OF HADJI BABA OF ISPAHAN. By JAMES MORIER. With an Introduction by E. S. BROWNE, M.A.

THE POEMS OF ROBERT BURNS. With an Introduction by W. E. HENLEY, and a Portrait. 2 vols.

THE LIVES OF THE ENGLISH POETS. By SAMUEL JOHNSON, LL.D. With an Introduction by JOHN HEPBURN MILLAR, and a Portrait. 3 vols.

Classical Translations

NEW VOLUMES

Crown 8vo. Finely printed and bound in blue buckram.

LUCIAN—Six Dialogues (Nigrinus, Icaro-Menippus, The Cock, The Ship, The Parasite, The Lover of Falsehood). Translated by S. T. IRWIN, M.A., Assistant Master at Clifton; late Scholar of Exeter College, Oxford. 3s. 6d.

SOPHOCLES—Electra and Ajax. Translated by E. D. A. MORSHEAD, M.A., late Scholar of New College, Oxford; Assistant Master at Winchester. 2s. 6d.

TACITUS—Agricola and Germania. Translated by R. B. TOWNSHEND, late Scholar of Trinity College, Cambridge. 2s. 6d.

CICERO—Select Orations (Pro Milone, Pro Murena, Philippic II., In Catilinam). Translated by H. E. D. BLAKISTON, M.A., Fellow and Tutor of Trinity College, Oxford. 5s.

University Extension Series

NEW VOLUMES. Crown 8vo. 2s. 6d.

THE EARTH. An Introduction to Physiography. By EVAN SMALL, M.A. *Illustrated.*

INSECT LIFE. By F. W. THEOBALD, M.A. *Illustrated.*

Social Questions of To-day

NEW VOLUME. Crown 8vo. 2s. 6d.

WOMEN'S WORK. By LADY DILKE, MISS BULLEY, and MISS WHITLEY.

Cheaper Editions

Baring Gould. THE TRAGEDY OF THE CAESARS: The Emperors of the Julian and Claudian Lines. With numerous Illustrations from Busts, Gems, Cameos, etc. By S. BARING GOULD, Author of 'Mehalah,' etc. *Third Edition. Royal 8vo.* 15s.

'A most splendid and fascinating book on a subject of undying interest. The great feature of the book is the use the author has made of the existing portraits of the Caesars, and the admirable critical subtlety he has exhibited in dealing with this line of research. It is brilliantly written, and the illustrations are supplied on a scale of profuse magnificence.'—*Daily Chronicle.*

Clark Russell. THE LIFE OF ADMIRAL LORD COLLINGWOOD. By W. CLARK RUSSELL, Author of 'The Wreck of the Grosvenor.' With Illustrations by F. BRANGWYN. *Second Edition. 8vo.* .6s.

'A most excellent and wholesome book, which we should like to see in the hands of every boy in the country.'—*St. James's Gazette.*

A 2

Fiction

Baring Gould. KITTY ALONE. By S. BARING GOULD,
Author of 'Mehalah,' 'Cheap Jack Zita,' etc. *3 vols. Crown 8vo.*
A romance of Devon life.

Norris. MATTHEW AUSTIN. By W. E. NORRIS, Author of
'Mdle. de Mersai,' etc. *3 vols. Crown 8vo.*
A story of English social life by the well-known author of 'The Rogue.'

Parker. THE TRAIL OF THE SWORD. By GILBERT
PARKER, Author of 'Pierre and his People,' etc. *2 vols. Crown 8vo.*
A historical romance dealing with a stirring period in the history of Canada.

Anthony Hope. THE GOD IN THE CAR. By ANTHONY
HOPE, Author of 'A Change of Air,' etc. *2 vols. Crown 8vo.*
A story of modern society by the clever author of 'The Prisoner of Zenda.'

Mrs. Watson. THIS MAN'S DOMINION. By the Author
of 'A High Little World.' *2 vols. Crown 8vo.*
A story of the conflict between love and religious scruple.

Conan Doyle. ROUND THE RED LAMP. By A. CONAN
DOYLE, Author of 'The White Company,' 'The Adventures of Sher-
lock Holmes,' etc. *Crown 8vo. 6s.*
This volume, by the well-known author of 'The Refugees,' contains the experiences
of a general practitioner, round whose 'Red Lamp' cluster many dramas—some
sordid, some terrible. The author makes an attempt to draw a few phases of life
from the point of view of the man who lives and works behind the lamp.

Barr. IN THE MIDST OF ALARMS. By ROBERT BARR,
Author of 'From Whose Bourne,' etc. *Crown 8vo. 6s.*
A story of journalism and Fenians, told with much vigour and humour.

Benson. SUBJECT TO VANITY. By MARGARET BENSON.
With numerous Illustrations. *Crown 8vo. 3s. 6d.*
A volume of humorous and sympathetic sketches of animal life and home pets.

X. L. AUT DIABOLUS AUT NIHIL, and Other Stories.
By X. L. *Crown 8vo. 3s. 6d.*
A collection of stories of much weird power. The title story appeared some years
ago in 'Blackwood's Magazine,' and excited considerable attention. The
'Spectator' spoke of it as 'distinctly original, and in the highest degree imagina-
tive. The conception, if self-generated, is almost as lofty as Milton's.'

Morrison. TALES OF MEAN STREETS. By ARTHUR
MORRISON. *Crown 8vo. 6s.*
A volume of sketches of East End life, some of which have appeared in the 'National
Observer,' and have been much praised for their truth and strength and pathos.

O'Grady. THE COMING OF CURCULAIN. By STANDISH
O'GRADY, Author of 'Finn and his Companions,' etc. Illustrated
by MURRAY SMITH. *Crown 8vo. 3s. 6d.*
The story of the boyhood of one of the legendary heroes of Ireland.

New Editions

E. F. Benson. THE RUBICON. By E. F. BENSON, Author of 'Dodo.' *Fourth Edition. Crown 8vo. 6s.*

Mr. Benson's second novel has been, in its two volume form, almost as great a success as his first. The 'Birmingham Post' says it is '*well written, stimulating, unconventional, and, in a word, characteristic*': the 'National Observer' congratulates Mr. Benson upon '*an exceptional achievement,*' and calls the book '*a notable advance on his previous work.*'

Stanley Weyman. UNDER THE RED ROBE. By STANLEY WEYMAN, Author of 'A Gentleman of France.' With Twelve Illustrations by R. Caton Woodville. *Fourth Edition. Crown 8vo. 6s.*

A cheaper edition of a book which won instant popularity. No unfavourable review occurred, and most critics spoke in terms of enthusiastic admiration. The 'Westminster Gazette' called it '*a book of which we have read every word for the sheer pleasure of reading, and which we put down with a pang that we cannot forget it all and start again.*' The 'Daily Chronicle' said that *every one who reads books at all must read this thrilling romance, from the first page of which to the last the breathless reader is haled along.*' It also called the book '*an inspiration of manliness and courage.*' The 'Globe' called it '*a delightful tale of chivalry and adventure, vivid and dramatic, with a wholesome modesty and reverence for the highest.*'

Baring Gould. THE QUEEN OF LOVE. By S. BARING GOULD, Author of 'Cheap Jack Zita,' etc. *Second Edition. Crown 8vo, 6s.*

The scenery is admirable and the dramatic incidents most striking.'—*Glasgow Herald.*

'Strong, interesting, and clever.'—*Westminster Gazette.*

'You cannot put it down till you have finished it.'—*Punch.*

Can be heartily recommended to all who care for cleanly, energetic, and interesting fiction.'—*Sussex Daily News.*

Mrs. Oliphant. THE PRODIGALS. By Mrs. OLIPHANT. *Second Edition. Crown 8vo. 3s. 6d.*

Richard Pryce. WINIFRED MOUNT. By RICHARD PRYCE. *Second Edition. Crown 8vo. 3s. 6d.*

The 'Sussex Daily News' called this book '*a delightful story,*' and said that the writing was '*uniformly bright and graceful.*' The 'Daily Telegraph' said that the author was a '*deft and elegant story-teller,*' and that the book was '*an extremely clever story, utterly untainted by pessimism or vulgarity.*'

Constance Smith. A CUMBERER OF THE GROUND. By CONSTANCE SMITH, Author of 'The Repentance of Paul Wentworth,' etc. *New Edition. Crown 8vo. 3s. 6d.*

School Books

A VOCABULARY OF LATIN IDIOMS AND PHRASES. By A. M. M. STEDMAN, M.A. 18*mo.* 1*s.*

STEPS TO GREEK. By A. M. M. STEDMAN, M.A. 18*mo.* 1*s.* 6*d.*

A SHORTER GREEK PRIMER OF ACCIDENCE AND SYNTAX. By A. M. M. STEDMAN, M.A. *Crown 8vo.* 1*s.* 6*d.*

SELECTIONS FROM THE ODYSSEY. With Introduction and Notes. By E. D. STONE, M.A., late Assistant Master at Eton. *Fcap. 8vo.* 2*s.*

THE ELEMENTS OF ELECTRICITY AND MAGNETISM. With numerous Illustrations. By R. G. STEEL, M.A., Head Master of the Technical Schools, Northampton. *Crown 8vo.* 4*s.* 6*d.*

THE ENGLISH CITIZEN : HIS RIGHTS AND DUTIES. By H. E. MALDEN, M.A. *Crown 8vo.* 1*s.* 6*d.*
A simple account of the privileges and duties of the English citizen.

INDEX POETARUM LATINORUM. By E. F. BENECKE, M.A. *Crown 8vo.* 4*s.* 6*d.*
An aid to Latin Verse Composition.

Commercial Series

A PRIMER OF BUSINESS. By S. JACKSON, M.A. *Crown 8vo.* 1*s.* 6*d.*

COMMERCIAL ARITHMETIC. By F. G. TAYLOR. *Crown 8vo.* 1*s.* 6*d.*

𝔑𝔢𝔴 𝔞𝔫𝔡 𝔕𝔢𝔠𝔢𝔫𝔱 𝔅𝔬𝔬𝔨𝔰

Poetry

Rudyard Kipling. BARRACK-ROOM BALLADS; And Other Verses. By RUDYARD KIPLING. *Seventh Edition. Crown 8vo. 6s.*

A Special Presentation Edition, bound in white buckram, with extra gilt ornament. *7s. 6d.*

'Mr. Kipling's verse is strong, vivid, full of character. . . . Unmistakable genius rings in every line.'—*Times.*

'The disreputable lingo of Cockayne is henceforth justified before the world; for a man of genius has taken it in hand, and has shown, beyond all cavilling, that in its way it also is a medium for literature. You are grateful, and you say to yourself, half in envy and half in admiration: " Here is a *book*; here, or one is a Dutchman, is one of the books of the year."'—*National Observer.*

' "Barrack-Room Ballads" contains some of the best work that Mr. Kipling has ever done, which is saying a good deal. "Fuzzy-Wuzzy," "Gunga Din," and "Tommy," are, in our opinion, altogether superior to anything of the kind that English literature has hitherto produced.'—*Athenæum.*

'These ballads are as wonderful in their descriptive power as they are vigorous in their dramatic force. There are few ballads in the English language more stirring than "The Ballad of East and West," worthy to stand by the Border ballads of Scott.'—*Spectator.*

'The ballads teem with imagination, they palpitate with emotion. We read them with laughter and tears; the metres throb in our pulses, the cunningly ordered words tingle with life; and if this be not poetry, what is?'—*Pall Mall Gazette.*

Henley. LYRA HEROICA : An Anthology selected from the best English Verse of the 16th, 17th, 18th, and 19th Centuries. By WILLIAM ERNEST HENLEY, Author of 'A Book of Verse,' 'Views and Reviews,' etc. *Crown 8vo. Stamped gilt buckram, gilt top, edges uncut. 6s.*

'Mr. Henley has brought to the task of selection an instinct alike for poetry and for chivalry which seems to us quite wonderfully, and even unerringly, right.'—*Guardian.*

Tomson. A SUMMER NIGHT, AND OTHER POEMS. By GRAHAM R. TOMSON. With Frontispiece by A. TOMSON. *Fcap. 8vo. 3s. 6d.*

An edition on hand-made paper, limited to 50 copies. *10s. 6d. net.*

'Mrs. Tomson holds perhaps the very highest rank among poetesses of English birth. This selection will help her reputation.'—*Black and White.*

Ibsen. BRAND. A Drama by HENRIK IBSEN. Translated by
WILLIAM WILSON. *Crown 8vo. Second Edition.* 3*s.* 6*d.*

'The greatest world-poem of the nineteenth century next to "Faust." "Brand"
will have an astonishing interest for Englishmen. It is in the same set with
"Agamemnon," with "Lear," with the literature that we now instinctively regard
as high and holy.'—*Daily Chronicle.*

"Q." GREEN BAYS : Verses and Parodies. By "Q.," Author
of 'Dead Man's Rock' etc. *Second Edition. Fcap. 8vo.* 3*s.* 6*d.*

'The verses display a rare and versatile gift of parody, great command of metre, and
a very pretty turn of humour.'—*Times.*

"A. G." VERSES TO ORDER. By "A. G." *Cr. 8vo.* 2*s.* 6*d.*
net.

A small volume of verse by a writer whose initials are well known to Oxford men.
'A capital specimen of light academic poetry. These verses are very bright and
engaging, easy and sufficiently witty.'—*St. James's Gazette.*

Hosken. VERSES BY THE WAY. BY J. D. HOSKEN.
Crown 8vo. 5*s.*

A small edition on hand-made paper. *Price* 12*s.* 6*d. net.*

A Volume of Lyrics and Sonnets by J. D. Hosken, the Postman Poet. Q, the
Author of 'The Splendid Spur,' writes a critical and biographical introduction.

Gale. CRICKET SONGS. By NORMAN GALE. *Crown 8vo.*
Linen. 2*s.* 6*d.*

Also a limited edition on hand-made paper. *Demy 8vo.* 10*s.* 6*d.*
net.

'They are wrung out of the excitement of the moment, and palpitate with the spirit
of the game.'—*Star.*

'As healthy as they are spirited, and ought to have a great success.'—*Times.*

'Simple, manly, and humorous. Every cricketer should buy the book.'—*Westminster
Gazette.*

'Cricket has never known such a singer.'—*Cricket.*

Langbridge. BALLADS OF THE BRAVE : Poems of Chivalry,
Enterprise, Courage, and Constancy, from the Earliest Times to the
Present Day. Edited, with Notes, by Rev. F. LANGBRIDGE.
Crown 8vo. Buckram 3*s.* 6*d.* School Edition, 2*s.* 6*d.*

'A very happy conception happily carried out. These "Ballads of the Brave" are
intended to suit the real tastes of boys, and will suit the taste of the great majority.
—*Spectator.*   'The book is full of splendid things.'—*World.*

General Literature

Collingwood. JOHN RUSKIN: His Life and Work. By W. G. COLLINGWOOD, M.A., late Scholar of University College, Oxford, Author of the 'Art Teaching of John Ruskin,' Editor of Mr. Ruskin's Poems. *2 vols. 8vo. 32s. Second Edition.*

This important work is written by Mr. Collingwood, who has been for some years Mr. Ruskin's private secretary, and who has had unique advantages in obtaining materials for this book from Mr. Ruskin himself and from his friends. It contains a large amount of new matter, and of letters which have never been published, and is, in fact, a full and authoritative biography of Mr. Ruskin. The book contains numerous portraits of Mr. Ruskin, including a coloured one from a water-colour portrait by himself, and also 13 sketches, never before published, by Mr. Ruskin and Mr. Arthur Severn. A bibliography is added.

'No more magnificent volumes have been published for a long time. . . .'—*Times.*

'This most lovingly written and most profoundly interesting book.'—*Daily News.*

'It is long since we have had a biography with such varied delights of substance and of form. Such a book is a pleasure for the day, and a joy for ever.'—*Daily Chronicle.*

'Mr. Ruskin could not well have been more fortunate in his biographer.'—*Globe.*

'A noble monument of a noble subject. One of the most beautiful books about one of the noblest lives of our century.'—*Glasgow Herald.*

Gladstone. THE SPEECHES AND PUBLIC ADDRESSES OF THE RT. HON. W. E. GLADSTONE, M.P. With Notes and Introductions. Edited by A. W. HUTTON, M.A. (Librarian of the Gladstone Library), and H. J. COHEN, M.A. With Portraits. *8vo. Vols. IX. and X. 12s. 6d. each.*

Clark Russell. THE LIFE OF ADMIRAL LORD COL-LINGWOOD. By W. CLARK RUSSELL, Author of 'The Wreck of the Grosvenor.' With Illustrations by F. BRANGWYN. *Second Edition. Crown 8vo. 6s.*

'A really good book.'—*Saturday Review.*

'A most excellent and wholesome book, which we should like to see in the hands of every boy in the country.'—*St. James's Gazette.*

Clark. THE COLLEGES OF OXFORD: Their History and their Traditions. By Members of the University. Edited by A. CLARK, M.A., Fellow and Tutor of Lincoln College. *8vo. 12s. 6d.*

'Whether the reader approaches the book as a patriotic member of a college, as an antiquary, or as a student of the organic growth of college foundation, it will amply reward his attention.'—*Times.*

'A delightful book, learned and lively.'—*Academy.*

'A work which will certainly be appealed to for many years as the standard book on the Colleges of Oxford.'—*Athenæum.*

Prior. CAMBRIDGE SERMONS. Edited by C. H. PRIOR, M.A., Fellow and Tutor of Pembroke College. *Crown 8vo.* 6s.

A volume of sermons preached before the University of Cambridge by various preachers, including the Archbishop of Canterbury and Bishop Westcott.

'A representative collection. Bishop Westcott's is a noble sermon.'—*Guardian.*

'Full of thoughtfulness and dignity.'—*Record.*

Beeching. BRADFIELD SERMONS. Sermons by H. C. BEECHING, M.A., Rector of Yattendon, Berks. With a Preface by CANON SCOTT HOLLAND. *Crown 8vo.* 2s. 6d.

Seven sermons preached before the boys of Bradfield College.

James. CURIOSITIES OF CHRISTIAN HISTORY PRIOR TO THE REFORMATION. By CROAKE JAMES, Author of 'Curiosities of Law and Lawyers.' *Crown 8vo.* 7s. 6d.

'This volume contains a great deal of quaint and curious matter, affording some "particulars of the interesting persons, episodes, and events from the Christian's point of view during the first fourteen centuries." Wherever we dip into his pages we find something worth dipping into.'—*John Bull.*

Kaufmann. CHARLES KINGSLEY. By M. KAUFMANN, M.A. *Crown 8vo. Buckram.* 5s.

A biography of Kingsley, especially dealing with his achievements in social reform.

'The author has certainly gone about his work with conscientiousness and industry.'— *Sheffield Daily Telegraph.*

Leaders of Religion

Edited by H. C. BEECHING, M.A. *With Portraits; crown 8vo.*

A series of short biographies of the most prominent leaders of religious life and thought of all ages and countries.

2/6 & 3/6

The following are ready— **2s. 6d.**

CARDINAL NEWMAN. By R. H. HUTTON. *Second Edition.*

'Few who read this book will fail to be struck by the wonderful insight it displays into the nature of the Cardinal's genius and the spirit of his life.'—WILFRID WARD, in the *Tablet.*

'Full of knowledge, excellent in method, and intelligent in criticism. We regard i as wholly admirable.'—*Academy.*

JOHN WESLEY. By J. H. OVERTON, M.A.

'It is well done: the story is clearly told, proportion is duly observed, and there is no lack either of discrimination or of sympathy.'—*Manchester Guardian.*

BISHOP WILBERFORCE. By G. W. DANIEL, M.A.
CARDINAL MANNING. By A. W. HUTTON, M.A.
CHARLES SIMEON. By H. C. G. MOULE, M.A.

3s. 6d.

JOHN KEBLE. By WALTER LOCK, M.A. *Seventh Edition.*
THOMAS CHALMERS. By Mrs. OLIPHANT. *Second Edition.*

Other volumes will be announced in due course.

Works by S. Baring Gould

OLD COUNTRY LIFE. With Sixty-seven Illustrations by
W. PARKINSON, F. D. BEDFORD, and F. MASEY. *Large Crown
8vo, cloth super extra, top edge gilt,* 10s. 6d. *Fourth and Cheaper
Edition.* 6s.
'"Old Country Life," as healthy wholesome reading, full of breezy life and movement, full of quaint stories vigorously told, will not be excelled by any book to be
published throughout the year. Sound, hearty, and English to the core.'—*World.*

HISTORIC ODDITIES AND STRANGE EVENTS. *Third
Edition. Crown 8vo.* 6s.
'A collection of exciting and entertaining chapters. The whole volume is delightful
reading.'—*Times.*

FREAKS OF FANATICISM. *Third Edition. Crown 8vo.* 6s.
'Mr. Baring Gould has a keen eye for colour and effect, and the subjects he has
chosen give ample scope to his descriptive and analytic faculties. A perfectly
fascinating book.'—*Scottish Leader.*

SONGS OF THE WEST: Traditional Ballads and Songs of
the West of England, with their Traditional Melodies. Collected
by S. BARING GOULD, M.A., and H. FLEETWOOD SHEPPARD,
M.A. Arranged for Voice and Piano. In 4 Parts (containing 25
Songs each), *Parts I., II., III.,* 3s. each. *Part IV.,* 5s. *In one
Vol., French morocco,* 15s.
'A rich and varied collection of humour, pathos, grace, and poetic fancy.'—*Saturday
Review.*

YORKSHIRE ODDITIES AND STRANGE EVENTS.
Fourth Edition. Crown 8vo. 6s.

STRANGE SURVIVALS AND SUPERSTITIONS. With
Illustrations. By S. BARING GOULD. *Crown 8vo. Second Edition.*
6s.

A book on such subjects as Foundations, Gables, Holes, Gallows, Raising the Hat, Old
Ballads, etc. etc. It traces in a most interesting manner their origin and history.

'We have read Mr. Baring Gould's book from beginning to end. It is full of quaint
and various information, and there is not a dull page in it.'—*Notes and Queries.*

THE TRAGEDY OF THE CAESARS: The
Emperors of the Julian and Claudian Lines. With numerous Illus
trations from Busts, Gems, Cameos, etc. By S. BARING GOULD,
Author of 'Mehalah,' etc. *Third Edition. Royal 8vo.* 15s.

'A most splendid and fascinating book on a subject of undying interest. The great
feature of the book is the use the author has made of the existing portraits of the
Caesars, and the admirable critical subtlety he has exhibited in dealing with this
line of research. It is brilliantly written, and the illustrations are supplied on a
scale of profuse magnificence.'—*Daily Chronicle.*

'The volumes will in no sense disappoint the general reader. Indeed, in their way,
there is nothing in any sense so good in English. . . . Mr. Baring Gould has
presented his narrative in such a way as not to make one dull page.'—*Athenæum.*

MR. BARING GOULD'S NOVELS

'To say that a book is by the author of "Mehalah" is to imply that it contains a
story cast on strong lines, containing dramatic possibilities, vivid and sympathetic
descriptions of Nature, and a wealth of ingenious imagery.'—*Speaker.*

'That whatever Mr. Baring Gould writes is well worth reading, is a conclusion that
may be very generally accepted. His views of life are fresh and vigorous, his
language pointed and characteristic, the incidents of which he makes use are
striking and original, his characters are life-like, and though somewhat exceptional people, are drawn and coloured with artistic force. Add to this that his
descriptions of scenes and scenery are painted with the loving eyes and skilled
hands of a master of his art, that he is always fresh and never dull, and under
such conditions it is no wonder that readers have gained confidence both in his
power of amusing and satisfying them, and that year by year his popularity
widens.'—*Court Circular.*

SIX SHILLINGS EACH

IN THE ROAR OF THE SEA: A Tale of the Cornish Coast.

MRS. CURGENVEN OF CURGENVEN.

CHEAP JACK ZITA.

THE QUEEN OF LOVE.

THREE SHILLINGS AND SIXPENCE EACH

ARMINELL: A Social Romance.

URITH: A Story of Dartmoor.

MARGERY OF QUETHER, and other Stories.

JACQUETTA, and other Stories.

Fiction

SIX SHILLING NOVELS

Corelli. BARABBAS: A DREAM OF THE WORLD'S TRAGEDY. By MARIE CORELLI, Author of 'A Romance of Two Worlds,' 'Vendetta,' etc. *Eleventh Edition. Crown 8vo. 6s.*

Miss Corelli's new romance has been received with much disapprobation by the secular papers, and with warm welcome by the religious papers. By the former she has been accused of blasphemy and bad taste; 'a gory nightmare'; 'a hideous travesty'; 'grotesque vulgarisation'; 'unworthy of criticism'; 'vulgar redundancy'; 'sickening details'—these are some of the secular flowers of speech. On the other hand, the 'Guardian' praises 'the dignity of its conceptions, the reserve round the Central Figure, the fine imagery of the scene and circumstance, so much that is elevating and devout'; the 'Illustrated Church News' styles the book 'reverent and artistic, broad based on the rock of our common nature, and appealing to what is best in it'; the 'Christian World' says it is written 'by one who has more than conventional reverence, who has tried to tell the story that it may be read again with open and attentive eyes'; the 'Church of England Pulpit' welcomes 'a book which teems with faith without any appearance of irreverence.'

Benson. DODO: A DETAIL OF THE DAY. By E. F. BENSON. *Crown 8vo. Fourteenth Edition. 6s.*

A story of society by a new writer, full of interest and power, which has attracted by its brilliance universal attention. The best critics were cordial in their praise. The 'Guardian' spoke of 'Dodo' as *unusually clever and interesting*; the 'Spectator' called it *a delightfully witty sketch of society*; the 'Speaker' said the dialogue was *a perpetual feast of epigram and paradox*; the 'Athenæum' spoke of the author as *a writer of quite exceptional ability*; the 'Academy' praised his *amazing cleverness*; the 'World' said the book was *brilliantly written*; and half-a-dozen papers declared there was *not a dull page in the book.*

Baring Gould. IN THE ROAR OF THE SEA: A Tale of the Cornish Coast. By S. BARING GOULD. *New Edition. 6s.*

Baring Gould. MRS. CURGENVEN OF CURGENVEN. By S. BARING GOULD. *Third Edition. 6s.*

A story of Devon life. The 'Graphic' speaks of it as *a novel of vigorous humour and sustained power*; the 'Sussex Daily News' says that *the swing of the narrative is splendid*; and the 'Speaker' mentions its *bright imaginative power.*

Baring Gould. CHEAP JACK ZITA. By S. BARING GOULD. *Third Edition. Crown 8vo. 6s.*

A Romance of the Ely Fen District in 1815, which the 'Westminster Gazette' calls 'a powerful drama of human passion'; and the 'National Observer' 'a story worthy the author.'

Baring Gould. THE QUEEN OF LOVE. By S. BARING GOULD. *Second Edition. Crown 8vo. 6s.*

The 'Glasgow Herald' says that 'the scenery is admirable, and one dramatic incidents are most striking.' The 'Westminster Gazette' calls the book 'strong, interesting, and clever.' 'Punch' says that 'you cannot put it down until you have finished it.' 'The Sussex Daily News' says that it 'can be heartily recommended to all who care for cleanly, energetic, and interesting fiction.'

Norris. HIS GRACE. By W. E. NORRIS, Author of 'Mademoiselle de Mersac.' *Third Edition. Crown 8vo.* 6s.

'The characters are delineated by the author with his characteristic skill and vivacity, and the story is told with that ease of manners and Thackerayean insight which give strength of flavour to Mr. Norris's novels No one can depict the Englishwoman of the better classes with more subtlety.'—*Glasgow Herald.*

'Mr. Norris has drawn a really fine character in the Duke of Hurstbourne, at once unconventional and very true to the conventionalities of life, weak and strong in a breath, capable of inane follies and heroic decisions, yet not so definitely portrayed as to relieve a reader of the necessity of study on his own behalf.'—*Athenæum.*

Parker. MRS. FALCHION. By GILBERT PARKER, Author of 'Pierre and His People.' *New Edition.* 6s.

Mr. Parker's second book has received a warm welcome. The 'Athenæum' called it *a splendid study of character*; the 'Pall Mall Gazette' spoke of the writing as *but little behind anything that has been done by any writer of our time*; the 'St. James's' called it *a very striking and admirable novel*; and the 'Westminster Gazette' applied to it the epithet of *distinguished.*

Parker. PIERRE AND HIS PEOPLE. By GILBERT PARKER. *Crown 8vo. Buckram.* 6s.

'Stories happily conceived and finely executed. There is strength and genius in Mr. Parker's style.'—*Daily Telegraph.*

Parker. THE TRANSLATION OF A SAVAGE. By GILBERT PARKER, Author of 'Pierre and His People,' 'Mrs. Falchion,' etc. *Crown 8vo.* 5s.

'The plot is original and one difficult to work out; but Mr. Parker has done it with great skill and delicacy. The reader who is not interested in this original, fresh, and well-told tale must be a dull person indeed.'—*Daily Chronicle.*

'A strong and successful piece of workmanship. The portrait of Lali, strong, dignified, and pure, is exceptionally well drawn.'—*Manchester Guardian.*

'A very pretty and interesting story, and Mr. Parker tells it with much skill. The story is one to be read.'—*St. James's Gazette.*

Anthony Hope. A CHANGE OF AIR: A Novel. By ANTHONY HOPE, Author of 'The Prisoner of Zenda,' etc. *Crown 8vo.* 6s.

A bright story by Mr. Hope, who has, the *Athenæum* says, 'a decided outlook and individuality of his own.'

'A graceful, vivacious comedy, true to human nature. The characters are traced with a masterly hand.'—*Times.*

Pryce. TIME AND THE WOMAN. By RICHARD PRYCE, Author of 'Miss Maxwell's Affections,' 'The Quiet Mrs. Fleming,' etc. New and Cheaper Edition. *Crown 8vo.* 6s.

'Mr. Pryce's work recalls the style of Octave Feuillet, by its clearness, conciseness, its literary reserve.'—*Athenæum.*

Marriott Watson. DIOGENES OF LONDON and other Sketches. By H. B. MARRIOTT WATSON, Author of 'The Web of the Spider.' *Crown 8vo. Buckram. 6s.*

'By all those who delight in the uses of words, who rate the exercise of prose above the exercise of verse, who rejoice in all proofs of its delicacy and its strength, who believe that English prose is chief among the moulds of thought, by these Mr. Marriott Watson's book will be welcomed.'—*National Observer.*

Gilchrist. THE STONE DRAGON. By MURRAY GILCHRIST. *Crown 8vo. Buckram. 6s.*

'The author's faults are atoned for by certain positive and admirable merits. The romances have not their counterpart in modern literature, and to read them is a unique experience.'—*National Observer.*

THREE-AND-SIXPENNY NOVELS

Baring Gould. ARMINELL: A Social Romance. By S. BARING GOULD. *New Edition. Crown 8vo. 3s. 6d.*

Baring Gould. URITH: A Story of Dartmoor. By S. BARING GOULD. *Third Edition. Crown 8vo. 3s. 6d.*

'The author is at his best.'—*Times.*
'He has nearly reached the high water-mark of "Mehalah."'—*National Observer.*

Baring Gould. MARGERY OF QUETHER, and other Stories. By S. BARING GOULD. *Crown 8vo. 3s. 6d.*

Baring Gould. JACQUETTA, and other Stories. By S. BARING GOULD. *Crown 8vo. 3s. 6d.*

Gray. ELSA. A Novel. By E. M'QUEEN GRAY. *Crown 8vo. 3s. 6d.*

'A charming novel. The characters are not only powerful sketches, but minutely and carefully finished portraits.'—*Guardian.*

Pearce. JACO TRELOAR. By J. H. PEARCE, Author of 'Esther Pentreath.' *New Edition. Crown 8vo. 3s. 6d.*

A tragic story of Cornish life by a writer of remarkable power, whose first novel has been highly praised by Mr. Gladstone.

The 'Spectator' speaks of Mr. Pearce as *a writer of exceptional power*; the 'Daily Telegraph' calls the book *powerful and picturesque*; the 'Birmingham Post' asserts that it is *a novel of high quality.*

Edna Lyall. DERRICK VAUGHAN, NOVELIST. By EDNA LYALL, Author of 'Donovan,' etc. *Crown 8vo. 3s. 6d.*

Clark Russell. MY DANISH SWEETHEART. By W. CLARK RUSSELL, Author of 'The Wreck of the Grosvenor,' etc. *Illustrated. Third Edition. Crown 8vo. 3s. 6d.*

Author of 'Vera.' THE DANCE OF THE HOURS. By the Author of 'Vera.' *Crown 8vo.* 3*s.* 6*d.*

Esmè Stuart. A WOMAN OF FORTY. By ESMÈ STUART, Author of 'Muriel's Marriage,' 'Virginie's Husband,' etc. *New Edition. Crown 8vo.* 3*s.* 6*d.*
'The story is well written, and some of the scenes show great dramatic power. — *Daily Chronicle.*

Fenn. THE STAR GAZERS. By G. MANVILLE FENN, Author of 'Eli's Children,' etc. *New Edition. Cr. 8vo.* 3*s.* 6*d.*
'A stirring romance.'—*Western Morning News.*
'Told with all the dramatic power for which Mr. Fenn is conspicuous.'—*Bradford Observer.*

Dickinson. A VICAR'S WIFE. By EVELYN DICKINSON. *Crown 8vo.* 3*s.* 6*d.*

Prowse. THE POISON OF ASPS. By R. ORTON PROWSE. *Crown 8vo.* 3*s.* 6*d.*

Grey. THE STORY OF CHRIS. By ROWLAND GREY. *Crown 8vo.* 5*s.*

Lynn Linton. THE TRUE HISTORY OF JOSHUA DAVIDSON, Christian and Communist. By E. LYNN LINTON. Eleventh Edition. *Post 8vo.* 1*s.*

HALF-CROWN NOVELS

A Series of Novels by popular Authors, tastefully bound in cloth. **2|6**

1. THE PLAN OF CAMPAIGN. By F. MABEL ROBINSON.

2. DISENCHANTMENT. By F. MABEL ROBINSON.

3. MR. BUTLER'S WARD. By F. MABEL ROBINSON.

4. HOVENDEN, V.C. By F. MABEL ROBINSON.

5. ELI'S CHILDREN. By G. MANVILLE FENN.

6. A DOUBLE KNOT. By G. MANVILLE FENN.

7. DISARMED. By M. BETHAM EDWARDS.

8. A LOST ILLUSION. By LESLIE KEITH.

9. A MARRIAGE AT SEA. By W. CLARK RUSSELL.

10. IN TENT AND BUNGALOW. By the Author of 'Indian Idylls.'

11. MY STEWARDSHIP. By E. M'QUEEN GRAY.

12. A REVEREND GENTLEMAN. By J. M. COBBAN.

13. A DEPLORABLE AFFAIR. By W. E. NORRIS.

14. JACK'S FATHER. By W. E. NORRIS.

Other volumes will be announced in due course.

Books for Boys and Girls

Baring Gould. THE ICELANDER'S SWORD. By S. BARING GOULD, Author of 'Mehalah,' etc. With Twenty-nine Illustrations by J. MOYR SMITH. *Crown 8vo.* 6s.

A stirring story of Iceland, written for boys by the author of ' In the Roar of the Sea.

Cuthell. TWO LITTLE CHILDREN AND CHING. By EDITH E. CUTHELL. Profusely Illustrated. *Crown 8vo. Cloth, gilt edges.* 3s. 6d.

Another story, with a dog hero, by the author of the very popular 'Only a Guard-Room Dog.'

Blake. TODDLEBEN'S HERO. By M. M. BLAKE, Author of ' The Siege of Norwich Castle.' With 36 Illustrations. *Crown 8vo.* 3s. 6d.

A story of military life for children.

Cuthell. ONLY A GUARD-ROOM DOG. By Mrs. CUTHELL. With 16 Illustrations by W. PARKINSON. *Square Crown 8vo.* 3s. 6d.

' This is a charming story. Tangle was but a little mongrel Skye terrier, but he had a big heart in his little body, and played a hero's part more than once. The book can be warmly recommended.'—*Standard.*

Collingwood. THE DOCTOR OF THE JULIET. By HARRY COLLINGWOOD, Author of 'The Pirate Island,' etc. Illustrated by GORDON BROWNE. *Crown 8vo.* 3s. 6d.

' "The Doctor of the Juliet," well illustrated by Gordon Browne, is one of Harry Collingwood's best efforts.'—*Morning Post.*

Clark Russell. MASTER ROCKAFELLAR'S VOYAGE. By W. CLARK RUSSELL, Author of 'The Wreck of the Grosvenor,' etc. Illustrated by GORDON BROWNE. *Second Edition.* *Crown 8vo.* 3*s.* 6*d.*

'Mr. Clark Russell's story of "Master Rockafellar's Voyage" will be among the favourites of the Christmas books. There is a rattle and "go" all through it, and its illustrations are charming in themselves, and very much above the average in the way in which they are produced.'—*Guardian.*

Manville Fenn. SYD BELTON : Or, The Boy who would not go to Sea. By G. MANVILLE FENN, Author of 'In the King's Name,' etc. Illustrated by GORDON BROWNE. *Crown 8vo.* 3*s.* 6*d.*

Who among the young story-reading public will not rejoice at the sight of the old combination, so often proved admirable—a story by Manville Fenn, illustrated by Gordon Browne? The story, too, is one of the good old sort, full of life and vigour, breeziness and fun.'—*Journal of Education.*

The Peacock Library

A Series of Books for Girls by well-known Authors, handsomely bound in blue and silver, and well illustrated. Crown 8vo. **3/6**

1. A PINCH OF EXPERIENCE. By L. B. WALFORD.

2. THE RED GRANGE. By Mrs. MOLESWORTH.

3. THE SECRET OF MADAME DE MONLUC. By the Author of ' Mdle Mori.'

4. DUMPS. By Mrs. PARR, Author of 'Adam and Eve.'

5. OUT OF THE FASHION. By L. T. MEADE.

6. A GIRL OF THE PEOPLE. By L. T. MEADE.

7. HEPSY GIPSY. By L. T. MEADE. 2*s.* 6*d.*

8. THE HONOURABLE MISS. By L. T. MEADE.

9. MY LAND OF BEULAH. By Mrs. LEITH ADAMS.

University Extension Series

A series of books on historical, literary, and scientific subjects, suitable for extension students and home reading circles. Each volume is complete in itself, and the subjects are treated by competent writers in a broad and philosophic spirit.

Edited by J. E. SYMES, M.A.,

Principal of University College, Nottingham.

Crown 8vo.   Price (with some exceptions) 2s. 6d.

The following volumes are ready :—

THE INDUSTRIAL HISTORY OF ENGLAND. By H. DE B. GIBBINS, M.A., late Scholar of Wadham College, Oxon., Cobden Prizeman. *Third Edition.* With Maps and Plans. 3s.

'A compact and clear story of our industrial development. A study of this concise but luminous book cannot fail to give the reader a clear insight into the principal phenomena of our industrial history. The editor and publishers are to be congratulated on this first volume of their venture, and we shall look with expectant interest for the succeeding volumes of the series.'—*University Extension Journal.*

A HISTORY OF ENGLISH POLITICAL ECONOMY. By L. L. PRICE, M.A., Fellow of Oriel College, Oxon.

PROBLEMS OF POVERTY: An Inquiry into the Industrial Conditions of the Poor. By J. A. HOBSON, M.A.

VICTORIAN POETS. By A. SHARP.

THE FRENCH REVOLUTION. By J. E. SYMES, M.A.

PSYCHOLOGY. By F. S. GRANGER, M.A., Lecturer in Philosophy at University College, Nottingham.

THE EVOLUTION OF PLANT LIFE: Lower Forms. By G. MASSEE, Kew Gardens. With Illustrations.

AIR AND WATER. Professor V. B. LEWES, M.A. Illustrated.

THE CHEMISTRY OF LIFE AND HEALTH. By C. W. KIMMINS, M.A. Camb. Illustrated.

THE MECHANICS OF DAILY LIFE. By V. P. SELLS, M.A. Illustrated.

ENGLISH SOCIAL REFORMERS. H. DE B. GIBBINS, M.A.

ENGLISH TRADE AND FINANCE IN THE SEVENTEENTH CENTURY. By W. A. S. HEWINS, B.A.

THE CHEMISTRY OF FIRE. The Elementary Principles of Chemistry. By M. M. PATTISON MUIR, M.A. Illustrated.

A TEXT-BOOK OF AGRICULTURAL BOTANY. By M. C. POTTER, M.A., F.L.S. Illustrated. 3s. 6d.

A MANUAL OF FRENCH COMMERCIAL CORRES-
PONDENCE. By S. E. BALLY, Modern Language Master at
the Manchester Grammar School. 2s.

COMMERCIAL GEOGRAPHY, with special reference to Trade
Routes, New Markets, and Manufacturing Districts. By L. D.
LYDE, M.A., of The Academy, Glasgow. 2s.

COMMERCIAL EXAMINATION PAPERS. By H. DE B.
GIBBINS, M.A. 1s. 6d.

THE ECONOMICS OF COMMERCE. By H. DE B. GIBBINS,
M.A. 1s. 6d.

A PRIMER OF BUSINESS. By S. JACKSON, M.A. 1s. 6d.

COMMERCIAL ARITHMETIC. By F. G. TAYLOR,
M.A. 1s. 6d.

Works by A. M. M. Stedman, M.A.

INITIA LATINA : Easy Lessons on Elementary Accidence.
Second Edition. Fcap. 8vo. 1s.

FIRST LATIN LESSONS. *Fourth Edition   Crown 8vo.* 2s.

FIRST LATIN READER. With Notes adapted to the Shorter
Latin Primer and Vocabulary. *Second Edition. Crown 8vo.* 1s. 6d.

EASY SELECTIONS FROM CAESAR. Part I. The Helvetian War. 18mo. 1s.

EASY SELECTIONS FROM LIVY. Part I. The Kings of
Rome. 18mo. 1s. 6d.

EASY LATIN PASSAGES FOR UNSEEN TRANSLATION.
Third Edition. Fcap. 8vo. 1s. 6d.

EXEMPLA LATINA : First Exercises in Latin Accidence.
With Vocabulary. *Crown 8vo.* 1s.

EASY LATIN EXERCISES ON THE SYNTAX OF THE
SHORTER AND REVISED LATIN PRIMER. With Vocabu-
lary. *Fourth Edition. Crown 8vo.* 2s. 6d. Issued with the consent of Dr. Kennedy.

THE LATIN COMPOUND SENTENCE RULES AND
EXERCISES. *Crown 8vo.* 2s. With Vocabulary. 2s. 6d.

NOTANDA QUAEDAM : Miscellaneous Latin Exercises on Common Rules and Idioms. With Vocabulary. *Second Edition. Fcap. 8vo. 1s. 6d.*

LATIN VOCABULARIES FOR REPETITION : Arranged according to Subjects. *Fourth Edition. Fcap. 8vo. 1s. 6d.*

A VOCABULARY OF LATIN IDIOMS AND PHRASES. *18mo. 1s.*

LATIN EXAMINATION PAPERS IN MISCELLANEOUS GRAMMAR AND IDIOMS. *Fourth Edition.*

A KEY, issued to Tutors and Private Students only, to be had on application to the Publishers. *Second Edition. Crown 8vo.* 6s.

STEPS TO GREEK. *18mo. 1s. 6d.*

EASY GREEK PASSAGES FOR UNSEEN TRANSLATION. *Fcap. 8vo. 1s. 6d.*

EASY GREEK EXERCISES ON ELEMENTARY SYNTAX.
[*In preparation.*

GREEK VOCABULARIES FOR REPETITION : Arranged according to Subjects. *Second Edition. Fcap. 8vo. 1s. 6d.*

GREEK TESTAMENT SELECTIONS. For the use of Schools. *Third Edition.* With Introduction, Notes, and Vocabulary. *Fcap. 8vo. 2s. 6d.*

GREEK EXAMINATION PAPERS IN MISCELLANEOUS GRAMMAR AND IDIOMS. *Third Edition.* KEY (issued as above). 6s.

STEPS TO FRENCH. *18mo. 8d.*

FIRST FRENCH LESSONS. *Crown 8vo. 1s.*

EASY FRENCH PASSAGES FOR UNSEEN TRANSLATION. *Second Edition. Fcap. 8vo. 1s. 6d.*

EASY FRENCH EXERCISES ON ELEMENTARY SYNTAX. With Vocabulary. *Crown 8vo. 2s. 6d.*

FRENCH VOCABULARIES FOR REPETITION : Arranged according to Subjects. *Third Edition. Fcap. 8vo. 1s.*

FRENCH EXAMINATION PAPERS IN MISCELLANEOUS GRAMMAR AND IDIOMS. *Seventh Edition. Crown 8vo. 2s. 6d.* KEY (issued as above). 6s.

GENERAL KNOWLEDGE EXAMINATION PAPERS. *Second Edition. Crown 8vo. 2s. 6d.* KEY (issued as above). 7s.

School Examination Series

Edited by A. M. M. STEDMAN, M.A.   *Crown 8vo.   2s. 6d.*

FRENCH EXAMINATION PAPERS IN MISCELLANE-
OUS GRAMMAR AND IDIOMS. By A. M. M. STEDMAN, M.A.
Sixth Edition.

A KEY, issued to Tutors and Private Students only, to be had on
application to the Publishers. *Second Edition. Crown 8vo. 6s.*

LATIN EXAMINATION PAPERS IN MISCELLANEOUS
GRAMMAR AND IDIOMS.   By A. M. M. STEDMAN, M.A.
Fourth Edition. KEY (issued as above). 6s.

GREEK EXAMINATION PAPERS IN MISCELLANEOUS
GRAMMAR AND IDIOMS.   By A. M. M. STEDMAN, M.A.
Third Edition. KEY (issued as above). 6s.

GERMAN EXAMINATION PAPERS IN MISCELLANE-
OUS GRAMMAR AND IDIOMS.   By R. J. MORICH, Manchester. *Third Edition.* KEY (issued as above). 6s.

HISTORY AND GEOGRAPHY EXAMINATION PAPERS.
By C. H. SPENCE, M.A., Clifton College.

SCIENCE EXAMINATION PAPERS. By R. E. STEEL, M.A.,
F.C.S., Chief Natural Science Master Bradford Grammar School.
In three vols. Part I., Chemistry ; *Part II.*, Physics.

GENERAL KNOWLEDGE EXAMINATION PAPERS.
By A. M. M. STEDMAN, M.A. *Second Edition.* KEY (issued as
above). 7s.

Primary Classics

With Introductions, Notes, and Vocabularies. *18mo. 1s. and 1s. 6d.*

FIRST LATIN READER. By A. M. M. STEDMAN, M.A. 1s. 6d.

EASY SELECTIONS FROM CAESAR—THE HELVETIAN
WAR. Edited by A. M. M. STEDMAN, M.A. 1s.

EASY SELECTIONS FROM LIVY—THE KINGS OF
ROME. Edited by A. M. M. STEDMAN, M.A. 1s. 6d.

EASY SELECTIONS FROM HERODOTUS—THE PER-
SIAN WARS. Edited by A. G. LIDDELL, M.A. 1s. 6d.

Milton Keynes UK
Ingram Content Group UK Ltd.
UKHW022021010124
435322UK00005B/234